Praise for *The Passionat*
What We Can Learn from Jesus (*Grief, Joy and Living Auth.* ### and Peter Wallace's Work

"To read this book is to experience the 'off-kilter sense of deep familiarity juxtaposed by newness' which Peter Wallace winsomely finds in the Gospel accounts—and in his real, embodied, Gospel-informed life. This is … for twenty-first-century people looking for a whole-body, whole-spirit faithfulness between the lines and within the words of the Bible."

—**Krista Tippett**, host/producer, *On Being*, American Public Media

"By exploring Jesus's emotions, Wallace helps us to understand our own. With personal stories and deep questions at the end of each chapter, we come to know a Jesus who has all the complex emotions we do. This book is a treasure for both the introspective reader in search of inner awareness and the friendly book group in search of a more lasting intimacy with one another and with God."

—**Lillian Daniel**, senior minister, First Congregational Church (UCC); co-author, *This Odd and Wondrous Calling*

"Through his own courageous story, Peter Wallace shakes us from hypocrisy and pretense. He breaks us free from a proper, suitable, 'freshly shampooed' Jesus and hits us in the solar plexus with a raw, firebrand messiah. This Jesus is a true composite of humanity; a Jesus in whom each of us sees a reflection of our broken soul; a Jesus that invites us into a fully integrated life of truth, intimacy and realness. Thank you, Peter Wallace, for inspiring us to rediscover Jesus—while rediscovering ourselves."

—**Rev. Susan Sparks**, senior pastor, Madison Avenue Baptist Church; author, *Laugh Your Way to Grace: Reclaiming the Spiritual Power of Humor*

"Eloquent … encourages us passionately to embrace the God who has so lovingly embraced us. Jesus called us to do more than to calmly think about him, consider him, or argue the merits of his way. In loving us, he called upon us to passionately love him. Peter's book helps us to do just that."

— thor and professor, sity Divinity School

"Masterful ... Wallace not only puts the claws back on the Lion, but adds a passionate—and compassionate—heart and soul along with it. From page to page, you find Jesus becoming more three-dimensional, more real and, frankly, more like someone you'd throw your heart and soul into following."

—**Rev. Eric Elnes, PhD**, senior minister, Countryside Community Church (UCC); author, *The Phoenix Affirmations*

"With style and grace ... takes us on a journey into a spiritual practice that is passionate, compassionate and courageous. Reminds us that a Jesus who feels deeply is our model to do the same and our truest guide to authentic life."

—**Greg Garrett**, author, *Faithful Citizenship* and *The Other Jesus*

"Peter Wallace is a beautiful thinker and a deep, humane soul."

—**Michael Chabon**, Pulitzer Prize winning author of *The Amazing Adventures of Kavalier & Clay* and *Telegraph Avenue*

THE Passionate Jesus

What We Can Learn from Jesus about Love, Fear, Grief, Joy and Living Authentically

THE REV. PETER WALLACE

Walking Together, Finding the Way ®
SKYLIGHT PATHS®
PUBLISHING
Woodstock, Vermont

The Passionate Jesus:
What We Can Learn from Jesus about Love, Fear, Grief, Joy and Living Authentically

2013 Quality Paperback Edition, First Printing
© 2013 by Peter Marsden Wallace

Unless otherwise indicated, scripture quotations are from the New Revised Standard Version Bible, copyright © 1989 by the Division of Christian Education of the National Council of the Churches of Christ in the USA. Used by permission. All rights reserved.

First names used in brief stories or quotations are not the actual names of the persons.

Library of Congress Cataloging-in-Publication Data

Wallace, Peter M.
  The passionate Jesus : what we can learn from Jesus about love, fear, grief, joy and living authentically / Peter Wallace. — Quality pbk ed.
    p. cm.
  Includes bibliographical references and index.
  ISBN 978-1-59473-393-2 (quality pbk. : alk. paper) 1. Jesus Christ—Example. I. Title.
  BT304.2.W35 2012
  232.9'03—dc23
                        2012036205

10 9 8 7 6 5 4 3 2 1

Manufactured in the United States of America

Cover Design: Heather Pelham
Cover art: © chiakto/fotolia modified by Heather Pelham
Interior Design: Tim Holtz

SkyLight Paths is creating a place where people of different spiritual traditions come together for challenge and inspiration, a place where we can help each other understand the mystery that lies at the heart of our existence.

SkyLight Paths sees both believers and seekers as a community that increasingly transcends traditional boundaries of religion and denomination—people wanting to learn from each other, walking together, finding the way.

SkyLight Paths, "Walking Together, Finding the Way," and colophon are trademarks of LongHill Partners, Inc., registered in the U.S. Patent and Trademark Office.

Walking Together, Finding the Way®
Published by SkyLight Paths Publishing
A Division of LongHill Partners, Inc.
Sunset Farm Offices, Route 4, P.O. Box 237
Woodstock, VT 05091
Tel: (802) 457-4000 Fax: (802) 457-4004
www.skylightpaths.com

Contents

Acknowledgments

T he author wishes to express his deep gratitude to the many people in the different circles of his life who have in various and numerous ways helped form and shape this book. Among these are his colleagues at the Alliance for Christian Media/ Day1, including the staff, members of the board of trustees and advisory board, and Day1 preachers; the bishops, clergy, and staff of the Episcopal Diocese of Atlanta, especially his discernment mentors and fellow postulants, and the clergy and members of St. Bartholomew's Episcopal Church; his children, grandchildren, siblings, and other family members; and his supportive friends, most of all Dan Le. Special thanks go to Emily Wichland, Henry Lowell Carrigan, and the staff of SkyLight Paths Publishing.

A Personal Word
of Introduction

I will rise and go to meet him,
and embrace him in my arms.
In the arms of my dear Jesus,
O he hath ten thousand charms.
—JOHN NEWTON HYMN, "MERCY, O THOU SON OF DAVID"

Life's Changing Landscape

One of my most beloved life rituals is to carve a few days out
of my schedule and take off to St. Simons Island, Georgia, for a
creative retreat. I started doing this about twenty years ago when
friends invited me to stay with them at a cottage they owned on
East Beach. Immediately I fell in love with the island.

Over the next several years, I would come during Lent to paint
one of the Stations of the Cross for a church project. I enjoyed
stepping out of my usual writing endeavors to pursue an entirely
different area of creativity. Though I wasn't a very good painter I
actually did better than I expected. I also read books, walked the
beach, watched old movies, and simply relaxed. But it was the
creative aspect of those island getaways that truly energized me.

After several years, however, my friends sold their cottage
and I let the practice slide. Eight years ago, in the wake of a

radical and painful shift in my life, I decided to rekindle my yearly affair with St. Simons Island, and eventually found a wonderful condo owned by some fellow Episcopalians a few blocks from the beach. In recent years I have come back to the island during Lent or around Easter to write, read, and relax. It is bliss. Much of this book was written there.

Each year I am surprised by the changes in the shoreline as I walk along the broad, white-sand beach. How many years have I walked along that seaside? And yet every year the shore is different. The sea breezes and tides have reformed the sand bars and the beaches. Gulls waddle in the shallows of new eddies waiting for their meals, eddies that weren't there the year before. It always throws me off a little.

Not only is the landscape different, but each year I realize I am different. I bring a different set of plans, worries, and experiences to the shore. I have lived through fresh heartaches, joys, and terrors in the months since I've been away. Even the cells of my body have changed. I have aged; my body is different. I hope I have learned and grown in some areas, and I hope I have noticed other areas that need attention. My spirit has been wounded in new ways, and cracked open for fresh growth if I have been willing. My own landscape, internally and externally, has changed as much as the seashore.

It is this same phenomenon—this off-kilter sense of deep familiarity juxtaposed with unique newness—that I experience when I read the four gospels in the Bible. I am familiar with the words and the stories, but each time I read them I try to see them with fresh eyes. A phrase I never noticed before shines with relevant meaning. A minor gesture of Jesus's suddenly generates a sea change in perspective. A troubling question or doubt arises, demanding attention. I know this landscape, but it is different, reformed by the changes in my own understanding, my own spirit and needs.

As I was dealing with the latest crises in my life during my visit to the island two years ago, I reread the gospels once again and, through the lenses of my emotional state at the time, noticed something different in the scriptural landscape. The emotions of Jesus started shining brightly on the pages, and I realized how passionate he truly was, how fully he experienced whatever he was feeling—living it, expressing it, not apologizing for it, but simply being who he was directly, wholly, and authentically.

This shattered my own comfortable presuppositions about Jesus. So often in classic theological interpretations, movie portrayals, or other fictionalized accounts, we see a Jesus who is utterly cool, calm, and collected. He is beyond emotion. Freshly shampooed and blue-eyed, enfolded by crisp, clean robes, he floats above the grit and grime of human existence. He doesn't hurt, he doesn't fear, he doesn't laugh, and most tragically he doesn't love very passionately. In fact, nothing about him is passionate. He seems not to feel at all.

Unconsciously, I once adopted this approach to emotions as "Christlike." I kept the edge off how I was feeling so as to avoid conflict or inappropriate behavior or even deep, honest love. But this kind of living is as far as one can get from being truly like Jesus.

The picture revealed in the biblical account is that Jesus was present, connected, and sometimes painfully direct with everyone with whom he came into contact. He was one who was "deeply moved" (John 11:33). He knew and embodied the emotions he felt and expressed them in honest, clear, and life-giving ways.

What I hope to do in this book is discover with you what we can learn from Jesus about our emotional authenticity. Sometimes what we already "know" about Jesus only gets in the way of our really *knowing* him. It is easy to be lulled by the familiar stories rather than to allow ourselves to be stimulated by the real life, full of emotions, that courses underneath the printed words of the gospels.

So as we meet Jesus again, as he weeps at the death of a beloved friend, or allows a heartbroken woman to massage his dirty feet with her oiled hair, or lashes out at the hypocrisy of the religious leaders, or speaks to a sorrowful thief on the cross next to him, we can truly experience the emotion of the moment with Jesus. We can sense reality breaking through our carefully constructed self-protections as our souls come alive with passionate wonder.

A Journey toward Authenticity

This journey toward authenticity with Jesus as guide is intensely personal. In my case, a dozen years ago it began to dawn on me that the way I had been living my life was dishonest, empty, exhausting, and ultimately impossible. As a person of faith I yearned for clean, clear integrity and wholeness in my relationships with God and with others. Yet I found myself as far away from that goal as the east is from the west. My faith, so carefully constructed on certain premises and misunderstandings, seemed useless. I was a total fraud.

Yet something within me, surely the Spirit of God, kept pushing me, guiding me throughout this unfolding transformation, and in hindsight I could see that God was with me every step of the way. I just hadn't taken my eyes off myself to notice it.

I came to understand how shallow, inhibited, and inauthentic my existence really was. I was disconnected from my true self, detached and unaware of whatever emotions coursed through my mind and heart, or else aware of them but denying them, smothering them. I realized I was not being myself, not acknowledging the reality of my soul. I was not really living. I was not *me*.

I decided to open my eyes and my heart to God's wisdom all over again. I tried to see anew where Jesus, who is at the center of my faith, could be found in all this, how he himself dealt with the emotional realities of his life, how he trusted God through them. I sought to grasp the wisdom he shared through his words and his actions. And I began to appreciate how passionately Jesus lived.

My quest for wholeness and authenticity actually began many years before this, when the disconnectedness of my life forced me to begin to reevaluate my beliefs, the structure of my faith, and how I was receiving it and expressing it. Through an agonizing emotional and spiritual process extending over several years, I found myself in the Episcopal Church.

There my questions about faith and doubt really began to surface in the light of honesty. There my pursuit of authenticity began, with baby steps perhaps, because there I found people who were utterly honest about their faith, doubts, fears, and failures. They seemed to know who they were, warts and all. But that didn't stop them from fleeing to the altar for the Eucharist every Sunday morning to join their sisters and brothers in celebrating their beloved Savior.

This sort of spiritually rarefied atmosphere starts to work on you after a while. It seeps into your subconscious, your heart, your very life. And so, before too many years had passed, I began to grasp that in order to be authentic with myself and my emotions, I had to acknowledge who I was, who I had always been but had denied and tried to silence behind many carefully locked doors. I had to accept myself as God created me: a gay man.

I had so vigilantly constructed my life that it wasn't an easy process to begin unlocking those doors, to face what was within and recognize I would have to deal with what came out. But this process, though long and complicated, became a holy sojourn for me. And ultimately, nine years ago, I approached several wise people whom I thought could advise me along the way. Despite my terror over where this would lead me, each one urged me to continue forward on this quest.

Ultimately I reached the point of no return. If I was to be true to myself and to the God who made me, I had to complete the journey. Such a decision had an infinite array of painful ramifications both personally and professionally. I faced reactions I had never encountered before, positive and negative, affirming and angry. Some friendships I thought were important simply vanished. My decision understandably caused vast pain in the lives of dear people I loved, to my regret. Even so, most people in my circles—family, friends, and colleagues—welcomed and accepted me.

Over the eight years since, I have been striving to keep moving forward on this journey to authenticity, a journey often experienced as three steps forward and two steps backward. In the process I have come to acknowledge that life in its passionate fullness can be lived only when I am open and honest with myself, with others, and especially with God. I still have a long way to go.

You may not be dealing with the issue of your sexual orientation, but if you're human you're dealing with something that hinders you from having a full and whole existence. Each of us wrestles with areas of our lives that push against our authentic selves, aspects of our identity that we skillfully manage to keep hidden or suppressed, even from ourselves. As we explore the realm of Jesus's emotions, I hope we can be open to the light of wisdom that Jesus can shed on these dark areas of our own self-deceit.

Jesus the Wisdom Teacher

Much has been written about Jesus as a wisdom teacher. My friend and Episcopal priest Beverley Elliott spoke of this approach in one of her sermons: "It is from this understanding of Jesus—Jesus as rabbi, wisdom teacher—that I suggest we listen to Jesus speaking to us. He is helping us to be transformed so that we might become more whole, more as God created us to be.... It is through our inner transformation that we naturally find love and compassion leading us out to participate with Christ in his work in the world."[1]

This Jesus is part of the ancient wisdom tradition that, as spirituality writer Cynthia Bourgeault describes it, serves as the "headwaters of all the great religious traditions of the world today. It's concerned with the transformation of the whole human being. Transformation from what to what? Well, for a starter, from our animal instincts and egocentricity into love and compassion; from a judgmental and dualistic worldview into a nondual acceptingness. This was the message that Jesus, apparently out of nowhere, came preaching and teaching, a message that was radical in its own time and remains equally radical today."[2]

Together we'll follow Jesus the wisdom teacher on our journey as he urges us, goads us, teaches us, shoves us, and cheers us on as he walks with us toward our goal. We'll search for the wisdom he reveals through his teachings and actions as they relate to his emotional life, coming to see how he expressed his emotions, how he shared and dealt with his feelings.

As we do, we'll grapple with some important questions, such as: Who is Jesus? What was it like to be with him as one of his followers, or as one he touched with his healing hands, or as one he argued, laughed, or wept with? What did he do or say that would shock us, challenge us, or give us hope or joy? I want to understand how his provocative approach to living authentically provided clarity for his followers, his opponents, and anyone else who came in contact with him.

As we wrestle with these questions, we can better grasp larger overarching truths about faithful living: How do we approach our circumstances as Jesus did? How do we see through Jesus's eyes, and feel with his heart? How do we learn to respond to the world with the same wholeness and healing love that he so generously demonstrated? At the end of each chapter, I have provided reflection questions—for personal meditation or small-group discussion—to help you explore each emotion in the context of your own life.

Jesus did not play games. He was as direct with people as anyone I have ever encountered. He didn't wear his emotions on his cloak sleeves, but he identified them, acknowledged them, and expressed them as honestly as possible, and then accepted the consequences.

Jesus's life is a model for authenticity and honesty, but it's more than that, too. As Bourgeault writes, "Jesus' life, considered from this standpoint, is a sacrament: a mystery that draws us deeply into itself and, when rightly approached, conveys an actual spiritual energy empowering us to follow the path that his teachings have laid out."[3]

For this to happen we must be with Jesus for a while. Rest in his presence. Spend time with him. See him, hear him, and feel him. Consider what Buddhist teacher Thich Nhat Hanh has written:

> Like many great humans, the Buddha had a hallowed presence. When we see such persons, we feel peace, love, and strength in them, and also in ourselves. The Chinese say, "When a sage is born, the river water becomes clearer and the mountain plants and trees become more verdant." They are describing the ambience surrounding a holy man or woman. When a sage is present and you sit near him or her, you feel peace and light. If you were to sit close to Jesus and look into His eyes—even if you didn't see Him—you would have a much greater chance to be saved than by reading His words. But when He is not there, His teachings are second best, especially the teachings of His life.[4]

The landscape of life has changed for me, and is always changing. And I hope it will change for you as we walk together through the gospels with our eyes, our minds, and our hearts open to how Jesus lived and expressed his emotions. We can learn much about being authentic if we will open ourselves fully to this passionate Jesus.

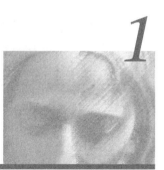

Understanding Our Emotions

W e are passionate creatures. Our feelings move us and shape us, and our hearts are in constant motion. We express our feelings with more meaning and force in some situations than in others. When we intentionally seek to track our feelings internally, we may be surprised at their mercurial and unpredictable nature. We churn from joy to sadness to anger, ever moving, expanding and diminishing, sometimes erupting.

Our emotions can reveal the truth about our beliefs and values, often in contradiction to what we may say or do. They reveal with clarity what drives and influences our relationships, our purposes, and our spiritual life.

We seekers of truth yearn to understand better what moves us and drives us emotionally in order to understand ourselves more deeply and to express ourselves more authentically. We want to develop our emotional capacities in order that we might respond naturally, immediately, spontaneously, wholly, and authentically with emotions that are appropriate to the circumstances in which we find ourselves.[1]

Our minds and hearts work interdependently to create this emotional consciousness. Often, however, we get sidetracked or confused by the apparent distinction between emotion and reason. We assume that reason is mere abstract rationalism, while emotion is often associated with passionate outbursts devoid of reason. But we must work to develop an authentic emotional life in order to experience an integrated humanity and an authentic spiritual life.[2]

This is why emotional authenticity is so vital for us: we draw not only our human identity from it but also our spiritual capacity. Our relationship with God is ultimately emotional, and so in order to experience that relationship to the utmost we must wrestle with our emotions, how we experience them and express them.

We must be able to give ourselves over to our passionate reality, to engage ourselves in all that we feel, to live in our emotions mindfully and wholeheartedly, and thus overcome the emptiness, meaninglessness, and impatience that so often hinder our living wholly with meaning and purpose.

This is the way of God that we seek. For, as the minister and author Dr. Matthew A. Elliott explains, "God is love. Love is the most basic of emotions, and God gives [God's self] this name. God is personal, God is emotional and God feels all the emotions that love can produce. This is central to the character of God. Our emotions are part of being made in the image of God; they are a good and integral part of human existence."[3]

"Passion" and "Heart"

The concept of "passion" is so intricately connected with emotions that the word *passions* is often used as a synonym for emotions. The word is also applied to particular and accustomed interests or concerns—for example, to have a passion for justice or peace, or for the arts, sports, or even comic books.

Out of our emotions flow our passions, determining the overarching character of our lives. Danish philosopher Søren Kierkegaard wrote of an "essential passion" in life, that is, a passion that, as Robert C. Roberts describes it, "defines not just some human being, but a *genuine* human being, one that is formed as human beings are supposed to be formed. Both essential and unessential passion give a person steadiness, reliability, a kind of transcendence of the ups and downs of immediate circumstances."[4]

Another concept frequently found in the scriptures is the "heart": an integration of our emotions, will, and intellect. The contemporary Sufi teacher Kabir Helminski defines heart this way: "Beyond the limited analytic intellect is a vast realm of mind that includes psychic and extrasensory abilities; intuition; wisdom; a sense of unity; aesthetic, qualitative and creative faculties; and image-forming and symbolic capabilities. Though these faculties are many, we give them a single name with some justification, because they are operating best when they are in concert. They comprise a mind, moreover, in spontaneous connection with the cosmic mind, the total mind we call 'heart.'"[5]

Both the Hebrew and the Christian Scriptures use *heart* to signify the integration of mind, will, and emotion. Heart refers to the innermost person, the very source of the soul and the spirit in the emotional, volitional, and rational life within each person.[6]

The heart that is integrated and authentic is the heart that is open fully to the way of Jesus. Jesus himself spoke about understanding and identifying the truly righteous—those whose lives align with the purposes of God—by looking at the condition of their hearts. Our state of righteousness is reflected in the responses of our mind, will, and emotion to the circumstances and needs around us.

For our purposes, we can conclude that emotions are a way of expressing our beliefs and values. They reflect our internal experience. The overall sense of the Bible's teachings is that emotions are an integral and natural aspect of our identity as persons created in the image of God, rather than forces that must be controlled or directed toward proper behavior. Furthermore, the emotions of those who are spiritually attuned should be "the most intense, most vibrant, and the most pervasive things we feel as they are based on the most important things in life,"[7] primarily our relationship to God. Indeed, our emotions will reveal the reality and depth of this spiritual relationship—a phenomenon manifest in Jesus's life.

All human beings experience love, anger, fear, grief, and joy, and most cultures have created stories and rituals for explaining the presence or lack of such feelings. The lens through which we examine them is the life of Jesus as recorded in the gospels of the Christian Scriptures. And Jesus, as we'll see, was an emotionally passionate human being.

Jesus and Emotions

Who was Jesus? I like the one-minute-and-fifteen-second answer that theologian Marcus J. Borg once gave on a live television interview:

> Jesus was from the peasant class. Clearly, he was brilliant. His use of language was remarkable and poetic, filled with images and stories. He had a metaphoric mind. He was not an ascetic, but world affirming, with a zest for life. There was a sociopolitical passion to him—like a Gandhi or a Martin Luther King, he challenged the domination system of his day. He was a religious ecstatic, a Jewish mystic, for whom God was an experiential reality. As such, Jesus was also a healer. And there seems to have been a spiritual presence around him, like that reported of St. Francis or the present Dalai Lama. And as a figure of history, Jesus was an ambiguous figure—you could experience him and conclude that he was insane, as his family did, or that he was simply eccentric or that he was a dangerous threat—or you could conclude that he was filled with the Spirit of God.[8]

Jesus's cultural training would have influenced his own emotional experience. As Borg puts it, "Jesus was deeply Jewish.... Not only was he Jewish by birth and socialization, but he remained a Jew all his life."[9] In the Jewish culture of Jesus's time people generally possessed a freedom of emotional expression. And yet there was an underlying assent to the proposition that the emotions of the faithful would reflect Jewish theology and spiritual understanding.

The God of the Hebrew Scriptures

A robust study of the Tanakh reveals that Yahweh is an intensely emotional God. God loves the nation and the people of Israel, yearns for their love, delights in their obedience, hates evil, and is angered by stiff-necked disobedience. Israel's theology considers God as a person in that God reacts to and is moved by human circumstances and events. To assume that God is without passion is to ignore the very heart of Jewish life and worship.[10]

Historian Diarmaid MacCulloch explains that the Jews conceived of their God "not simply as all-powerful, but as passionately concerned with their response to him, in anger as well as in love. Such an intensely personal deity, they began to assert, was nevertheless the God for all humanity."[11] Unfortunately, in many strains of Christian theology the passionate God of the Hebrew faith has been expunged, as some theologians throughout history have argued that God is above and beyond mere emotions.

Yet it is clear that Jesus was as human as you or I. Through his own emotional strength and authenticity his life reflected a deep belief in a personal, passionate God. As essayist Andrew Sullivan writes: "The mystery that Christians are asked to embrace is not that Jesus was God but that he was God-made-man, which is to say, prone to the feelings and doubts and joys and agonies of being human. Jesus himself seemed to make a point of that.... He told stories. He had friends. He got to places late; he misread the actions of others; he wept; he felt disappointed; he asked as many questions as he gave answers; and he was often silent in self-doubt or elusive or afraid."[12]

One biblical scholar found himself spellbound by the intensity of Jesus's emotions: Jesus expressed "not a twinge of pity, but heartbroken compassion; not a passing irritation, but terrifying anger; not a silent tear, but groans of anguish; not a weak smile, but ecstatic celebration."[13]

As we'll see, Jesus possessed an extra dimension of life, a fullness, a trueness—not because he was also divine, but because he was fully realized in his humanity. We can learn how to experience that fullness and trueness in our lives as well, in part by discovering how Jesus experienced, expressed, and responded to his very human emotions.

The Focus of Our Study

The four gospels—Matthew, Mark, Luke, and John—are our resource for this study, and though we may not have realized it before, Jesus's emotional life is vibrantly presented in them, albeit sometimes between the lines.

These accounts certainly present their difficulties in enabling us to grasp a genuine sense of Jesus's emotional life. They were written several decades after the events they record. In testifying to the life of Jesus, each writer offers a certain perspective, perhaps even has a particular theological axe to grind. Much of the content has undoubtedly been added and revised by later editors in order to "correct" certain teachings and bring some concepts more closely in line with what had become official dogma.[14]

For our purposes in this meditative approach to understanding the emotional life of Jesus, we will explore how the gospel writers portray Jesus as he interacts with his friends and loved ones, as well as with his opponents and mere curiosity seekers. We'll discover how consistent, or inconsistent, Jesus was in his emotional responses to various situations. And we'll wrestle with the notion of whether we would benefit personally by following his example, by imitating his emotions, in order to become more authentic persons—thus applying the time-honored spiritual practice of *imitatio Christi*, seeking to follow his example.

We'll do this because fully grasping the passionate emotions of Jesus is essential if we are to experience genuine discipleship and spiritual renewal.

Overcoming Misconceptions about Jesus

When we explore the passionate Jesus within the pages and between the lines of the gospels, we may find ourselves surprised and even shocked by the gritty reality we discover. Jesus will become more real to us than perhaps ever before. I know I was amazed by such readings mainly because of my own lifelong misunderstandings of Jesus's identity. It is difficult to sense the passion behind his words and deeds when reading the black and white (and occasionally red) texts in the Bible. And the classic motion picture versions of Jesus that I grew up with, starring cool, understated actors such as Jeffrey Hunter and Max von Sydow, don't help. The Jesus we'll discover in the four gospels possesses many contrasting features. As Quaker theologian and historian Elton Trueblood writes, "He is a Man of Sorrows, but He is also a Man of Joys; He uses terribly rough and blunt language; He expresses blazing anger; He teases; He foregathers with a gay crowd. How, for example, could we ever miss the fact that His words and behavior surprised His contemporaries?"[15]

Our misconceptions regarding the character of Jesus may arise out of a general desire developed over centuries to make the Christian faith as orderly, safe, and, yes, nice as possible. So we impose those attributes upon our image of Jesus as we read the gospels. Many of us have failed utterly to grasp who Jesus really was, how he felt, how he expressed his feelings, and how his authentic presence continues with us today if we are open to the Spirit of God. I know I have. British author Dorothy L. Sayers put it this way: "We have very efficiently pared the claws of the Lion of Judah, certified him 'meek and mild,' and recommended him as a fitting household pet for pale curates and pious old ladies. To those who knew him, however, he in no way suggests a milk-and-water person; they objected to him as a dangerous firebrand."[16]

Rarely has Jesus been examined through the lens of human emotion. One reason may be that there are relatively few specific references to his emotions in the gospels. In fact, most scholars cite about sixty such citations,[17] most of them in the gospel of John.

But, when you consider carefully what Jesus says and to whom he says it, how he acts and why, you can't help but discern the emotions behind his recorded words and deeds. So while the gospel writers may not often apply specific emotional language to the events they are recounting, we nevertheless can see that Jesus demonstrated the physical traits related to emotion: he groaned and sighed in grief, he cried out in rage, he enjoyed the merry company of fellow partygoers. In every way, we see that Jesus's emotional life was very human.

Furthermore, Jesus responds to the emotions of those around him with understanding, acceptance, and compassion. He doesn't let emotional outbursts of grief or anger rattle him or lure him into meaningless conflict. Rather, through his transformative ministry he lifts the emotions of those around him. He makes friendships, even deeply close relationships with certain others like Mary and Martha, Lazarus, and one described as the "disciple whom Jesus loved."

It is important to us as spiritual beings who seek the richest possible relationship with God to see the radiant kaleidoscope of emotions the gospel writers reveal in Jesus. When we do, we can acknowledge more fully Jesus as being wholly human in God's image. Through his life Jesus reveals with perfect clarity a passionate God. As we contrast our own passions and emotions with his, we become aware of our need for a more authentic emotional and spiritual life. When we encounter the passionate, fully human Jesus in the gospels, we can begin the journey toward our own fully realized humanity and a more meaningful and vibrant spiritual life.

The First Step of the Journey

There is an overarching purpose for us to experience a richer, more authentic emotional life as Jesus did: we will be driven, and liberated, to act in passionate, wholehearted faith in service to others. The classic devotional writer Robert Law encourages us toward this goal: "In the complex working of our nature, emotion has but one purpose, to move the will to action. Good feelings are given us not that we may enjoy feeling them, but that we may do good actions, do with a warm heart what we could not do, or could not so effectually do, with a cold heart. They are the tide which floats the ship over the harbor bar on which otherwise it would be stranded. And in this we see our perfect example in the compassion of Jesus."[18]

The first step in this journey with Jesus toward emotional authenticity is to accept the notion that Jesus's coming to earth in the first place was not about the fall of the human race, about our guilt and our shame, but rather "about goodness, solidarity, and our own intimate participation in the mystery of love at the heart of all creation."[19] With this as a foundation, we can reflect on what emotions are, how they are formed, experienced, expressed, and channeled, in order to become better equipped and enabled to nurture those with whom we live and whom we serve.

Our goal in examining the emotions experienced and expressed in the life of Jesus is to integrate true spirituality into our lives—a spirituality that can't help but flow through us to all around us.

An Invitation to Life

One of the richest and clearest descriptions of a full emotional life in the Hebrew Scriptures is found in Ecclesiastes 3:1–8:

For everything there is a season,
and a time for every matter under heaven....
a time to weep, and a time to laugh;
a time to mourn, and a time to dance;...
a time to embrace, and a time to refrain from
embracing;
a time to seek, and a time to lose;...
a time to keep silence, and a time to speak;
a time to love, and a time to hate;
a time for war, and a time for peace.

In this passage emotions are revealed to be an integral part of human life, a natural part of the theology of the Hebrew Scriptures. There is a rhythm of life through which our emotions carry us. God calls us to embrace our emotions, to accept them, express them authentically, and allow them to empower us for a richer, deeper spiritual life, a life that gives itself to others.

This is how Jesus lived his life, and it is the life he invites us to live with him: "Let anyone who is thirsty come to me, and let the one who believes in me drink. As the scripture has said, 'Out of the believer's heart shall flow rivers of living water'" (John 7:37–38). Jesus invites us to come to him and drink deeply of the life he offers us, to be set free by his spirit so that our lives may be lived as fully, richly, and authentically as his was.

Exploring Emotions

How would you describe yourself as an emotional being? What bothers you about the way you describe yourself? What encourages you?

What would you say are your passions in life? What passions do you hope to develop? What is hindering you from pursuing those passions?

When you think of Jesus, what image comes to your mind? How accurate do you think your image is? What misconceptions about Jesus do you think you're holding on to? Why do you think it is helpful to see Jesus as an emotional human being?

2

Love

The Centerpiece of Life

Love is perhaps the crucial issue of life, because it undergirds and liberates our faith, our hope, and our joy. It shapes our daily existence. It perfumes every breath we take. It can be powerfully positive, or it can break us and lead us into emptiness and despair.

The truth is, I can't remember a time I did not believe that God loved me, and yet this belief could be in many ways merely an agreement with a theological proposition. For long years before I came to terms with my sexual identity, I never felt free or honest in that love, and so I was never really able to fully, authentically love anyone else. I lived on the surface, afraid to plunge too deeply into another's life, let alone my own. I was simply going through the motions with a meaningless smile.

I had painted myself into an existential corner. I had gone way too far down the path of what I presumed others—my parents, my family, my friends, my church, my God—expected of me. I was shutting down and living life with little depth or authentic emotion. Without even realizing it, I was self-destructing—and harming other dear people in the process.

Through several years of trying to find that one friend to love who would make things right for me, the goal only seemed to move further away and my life became even more desperately imbalanced. Finally, I came to realize that experiencing wholeness did not mean finding that one perfect friend, but finding *myself*—knowing and accepting the real me. This was a treacherous and frightening path, but one that has led me ultimately to a new life, one that I hope is always becoming more self-accepting, other-accepting, liberating, and loving. That is my goal and my hope.

When we find ourselves in God's love, then we can reach out in that love to others. But I have come to realize that I need to understand, accept, and enjoy myself as a starting point. I need to love myself. And even more importantly, I need to understand, accept, and enjoy God's love for me, and be willing to love God to the same lengths that I want to be loved.

How do we do that? Jesus has given us the model. It starts with being honest and authentic with ourselves, with others, and with God.

How long have you searched for a place where you can love and be loved? How deeply frustrated have you become after reaching yet another dead end in experiencing real love? How intensely have you felt love's absence in your heart? How numb have you made yourself to compensate for the lack of it?

Jesus can help us wrestle with all these questions and more as we discover whom he loved, how he offered love, and how he received love. He does not promise an easy journey; in fact, his own heart was broken time and again by those with whom he surrounded himself, those he loved. But he does offer us a depth of meaning and purpose in our experience if we can learn from, and live into, his love.

What Is Love?

The problem with understanding love is that we often confuse it with all sorts of other feelings: Infatuation. Pleasure. Romance. Arousal. Lust. We tend to identify love with the rushing release of endorphins we experience when we are in the presence of someone we care deeply about. These wonderful feelings can dupe us into thinking they are love. We assume that if we love and are loved, then we will always feel warm, happy, and full. But this is not the kind of love we witness in Jesus's life.

Love can be defined in a variety of ways. Essentially, "Love is most generally an attraction towards an object. This attraction is the result of seeing a quality in an object that is good, valuable, or desirable."[1] Love is a state of being, not a fleeting feeling. It is an orientation toward goodwill, benevolence, kindness, and acceptance toward the whole of creation, including yourself, regardless of the circumstances of life.

Considered in this way, love can be understood as the root of all other positive emotions. Love forms the foundation and the core for all of Christian ethics, as Jesus taught. Love is the heart of the Christian faith. It spurs us to action. It empowers joy and hope and ignites the desire to overcome faults and weaknesses. It encompasses all righteous passions.[2]

Love in Jewish Culture

The core of the Jewish faith is found in the *Shema*: "Hear, O Israel: The Lord is our God, the Lord alone. You shall love the Lord your God with all your heart, and with all your soul, and with all your might" (Deuteronomy 6:4–5). Thus, in the Hebrew Scriptures loving God involves the whole person. God desires of us the fullest, deepest, richest love possible involving every aspect of our being, and God is eager to offer the same love in return with no strings attached. And there is a natural corollary to this sort of love: "You shall love your neighbor as yourself" (Leviticus 19:18). The love of God empowers and compels us to love others as well as ourselves.

Jesus grew up and lived within the Jewish culture of his time, learning through his faith how one can have a love-based relationship with God. He surely believed that the righteous— those who choose to live in the ways of God and pursue God's mission—are those who love God. Those who know and obey God can joyfully celebrate the love and wisdom of God. As a result, they desire to do good, to serve God, and they appreciate the blessings this life brings.

Shades of Meaning

The Bible uses several words that are translated as *love* in English. Dr. Martin Luther King Jr. preached about these kinds of love in his 1957 speech "The Power of Non-Violence":

> The Greek language uses three words for love. It talks about *eros*. *Eros* is a sort of aesthetic love. It has come to us to be a sort of romantic love and it stands with all of its beauty.... The Greek language talks about *philia* and this is a sort of reciprocal love between personal friends. This is a vital, valuable love. But when we talk of loving those who oppose you and those who seek to defeat you we are not talking about *eros* or *philia*. The Greek language comes out with another word and it is *agape*. *Agape* is understanding, creative, redemptive good will for all [people]. Biblical theologians would say it is the love of God working in the minds of [people]. It is an overflowing love that seeks nothing in return. And when you come to love on this level you begin to love [others] not because they are likeable, not because they do things that attract us, but because God loves them....[3]

The writer of 1 John tells us simply that "God is love" (4:8). That is perhaps as simple a definition as has ever been written of God. Our human minds can easily be overwhelmed by all the facets of God's being as all-powerful, all-knowing, and all-loving Creator. Yet the writer of 1 John boils it all down to one word: *love*. It is *agape* love, the kind of love that is unconditional and sacrificial. It costs. It is active and thoughtful on behalf of others, regardless of their response. It is constant and unwavering. It is purely volitional—one must choose to love this way. It is pure, offered without expectation of anything in return. It consumes and drives us. It is limitless.

Agape is the sort of love Jesus shared so freely. But it is not merely a Christian sort of love. "Agape love means feeling and expressing pure, unlimited love for every human being with no exception.... As the Dalai Lama has stated, 'All the major religions of the world have similar ideals of love, the same goal of benefiting humanity through spiritual practice, and the same effect of making their followers into better human beings.'"[4]

Love and Compassion

Another concept we will encounter when following Jesus through the gospels is *compassion*. In Hebrew and Aramaic, the word we translate typically as "compassion" is related to the word for "womb." In the Hebrew Scriptures, compassion comprises both an emotion and a way of being that arises from that emotion. According to the Jewish writers we literally feel compassion in a particular part of the body: our loins.[5]

The word *compassion* is our translation for the Greek word *splanchnizomai*, a verb expressing strong emotion. Its root refers to our inner organs, our guts, which the Greeks considered the seat of emotions. This Greek word is used a dozen times in the Christian Scriptures, always with reference to Jesus; he used it in his teaching, or the gospel writer used it to describe his feelings. The word means to have great affection, love, and concern for another. We know compassion when we feel it, for as it moves us we can feel it stir in our gut.

Compassion is as an outgrowth of love, but is different from other forms of love because of its object. One can experience love with a friend, family member, spouse, or other human beings; however, one has compassion with those who are suffering or in need.[6] So Jesus, out of his love for all, experienced compassion for a wide array of people he came in contact with, including a leper (Mark 1:40–41), two blind men (Matthew 20:34), and a widow mourning the loss of her only son (Luke 7:13).

Jesus also experienced compassion for whole crowds of people massing around him, yearning for his healing touch and his hopeful yet radical message. Matthew tells us he had compassion for the crowds "because they were harassed and helpless, like sheep without a shepherd" (9:35–36). Twice Jesus's compassion for the crowds led to miracles of feeding these vast numbers even though only a few fish and loaves of bread were initially proffered (see Matthew 15:29–38 and Mark 7:31–8:9).

Jesus's compassion was stirred by the physical and spiritual needs of those around him. His heart broke when people who were oppressed and distressed confronted him, and his compassionate love drove him to minister to those who needed healing. Transparent, truthful love is the basis for Jesus's entire emotional life. This is what empowers and guides the whole range of his passions.

Who Jesus Loves

A stone is tossed into a still pond, and from its point of entry ripples and wavelets circle out, wider and wider. In the same way, Jesus enters human existence, piercing the surface between the eternal and the here-and-now, and love washes continually from him in wave after wave, flowing out beyond him, touching all in its path, ultimately encircling the whole of creation. God's love surges through Jesus in every direction.

Jesus is not stingy with his love. The gospel writers make that clear. The writer of John in particular remarks often about Jesus's love for someone or other. To help us gain an understanding of the wide variety of people Jesus loved, we'll explore some of his most intimate relationships.

Jesus Loves God the Father/Mother

Love is abundantly manifest in the mutual relationship between Jesus and God the Father/Mother. God loves Jesus because Jesus is God's own (see Matthew 3:17, 17:5; Mark 12:6). God declares,

"You are my Son, the Beloved; with you I am well pleased" (Mark 1:11). John's gospel reveals a unique bond of love between the divine Parent and the Son: "The Father loves the Son" (John 3:35 and 5:20). It is a deeply passionate relationship, one that overflows into the lives of those who love God, as Jesus told his beloved disciples: "For the Father himself loves you, because you have loved me and have believed that I came from God" (John 16:27).

Roman Catholic priest and writer Henri Nouwen wrote of the source of Jesus's words and works:

> This eternal community of love is the center and source of Jesus' spiritual life, a life of uninterrupted attentiveness to the Father in the Spirit of Love. It is from this life that Jesus' ministry grows. His eating and fasting, his praying and acting, his traveling and resting, his preaching and teaching, his exorcising and healing, were all done in the Spirit of Love. We will never understand the full meaning of Jesus' richly varied ministry unless we see how the many things are rooted in the one thing: listening to the Father in the intimacy of perfect love.[7]

Jesus did what he did "so that the world may know that I love the Father" (John 14:31). God the loving Parent gave Jesus the difficult, nigh impossible, task of showing the world how to love. It meant overturning cherished theological notions and practices, revolutionizing our way of life, putting aside self for the benefit of others. It ultimately cost Jesus his life, so that the glory of what he taught and how he lived could be better seen against the dark backdrop of vicious human self-interest.

"For this reason the Father loves me, because I lay down my life in order to take it up again," Jesus said (John 10:17), revealing his own assurance that the holy Parent loved him, as well as his realization of how much that love would cost—and why it was worth that very dear price.

To leave it at this would base the relationship ultimately on actions, as though God the Parent loves Jesus only because of what he does, not because of who he is. The reality of this loving relationship can be glimpsed in the ways Jesus talks to God in prayer.

Consider for example Jesus's prayer after spending time with his disciples in the "upper room," just before his arrest. His conversation with his loving Parent here is marked by a passionate intimacy: "I glorified you on earth by finishing the work that you gave me to do. So now, Father, glorify me in your own presence with the glory that I had in your presence before the world existed" (John 17:1–26). Jesus alludes to the ineffable relationship he and his Father have always experienced outside of time and place. They share a gloriously intimate bond beyond what we can ever understand or even imagine. It was out of this bright and holy union that Jesus came to enlarge the relationship between God and humanity, in order to welcome us all into the divine presence.

Jesus speaks to his beloved Father/Mother of the close relationship he has built with his disciples, who were already within God's loving possession, as all humanity is: "I have made your name known to those whom you gave me from the world. They were yours, and you gave them to me, and they have kept your word." The relationship among them is ever growing, as they all belong to one another. As Jesus puts it, "All mine are yours, and yours are mine; and I have been glorified in them." The same relationship between Jesus and the holy Parent has been extended to his disciples, and from there it is passed on and on, even to you and me.

Jesus prays with his disciples in that upper room, asking God to "protect them in your name that you have given me, so that they may be one, as we are one. While I was with them, I protected them in your name that you have given me.... But now I am coming to you, and I speak these things in the world so that they may have my joy made complete in themselves." You can sense Jesus's deep desire to return to his loving Father/

Mother. Twice in this prayer he tells God, "I am coming to you," as though he can't wait to return to the holy presence. Yet he will not leave his beloved ones unprotected and alone here. He has done all he can to ensure they have access to all the love and joy he can make available.

Jesus expands his vision beyond his band of followers to all those, including you and me, who will believe in God through their words and deeds: "I ask not only on behalf of these, but also on behalf of those who will believe in me through their word."

The goal is clear: that we may all be one. "As you, Father, are in me and I am in you, may they also be in us, so that the world may believe that you have sent me. The glory that you have given me I have given them, so that they may be one, as we are one, I in them and you in me, that they may become completely one, so that the world may know that you have sent me and have loved them even as you have loved me."

Count how many times Jesus uses the word *one* in this prayer. Unity of the spirit is foremost on his heart; he wills that all of us be brought together in the unshakable, protective, and healing love relationship just as he and his Father/Mother have and always will have. *"I in them and you in me"*—this is the deep and consuming unity of love, all with the goal of sharing the love of God with one another.

Of course it is difficult to consider Jesus's relationship with his loving Parent without thinking of your own parents. A few years ago my parents died within months of each other after long, rich lives, and I deeply miss their presence. I yearn to have a conversation with them again in this world, and sometimes I will talk with them as though they can hear me. I want their advice, their comfort, their understanding and encouragement. I fondly recall their quirks, and what brought them joy and pleasure. I desire their presence.

I seem always to keep an eye out for a sign that they are watching, that they are with me. One day not long after my mother passed away, I shared with a close friend that I had noticed so many cardinals throughout that day, and that the cardinal was my mother's favorite bird. My friend wisely said, "I think your mother is sending those cardinals to you to say hello, to tell you she's thinking of you and loves you." Now every time I see a cardinal I think of that connection, especially in moments when I really need some loving reassurance.

My relationship with my late parents pales in comparison with Jesus's relationship with his heavenly Parent, which surges with passion. Jesus's prayer in that upper room goes on and on—as though he can't get enough of the loving presence of his holy Mother/Father. He yearns for wisdom, for acceptance, for closeness, for fulfillment of all that God has planned. Their love for each other is palpable, lifting itself above the pages of the Bible and weaving its way into our lives as an example of an authentically loving relationship.

Jesus Loves the Disciples

Jesus also demonstrates love for his disciples, the twelve men he gathered around him to teach through his word and example. He commissioned them to share his wisdom and works with others within their spheres of life and ultimately throughout the world—not to build an empire, but to bring all together as one loving human family: "This is my commandment, that you love one another as I have loved you" (John 15:12). It doesn't get much clearer than that. Jesus has loved his companions selflessly and limitlessly, and he commands them—and all who claim to follow him—to love one another in the same way.

The last meal Jesus shared with his disciples was saturated with love (Matthew 26:26–30; Mark 14:22–26). We remember Jesus's sacrificial love even today through the sacrament of the Eucharist, the broken bread and the wine through which Jesus offers his very life essence, his body and blood, in love. Every time we eat the bread and drink the wine, we remember him, we honor his sacrificial love for us, and we draw strength to go forth to serve in his name.

Jesus and the Beloved Disciple

Jesus expressed his love for all his disciples and longs deeply for their companionship (see Luke 22:15). But one disciple, who many assume was John, seemed to have a uniquely intimate relationship with Jesus. Numerous times in the gospel that bears his name he is referred to as "the disciple whom Jesus loved." Whether it was a close bond of love or a big brother/little brother–type relationship, John named and claimed a special relationship with Jesus.

There is a glimpse of this close connection between Jesus and this disciple during the final meal Jesus had with his disciples in the upper room (John 13:21–26). For several chapters the writer recounts what Jesus says and prays during those final evening hours together. Jesus washes his disciples' feet and explains that he is thereby giving them an example of sacrificial servant-love, the kind of love that is willing to get down and dirty to help others. Then, as he reclines with his companions at the Passover dinner table, Jesus becomes troubled in spirit and declares, "Very truly, I tell you, one of you will betray me."

A shockwave of concern trembles through the disciples gathered around the table. They look at each other, wondering who this betrayer might be. In the midst of this intense moment the writer slips in an interesting detail: "One of his disciples—the one whom Jesus loved—was reclining next to him; Simon Peter therefore motioned to him to ask Jesus of whom he was speaking. So while reclining next to Jesus, [the one whom Jesus loved] asked him, 'Lord, who is it?'" And Jesus indicates it is Judas by handing him a dipped piece of bread.

As they are dining together, during a moment heavy with emotion and confusion, the beloved disciple pulls closer to Jesus and lays his head back on his rabbi's chest. As Jesus speaks, the timbre of his voice resonates within his chest; his breath stirs the disciple's hair. The original Greek indicates that this beloved disciple "was reclining … in the bosom of Jesus" (John 13:23).

"In the bosom of Jesus." The disciple's head rests serenely on his master's chest; he trusts in his love, and rests in the safety of his easy embrace. That is a place of acceptance and safety,

a place of supreme trust and unashamed love. Author Brennan Manning captures it beautifully:

> John lays his head on the heart of God, on the breast of the Man.... Have we ever seen the human Jesus at closer range?
>
> Clearly, Jesus did not intimidate John. He was not afraid of his Lord and Master. John was deeply affected by this sacred Man....
>
> As John leans back on the breast of Jesus and listens to the heartbeat of the Great Rabbi, he comes to know Him in a way that surpasses mere cognitive knowledge. What a world of difference lies between *knowing about* someone and *knowing Him!*
>
> In a flash of intuitive understanding, John experiences Jesus as the human face of the God who is love. And in coming to know who the Great Rabbi is, John discovers who he is—*the disciple Jesus loved.*[8]

This vignette offers us a breathtaking message: Jesus welcomes our affectionate devotion. In our mind, our spirit, our heart, our innermost being, we too can express our love by resting against the bosom of our Lord, and he will not push us away. He will welcome us into his embrace. It is a symbiotic relationship of loyal love and trust, one that is true now and forever will be true. The more you can imagine it, the more you can experience it.

This is the love Jesus lived with his disciples: It was easy, honest, and clear. It was passionate without shame or restraint. Jesus expressed a wide range of emotions with his followers, but love was the foundation of them all. It was all part of the complete package of authentic emotions that Jesus felt and expressed.

Jesus Loves Mary, Martha, and Lazarus

There was a wider circle of loved ones in Jesus's life as well, including three siblings: Mary, Martha, and Lazarus. We meet them in John's gospel (11:1–44). The writer puts it simply: "Jesus loved Martha and her sister and Lazarus." The relationship between them must have been strongly forged before this account, but those details and reasons are lost to us and ignored by the gospel writers.

When the writer of John introduces them, Lazarus is sick and his sisters send word to Jesus: "Lord, the one you love is sick." Notice that: *another* person is described as "the one" Jesus loves. Oddly, Jesus hears this news and proclaims to his disciples that Lazarus's illness will not lead to death, that this is an opportunity to reveal the power of God. So he stays where he is for two more days. His behavior must have stymied the disciples, because obviously Jesus loves this man who is now dying, yet is doing nothing about it, and they know he can. Is he distracted by other matters? Is he afraid to go back to Judea because of threats of violence (see John 8:59; 10:31)? Or does he have something up his supernatural sleeve?

Eventually, Jesus announces to his disciples that they are going to Judea. He tells them, "Our friend Lazarus has fallen asleep, but I am going there to awaken him." As is typical, his disciples misunderstand what Jesus is saying. So Jesus tells them plainly, "Lazarus is dead. For your sake I am glad I was not there, so that you may believe. But let us go to him."

After a journey on foot, Jesus and his band arrive only to find that Lazarus has indeed been dead and entombed for four days. Many friends and neighbors have gathered to offer solace and support. Word reaches the siblings' house that Jesus is coming, so Martha goes to meet him outside their village; Mary—perhaps too grief-stricken and upset with their slow-to-respond so-called friend—stays home.

Martha gives Jesus a piece of her mind: "Lord, if you had been here, my brother would not have died." There is a lot of emotion in those simple words, though she continues, "But even now I know that God will give you whatever you ask of him." Perhaps Martha will give him the benefit of the doubt, but it isn't easy. Jesus explains, "Your brother will rise again." Martha takes that cryptic comment as a theological lesson about the resurrection of the body at the last days. But Jesus sets her straight: "I am the resurrection and the life," he says. This isn't a theology lesson regarding the afterlife. Jesus proclaims himself to be the power of life, the agent of renewal. *Now.* "Do you believe this?" he asks Martha. And Martha answers affirmatively, whether she truly understands what he is saying or not.

Martha runs back home to tell her sister, Mary, that the rabbi is coming. Mary quickly goes to Jesus, still outside the village. She falls at Jesus's feet, inconsolable, and she, just as her sister had, expresses her frustration and despair over Jesus's apparent carelessness.

Now Jesus is surrounded by a group of grieving people, including his beloved friends Mary and Martha. They are wailing over the untimely loss of Lazarus, who after all was "the one" Jesus loved. It seems that only then the emotion of the moment hits Jesus: "He was greatly disturbed in spirit and deeply moved." He is angry that death could cause so much sorrow in the family of humanity, and in this family whom he loved in particular.

Jesus asks where Lazarus has been laid. "Lord, come and see," they reply. Then comes one of the most powerful verses in the entire Christian Scriptures. It gathers together in two brief words all the passionate love and care and grief and even joy that Jesus feels in that moment: "Jesus wept."

Jesus has already announced to his disciples and to Martha that he would bring Lazarus back to life. Yet he begins weeping deeply, "bursting into tears," as the original text might be more accurately rendered.[9] He is feeling the love he has for this man, perhaps knowing that, even though Lazarus will be raised, it is only a temporary fix, that life will go on, that they both will die, that relationships are always only temporary, and yet above and beyond that temporary nature is a reality that lasts forever—the reality of love.

Jesus sheds the tears of a man who loves another man now dead. But perhaps he also weeps in hope, in the knowledge that death is but a temporary separation, that the love they had known would last forever. Perhaps, among the bitter tears of grief, there are also tears of joy and gratitude. Those gathered around Jesus know what he is feeling: "See how he loved him!" they whisper among themselves, for Jesus does not hide his feelings.

Jesus, "once more deeply moved," approaches the tomb where his loved one lies, a cave whose opening is closed by a large stone. He wipes the tears from his cheeks, the snot from his nose and beard, and orders the stone to be moved away. This is a shocking request—not only would it cause ritual defilement to come in contact with the dead, but as Martha points out, Lazarus has been in there four days already: "There is a stench." Jesus has to remind Martha, "Did I not tell you that if you believed, you would see the glory of God?"

The stone is moved away. Those gathered, even Jesus's friends and followers, must surely be staring at him wondering about this crazy man who may or may not, here and now, do something never before witnessed. Jesus looks up and prays to God the loving Parent. Then he cries out with a loud voice, "Lazarus, come out!" Immediately the dead man, wrapped with strips of linen like a mummy, with a cloth around his face, walks out of the tomb.

The writer doesn't record much detail here. We are left to our imaginations. Surely the crowd falls back, screaming in shock and relief. Jesus calmly instructs them, "Unbind him, and let him go." Set him free! Let him loose, back into life and love, fully and without hindrance. By doing so the community becomes part of the life-giving miracle of setting Lazarus free from death.

Jesus had fostered a strong, loving relationship with this man and his sisters. We don't know how it began, what it looked like, or how it was expressed. All we know is that Jesus took an opportunity to make clear to the people, as well as to the religious authorities, who he was and what he was about. And it centered on love, a love that forced Jesus's hand to reveal the truth about his mission. A love that caused him deep distress, that brought him to tears when it was temporarily torn apart by death. It was a passionate love.

Jesus Loves His Mother, Mary

There's relatively little information about Jesus's mother, Mary, in the gospels. Yet there are glimmers of a relationship that is unmistakably loving and also rather normal as far as mother-son relationships go, such as in the story of the wedding in Cana (John 2:1–5): "On the third day there was a wedding in Cana of Galilee, and the mother of Jesus was there. Jesus and his disciples had also been invited to the wedding. When the wine gave out, the mother of Jesus said to him, 'They have no wine.' And Jesus said to her, 'Woman, what concern is that to you and to me? My hour has not yet come.' His mother said to the servants, 'Do whatever he tells you.'"

Mary knows Jesus is special. That's clear. She has given birth to him, raised him, and guided him as all good mothers do. She has lived with Jesus for three decades. She knows he can fix the slightly embarrassing situation in which their wedding hosts find themselves. After all, he's at a party. He has just called and gathered his disciples, those who would live with him and follow him, preparing for the next step. He's come to honor the occasion of marriage, to have fun with some friends, and now this.

Notice, though, that Jesus doesn't call Mary *mother*. He calls her *woman*. There's a playfulness about this exchange that we may overlook, but there's also a deeper level to this exchange. Jesus is not being curt with her. He's simply recognizing who Mary is and who he is. He realizes that he is moving on, knowing he is about to start something new. His destiny is about to unfold, his identity about to be revealed. Mary's son is about to grow up.

Is he ready? Are his followers? Is he hesitant to step forward as someone special, someone God has sent to proclaim the way of love? Is this why Jesus tells her, "This isn't my time"?

It doesn't appear as though Mary pays much attention to his rebuff. The very next moment she's instructing the servants, "Do whatever he tells you." Before you know it, perhaps because of a mother's loving nudge, Jesus performs his first public miracle, transforming earthenware jugs of water into carafes of the finest wine.

Mary knows, trusts, and loves her son, and she is aware of what he has come to do. And, certainly, so is Jesus. He is ready to unleash God's miraculous love on a world that needs it. He is prepared to fulfill his purpose: to share a new way of life that will change all the rules—even those of physics, medicine, and theology.

Cana is the place where Jesus finds himself ready to pour out the wine of divine love into the world, and into each one of us, through his death. But without the faith and guidance of his mother—and that loving nudge—what might have happened?

Time and again Jesus brings people together in loving relationships, in families of faith that go beyond the routine. We see this at the cross when, breathing his final breaths, he tells the beloved disciple that Mary is his mother, and tells Mary that this disciple is her son (John 19:25–27). In doing so, he encourages us to love a woman as we would our mother, to love a young man as we would a son or a brother.

When we accept Jesus's invitations to enter into loving relationships like these, we create a home of loving care and nurture that can heal our lonely wounds, fill our empty hearts, water our dry souls. Indeed, we forge a bond of care that compels us to expand the boundaries of our homes to welcome still more in, even those who are different from us. In Jesus we are brought together, our hearts bound as one in God's love.

Jesus Loves a Stranger

Jesus surely loved his friends and family, and yet Jesus is also said to "love" a stranger, someone with whom he apparently had no regular contact, perhaps didn't even know at all.

The gospels of Matthew, Mark, and Luke recount a very similar story about a man—Luke says he was a ruling official of sorts, but in all cases a person of means—who approaches Jesus with a question. Addressing Jesus as "Good Teacher," the man asks what he must do to inherit eternal life. Jesus answers his question rather straightforwardly: follow the commandments. The man responds, "Teacher, I have kept all these since my youth" (Mark 10:17–31).

Here Mark adds an interesting tidbit not found in the later accounts, perhaps because it is so peculiar: "Jesus, looking at him, loved him...." There is a clear intentionality to Jesus's gaze. Jesus pauses during this casual conversation between himself and a man who seems so intent on doing what's right, and looks deep into the stranger's eyes and down into his soul. And that gaze causes him to love the man.

Perhaps in looking Jesus could understand how difficult true discipleship can be to someone who possesses authority and wealth—as it can be even to those who do not. Perhaps Jesus could see how desperately the man wanted to follow him, and yet the responsibilities of his life kept forcing him to the sidelines. Whatever Jesus saw deep within the man's soul, his passionate response was to love him with unselfish, caring love.

In doing so, Jesus sees the man's problem, the issue that would trip up the freedom of heart and spirit that would enable him to love in the same way: "You lack one thing; go, sell what you own, and give the money to the poor, and you will have treasure in heaven; then come, follow me."

It doesn't seem fair: The man has carefully obeyed all the commandments. He has not murdered, committed adultery, stolen, or lied, and despite his potentially lucrative position of authority he has not cheated anyone. He could check off all Ten Commandments as proof that he is wholly acceptable to God. But looking deeper, gazing intensely into his soul, Jesus sees the spiritual blockage in the man's heart.

Regrettably for the man, this is a blockage that remains too huge to move: "When he heard this, he was shocked and went away grieving, for he had many possessions." The man realizes with astonishment the unalterable selfishness of his own heart, and it devastates him.

Jesus uses this encounter as a teaching moment with his disciples, showing them how hard it is for those who possess wealth to enter God's reign. This revelation astounds the disciples and they exclaim, "Then who can be saved?" If this man—who is obedient and humble, who clearly knows the ways of God and even honors Jesus—can't do it, who possibly can?

That's when Jesus holds out some hope: "For mortals it is impossible, but not for God; for God all things are possible." In other words, we ourselves can never get to the place where we live in a way that fully and passionately reflects God's values, God's love and care for all. As much as we struggle to follow Jesus, we simply cannot do it on our own. Only with the loving Spirit of God within us can we come anywhere near that goal.

What if that wealthy young man, whom Jesus "loved," had heard this? Would he have had some hope? Or was his dependence on wealth and position so deep-rooted that he could never ultimately come to a place of surrender to the ways of God?

Following Jesus authentically costs us everything. Every prop we have to hold up our ego must be kicked out from under us. Every safety net we have carefully woven around us to ensure our security, our position, and our identity must be cut, so that we fall naked into God's arms, clutching nothing in our rigid grasp, but opening our whole being to God's love and will for us.

How have we responded to Jesus's call to let go of everything we grasp desperately to give us what we thought was meaning and purpose in life? What is it about our identity that we have relentlessly held on to despite the fact that we know deep down that it is false, and that we have carefully constructed to protect ourselves, even though it keeps us from fully knowing or being known by someone else?

Jesus looks hard into our eyes: What does he see that is holding us back? He is looking at us with eyes of love, the deepest, most sincere, most authentic love. What does he see?

I have known many people who, when confronted by Jesus about the "one thing" that is keeping them from experiencing God's liberating, loving reign in their lives, did not go away in grief, but instead listened to Jesus and let go. You know people like that, too. Perhaps it is a call to show love to a special stranger, or to reach out to someone who is outcast and in need.

Perhaps it is a call to tear down the self-protective walls of a false identity and let God liberate you.

Too many people turn away from the opportunity to grow and serve, and they walk away in grief because their assumptions were wrong or their expectations weren't met. For many who turn from Jesus's way, the "one thing" is a theological or biblical tenet they simply can't get beyond despite the Spirit's prodding. Jesus invites us all into a life of lovingly serving others, but too many of us find excuses that may even sound "righteous" and avoid answering the call with holy abandonment. The only way that will change is if we surrender to the love of God.

How Jesus Receives Love

Both the giving and the receiving of love are vitally important aspects of experiencing this emotion authentically and passionately. We need this continuing ebb and flow of love in our lives to experience wholeness, so we need to know how to accept and embrace the loving words and gestures that are offered to us, as Jesus did.

One of the most moving expressions of loving service in the Bible is recorded in three of the four gospels: a woman lovingly pours precious oil on Jesus's feet, washing them not only with aromatic oil but also with her hair and her tears. It's unclear whether these three accounts (Matthew 26:6–13, Luke 7:36–50, and John 12:1–8) are variations on the same experience or separate occasions involving different women.

We'll explore Luke's account, where the occasion is a dinner at the home of Simon the Pharisee, a religious leader who apparently was intrigued by Jesus's bold teachings. "And a woman in the city, who was a sinner, having learned that [Jesus] was eating in the Pharisee's house, brought an alabaster jar of ointment. She stood behind him at his feet, weeping, and began to bathe his feet with her tears and to dry them with her hair. Then she continued kissing his feet and anointing them with the ointment."

Notice that she "began" and "continued" the loving ablutions, which must have gone on for some time as the woman softly weeps in response to the hope of freedom and purpose that Jesus has offered, knowing her need for cleansing. She desires to show Jesus that he has made a deep impact on her soul, far beyond what other men have done with her.

Notice Jesus's response: Jesus quietly, patiently, willingly lets the woman perform her intimate and sacrificial service, accepting it with understanding and appreciation. He doesn't stop the act out of embarrassment or propriety, and no inappropriate limit is crossed. He doesn't hurry it up. He lets it play out. He seems to enjoy it and to appreciate the depth of meaning behind it. He doesn't seem concerned at all about what others may think. He revels in the lavish, loving attention.

Can you imagine the shock and discomfort among the dinner guests? Jesus's host, witnessing this scandalous scene in his own righteous home, says to himself under his breath, "If this man were a prophet, he would have known who and what kind of woman this is who is touching him—that she is a sinner."

Jesus knows this woman's story; he can likely see it etched on her face. He knows what has happened in this woman's heart, a change that has emboldened her to express her love for Jesus perhaps in the only way she knew how. Jesus overhears his host's muttering and tells Simon he has something to say. But rather than blast Simon for his small-minded, sanctimonious assumptions, he tells a story; the impact is even more powerful.

"A certain creditor had two debtors; one owed five hundred denarii, and the other fifty. When they could not pay, he canceled the debts for both of them. Now which of them will love him more?" Simon answers, "I suppose the one for whom he canceled the greater debt." And Jesus says to him, "You have judged rightly." Jesus lets Simon come to the natural conclusion that her actions, though stunning in their boldness, are simply her way to express the vast love she has for the one who has set her free.

Then Jesus tenderly turns toward the woman and says to Simon, with a much clearer message: "Do you see this woman? I entered your house; you gave me no water for my feet, but she has bathed my feet with her tears and dried them with her hair.

You gave me no kiss, but from the time I came in she has not stopped kissing my feet. You did not anoint my head with oil, but she has anointed my feet with ointment. Therefore, I tell you, her sins, which were many, have been forgiven; hence she has shown great love. But the one to whom little is forgiven, loves little."

The woman's love for Jesus is great because she has been so detached from true love for so long. She has been living a life that was not her own; it was inauthentic, unnatural, unfulfilling, dishonest, and as far from truly loving as one can get. But, attracted by the liberating message of Jesus and by the challenge of following him in the reign of God, she has sought forgiveness and cleansing, and receives it wholly. She demonstrates her love for Jesus viscerally, wholeheartedly, without holding back. And Jesus accepts it in the very same way.

Then Jesus gently turns up her tear-streaked, emotion-swollen face to look deeply in her dark eyes—eyes that have seen so much of life's degradation and emptiness. He says with loving clarity, "Your sins are forgiven…. Your faith has saved you; go in peace."

How powerfully she must have felt those gracious words wash over her soul. In the midst of the grace-filled interaction, however, the others who are there—likely other religious leaders and their cronies—begin to mutter among themselves, "Who is this who even forgives sins?" They miss the entire point of the encounter because of their shortsighted, loveless beliefs. They can't get over the authority Jesus possesses and the way he expresses it: in love without limits. Tragically, they are offended by the authentic giving and receiving of liberated love.

What Jesus Teaches about Love

Jesus's teaching is saturated with love. He continually speaks to the crowds of God's love for them, urging them to respond in loving, sacrificial service.

One night Jesus has an illuminating conversation with Nicodemus, a religious leader who is curious about Jesus's teachings and comes to him secretly (John 3:1–21). Jesus tells him one can only see the kingdom of God by being born from above, born of water and Spirit.

Seeing Nicodemus's confusion about this teaching, Jesus clarifies the meaning of his own words: "For God so loved the world that he gave his only Son, so that everyone who believes in him may not perish but have eternal life." God reveals God's love for all of us by sending Jesus to show the way to whole, meaningful, everlasting life. "Indeed," Jesus continues, "God did not send the Son into the world to condemn the world, but in order that the world might be saved through him."

Jesus is revealing the ways of God, inviting us to enter into a life of love forever. This invitation arises from God's generous, self-giving love. God's very reality was enfolded in human flesh and offered to us all in order that we might learn how to live a life of meaning and purpose—a life of self-giving love like Jesus's—forever. Notice, too, that in this beloved passage Jesus is careful to point out that he comes not to condemn or judge the people of the world, but to rescue them from their own self-centeredness and self-destruction. It's all about love.

The First Commandment

An interaction with the religious elite in Mark 12:28–34 clarifies the heart of Jesus's teaching. Feeling threatened, the hypocritical religious leaders surround him after he has been teaching at the temple and attempt to trap him into implicating himself by uttering false claims regarding his own identity and mission. As they argue and dispute with him, a scribe hears Jesus's wise answers and asks him, "Which commandment is the first of all?"

Quoting key texts in the Hebrew Scriptures, including the *Shema*, Jesus answers, "The first is, 'Hear, O Israel: the Lord our God, the Lord is one; you shall love the Lord your God with all your heart, and with all your soul, and with all your mind, and with all your strength.' The second is this, 'You shall love your neighbor as yourself.' There is no other commandment greater than these."

The scribe—who may or may not have been testing Jesus in the same way as the other religious leaders were—responds, "You are right, Teacher; you have truly said that 'he is one, and besides him there is no other'; and 'to love him with all the heart, and with all the understanding, and with all the strength,' and 'to love one's neighbor as oneself,'—this is much more important than all whole burnt offerings and sacrifices." Recognizing the scribe's wisdom, Jesus replies, perhaps with a chuckle, "You are not far from the kingdom of God." He has gotten a scribe, part of the self-protective religious elite, to make his very point. And as a result, "After that no one dared to ask him any question."

In a similar story in Luke 10:25–37, one of the religious experts on the law stands up "to test Jesus," asking him, "What must I do to inherit eternal life?" Jesus points to the Jewish law to love God with heart, soul, strength, and mind, and your neighbor as yourself. "Do this, and you will live."

But this lawyer doesn't give up; he pushes the issue: "And who is my neighbor?" In response Jesus tells a parable that would have angered these leaders, because the hero is a Samaritan—one of their religious enemies whom they considered religiously inferior. And the villains include a priest and a Levite, men of their own class.

A man, Jesus says, is attacked by robbers and left for dead. The priest and the Levite avoid the grievously wounded man lying on the roadside, but a Samaritan stops and cares for him, taking him to an inn to heal and paying for his stay. Then Jesus asks the contentious lawyer, "Which of these three, do you think, was a neighbor to the man who fell into the hands of the robbers?" The man replies, "The one who showed him mercy." And Jesus tells him, "Go and do likewise."

That's how you love your neighbor as yourself. Although the parable makes no mention of love, the Samaritan acts with loving care for his neighbor, binding his wounds, carrying him to a doctor, and even paying for the victim's care. This is the kind of love Jesus calls for. It is sacrificial; it costs us. It is active no matter what the circumstances. This kind of love does not base its actions on the identity of those in need. We are to care for them regardless of their circumstances, their identity, or their physical and emotional states of being.

Love Your Enemies

Jesus also taught that we are not to pay back our enemies according to what they do to us. Rather, we are to love them no matter what (Luke 6:27–36). "But I say to you that listen, Love your enemies, do good to those who hate you, bless those who curse you, pray for those who abuse you. If anyone strikes you on the cheek, offer the other also; and from anyone who takes away your coat do not withhold even your shirt. Give to everyone who begs from you; and if anyone takes away your goods, do not ask for them again. Do to others as you would have them do to you."

Such a teaching must have shocked the listening crowd; perhaps some even laughed at it. Who could do such things? Jesus's way of love is utterly counter to the ways of the world. He sets the bar for a fulfilling life of love far higher than we might set it.

Jesus explains why he encourages this radical lifestyle: "If you love those who love you, what credit is that to you? For even sinners love those who love them. If you do good to those who do good to you, what credit is that to you? For even sinners do the same." In other words, our loving those who love us is only natural. But Jesus calls us to a higher, a supernatural love: "Love your enemies, do good, and lend, expecting nothing in return. Your reward will be great, and you will be children of the Most High; for he is kind to the ungrateful and the wicked. Be merciful, just as your Father is merciful." We are to live as merciful people, as loved and loving people, following the example of Jesus.

Love One Another

In John 13–17, Jesus offers his disciples exquisite words of love in his final teachings in the upper room. Cynthia Bourgeault sets the scene: "With his betrayal and arrest imminent, Jesus gathers his disciples one last time to share his final instructions.

What flows forth from this moment is an extraordinary series of teachings whose entire message is of love brought to its glorious fruition. These discourses contain, first and foremost, some of Jesus' most beautiful descriptions of indwelling love."[10]

Jesus knows the end is coming, and the love in his heart gushes for those who have sacrificed much for him, and who would endure much for the reign of God in the days to come. The gospel writer observes, "Having loved his own who were in the world, he loved them to the end." Jesus opens his heart to them completely, in every way, revealing the full extent of his love.

After washing his disciples' feet in a sacrificial display of caring concern, he begins sharing with his companions about the love that drives his works, his teachings, and his very life: "I give you a new commandment, that you love one another. Just as I have loved you, you also should love one another. By this everyone will know that you are my disciples, if you have love for one another."

Love characterizes everyone who follows the way of Jesus, and those who wish to follow Jesus into passionate living will follow his teachings: "Those who love me will keep my word, and my Father will love them, and we will come to them and make our home with them." It's a beautiful image of the relationship between us and our loving God. Those who love Jesus are those who are loved by God, and God will dwell within them.

Jesus's words of love continue to pour forth, comforting and strengthening his weary and worried disciples: "As the Father has loved me, so I have loved you; abide in my love. If you keep my commandments, you will abide in my love, just as I have kept my Father's commandments and abide in his love.... This is my commandment, that you love one another as I have loved you." If we live according to Jesus's command to love, we can rest forever in his love.

Knowing the fate that awaits him, Jesus speaks of the depth of his love for his friends: "No one has greater love than this, to lay down one's life for one's friends." The love Jesus commands us to share is sacrificial and costly, but it lasts forever.

Jesus explains what his friends are about to endure, and why. He closes with an intimate and luminous prayer to his loving God. In praying for his disciples, he also includes us in his prayer: "I ask not only on behalf of these, but also on behalf of those who will believe in me through their word, that they may all be one. As you, Father, are in me and I am in you, may they also be in us, so that the world may believe that you have sent me. The glory that you have given me I have given them, so that they may be one, as we are one, I in them and you in me, that they may become completely one, so that the world may know that you have sent me and have loved them even as you have loved me."

Even as Jesus anticipates his death, his words are breathtakingly intimate and overwhelming with love: "I in them and you in me, that they may become completely one," with the goal that through our love the world may experience the love God has for each of us, which is as full and rich as God's love for Jesus.

Do You Love Me?

After his resurrection, Jesus appears a third time to most of the disciples as they are fishing at the Sea of Tiberias (John 21:1–19). A beleaguered Peter is ready to go back to his fishing, and his friends go with him. They sail out into the night but catch no fish.

As dawn breaks over the horizon, the disciples see a man standing on the beach. He calls to them, "Children, you have no fish, have you?" These grizzled, hardy "children"—a term of warm affection—answer him grumpily, "No." The man on the shore yells for them to cast their fishing nets on the right side of their boat. When they do, they are unable to haul in the load of fish that fills the nets.

"The disciple whom Jesus loved" realizes who the man is, and tells Peter, "It is the Lord!" The disciples quickly bring the boat to shore, and as they arrive they find that Jesus has built a charcoal fire and is preparing breakfast. When Jesus asks them for some of the fish they have caught, Peter pulls the heavy net ashore; in spite of its huge load of large fish, the net does not tear.

They all gather around. "Jesus came and took the bread and gave it to them, and did the same with the fish." This meal is a glorious counterpart to the last meal of bread and wine they shared with Jesus before his death. Now it is time for nourishment for the new day.

After breakfast, Jesus has a riveting personal conversation with Peter, who no doubt carries a heavy burden of guilt and grief after denying even knowing Jesus while his rabbi was being questioned and ultimately put to death (John 18:15–18; 18:25–27). Jesus asks him, "Simon son of John, do you love me more than these?" Peter replies, "Yes, Lord; you know that I love you." In the Greek, *agape* is the word for love that Jesus utters, while *phileo* is the word for love that Peter uses, referring to the mutual relationship of friends; Peter cannot bring himself to use the same word for love as Jesus has after failing his master so miserably. Yet Jesus says simply, "Feed my lambs," encouraging Peter to serve the children of God.

But then Jesus repeats the question: "Simon son of John, do you love me?" And Peter replies, "Yes, Lord; you know that I love you." Again they use different verbs for "love." Again Jesus challenges Peter to serve his sheep.

Finally, in a reflection of Peter's three earlier denials, Jesus asks him a third time, "Simon son of John, do you love me?" Here the writer observes, "Peter felt hurt because he said to him the third time, 'Do you love me?'" Jesus is not making this easy. Peter blurts out in his pain, "Lord, you know everything; you know that I love you." So, Jesus tells him again, "Feed my sheep." This time, the word *phileo* appears in both Jesus's and Peter's response to each other—and this may emphasize Peter's shameful hurt, for Jesus has in a subtle way lowered the standard regarding the love he asks of Peter. Even so, Jesus then encourages Peter by indicating that he knows Peter's faith would become so strong that he would ultimately die a martyr's death for his rabbi.

And then in this teaching moment, his voice no doubt filled with love for his very human friend, Jesus says, "Follow me." Jesus is offering this failed disciple another chance, giving him a new invitation to live as Jesus lived by sacrificially serving others, and to love as Jesus loved by tending his sheep and feeding his lambs. We can only imagine the healing relief and joy that filled Peter's heart.

Love is clearly the centerpiece, the heart, of life for Jesus, and he invites those who wish to live fully and authentically to follow him in the passionate way of love.

Living in Love

We've considered only a few of the many rich examples of love revealed in the gospels: Jesus loves his Father/Mother. Jesus loves the disciples upon whom he chose to personally impress his way. Jesus loves a stranger whose heart is tender, but who wrestles with the tough choices of real life. Jesus loves his mother even to the very end.

And as you think back through these examples, consider *how* Jesus shared his love:

Jesus's love is uninhibited and freely shared. You know he loves you simply from his gaze, his touch, his words, his warmth, his very presence.

Jesus's love is actively expressed—with acts of service, with healing, with sacrifice. It means something. It isn't merely an emotion felt; it is an action fulfilled.

Jesus's love is authentic, real, and trustworthy. There is no doubt, no uncertainty. He doesn't offer his love with ulterior motives. His love is clean, clear, and true.

Jesus's love is forever, from the beginning of time to the end of infinity. Unwavering. Unshakable. Undiminished. Eternal.

So what sort of love does Jesus call us to experience and share throughout the gospels? We have seen that this love involves compassionately serving anyone who is in need. It involves actively doing good to everyone, even our enemies. It involves avoiding the self-approving judgment of others who are different. It involves forgiveness and reconciliation. It involves sharing all our resources with those with whom we live in community.

But this love is more than that. As we have seen in the gospels, Jesus possesses a heart of love full to bursting. He wholly knows the character of God, and he knows that all men and women are made in God's image. Out of that knowledge flows a love that must be expressed, given away, multiplied.

The basis for Jesus's entire ministry was a sacrificial, healing love for others deeply rooted in the Jewish understanding of God's compassion for all who are created in God's image. This sort of love is not a general, ethereal, otherworldly love for all humanity; it is a genuine love for each person Jesus encountered, because Jesus saw his or her infinite value in God's heart.

It is not enough to know whom and how Jesus loved, or what he taught about love. It is not even enough to accept the reality that Jesus loves us even now. This love is not a one-way street. It must have an outlet. We must follow Jesus's example in expressing our holy love passionately, in sharing it, receiving it, and living in and through it.

Think about how you share love with those in your circles of life. Your lover. Your family. Your friends. Your colleagues. Your fellow congregants. Your neighbors. Strangers on the street. On and on in outwardly rippling circles. How free and uninhibited and healing is your love? How actively and sacrificially is it given? How authentic and real and trustworthy is it? How long will it last? In short, what kind of love is Jesus passionately calling all of us to experience and share?

This kind of love is sacrificial and giving; it is meant to build up the other person, not to use him or her for some ulterior selfish purposes. It involves caring and serving. It is passionate and holy work. It is not mere romance or friendship, or any of our culture's weak and empty fabrications of love. We must know in our hearts that this love is the most genuine reality in the universe.

This kind of love demands honesty and authenticity. It is expressed fully and openly without holding back. As a result, it can overturn cherished notions and practices. It offers a revolutionary way of life, of putting aside self for others, for the common good, for Jesus's sake.

This kind of love puts us together into families of faith. Jesus brought people together to love and support and teach and learn from one another, to serve one another no matter what. Jesus puts people together in loving relationships that go beyond the routine and the expected. Our Jesus-like love is multiplied exponentially when it is channeled through families of faith, our congregations, our efforts to serve, our important relationships.

This kind of love costs us everything. Jesus demands all—every part of us—not that we become imprisoned by standards of behavior we don't want to or can't fulfill. Rather, Jesus frees us to become all we were created to be. He enables us to engage life passionately at every level, even when we know that such engagement often involves tremendous risk. Ultimately we are in God's hands, but the traditional, worldly understanding of safety and security—often involving wealth and possessions—evaporates in the loving will of God.

This kind of love is radiated through our every word and deed. In Jesus's case, his love colors every emotion he felt and expressed, even his anger and fear. Love is the foundation of all the other passions. Love seeps into every breath he took, every gesture he made, every word he spoke, and it can do so with us as well.

We can follow Jesus's example of selfless, sacrificial, authentic love. We can gratefully, with understanding and appreciation, accept that kind of healing love when it is shared with us.

We can find ourselves in the big picture of eternity and universality, part of the web of loving care God has spread throughout all existence.

We can live in love forever.

EXPLORING EMOTIONS: LOVE

Have you ever felt unloved? What was the cause? Do you recall how lonesome, perhaps desperate, you felt? Can you identify individuals in your community, your workplace, your religious community who are unloved? What would it mean for you to love those individuals as Jesus loves us?

Can you recall a time when you failed in love? Has a lover ever failed you? How did you learn to love again?

Have you ever fallen out of love with God? What was the cause? Have you found your way back to God's full embrace? How did that happen, or how do you think it might happen?

When was the last time you embraced lovingly an enemy or an unlovely and unloving person? What would enable you to embrace that person?

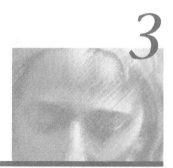

3

Anger
In Defense of Justice

As a journalism major in college, I worked in a variety of ways on the daily campus newspaper. While I took news writing and editing classes, I was also the staff editorial cartoonist, a job I loved, and earned money by pasting up ads for the paper, a job that no longer exists thanks to computerization. One semester when I was the features editor, I helped put the paper together every night so that bundles could be delivered around campus the next morning.

Our editor-in-chief that year was an earnest, bespectacled, bearded young man with definite opinions on just about everything. He and the entertainment reporter frequently butted heads. Their personalities were like oil and water, or perhaps kindling and matches.

One evening the entertainment reporter had written a rather negative review of a controversial performer of the day, submitting it as usual for the editor-in-chief's approval. As I was busy finalizing the features page in the paste-up area, I glanced at the editor, who was ensconced in his glass-walled office adjacent to the large newsroom, bustling with the sounds of people talking and the clatter of electric typewriters.

The editor called the entertainment reporter into his office, and almost immediately we in the newsroom could see through the editor's windows that they were arguing with furious gestures and red faces. Finally, we watched in surprise as the editor ripped the reporter's carefully typed story into shreds in front of the reporter's enraged face; this was in the days when you couldn't simply reprint a typed document.

The entertainment reporter stormed out of the office into the newsroom, and we could almost see the steam blowing out of his ears. He stood staring off into the distance for a moment, muttering to himself. Suddenly, he grabbed one of the heavy electric typewriters from a nearby desk, yanked its plug out of the socket, and threw it through the huge glass window right at the editor, who saw it coming and jumped out of the way.

The sudden cacophony of the shattering glass and the typewriter's impact on the editor's desk startled the wits out of everyone in the newsroom. An eerie quiet descended as we stared in shock at the entertainment reporter, who collapsed to the floor and lay there in a catatonic stupor. Several of us rushed to check on him, and ultimately an ambulance team took him away while the rest of us, the stunned editor included, tried to make some sense of what had happened. Needless to say, the entertainment reporter lost his position.

What causes people to explode in anger like that?

When we read the gospels with open eyes, we're often quite surprised to find Jesus getting angry, even expressing his anger in an explosive way himself. In our study of the anger of the passionate Jesus, we'll discover whom Jesus was angry with, and how he expressed that anger. We'll see how he responded to anger, and what he taught about it. Finally, we'll learn how we can live more authentically as passionate followers of God's way, expressing our anger in authentic but safe ways for all the right reasons and none of the wrong ones.

What Is Anger?

We are surrounded by anger in our society: vicious arguments about political and moral views on radio and cable news programs; honking horns and rude gestures on a traffic-choked freeway, sometimes leading to road rage; mean-spirited, rude, and sometimes anonymous comments blowing up on your Facebook page, Twitter feed, or blog; a silly disagreement with a family member, coworker, or even a loved one which suddenly becomes fueled by deep stress or fear and ignites into a nearly violent altercation.

What is anger? Where does it come from? What does it mean? More importantly, how can we identify it, evaluate it, and deal with these feelings in constructive ways? And how can Jesus help us do that?

Aaron Ben-Ze'ev, codirector of the Center for Interdisciplinary Research on Emotions at the University of Haifa, Israel, offers this definition: Anger is "a specific negative emotional attitude toward another agent who is considered to have inflicted unjustified harm upon us." Anger can be caused by a belief that the object of anger "has committed a blameworthy act; a perceived threat to something of value to the subject; a belief that the object's act has undesirable consequences for the subject; a belief that the object deserves to be punished."[1]

Anger has been called the combative emotion. It is "an explosive liberation of psychical force,"[2] which in the moment it hits us can pull us out of our normal self. Anger can be a dangerous emotion, even evil in its destructiveness. It can confuse our judgment and our understanding of reality. When we are in the grip of anger we rarely see clearly and often miss the big picture of what's happening.

In religious circles, some pastors and teachers consider anger sinful, an overwhelming feeling that must be quenched, presumably in spiritual ways. Psychologists, on the other hand, suggest that releasing anger is healthy in a variety of circumstances, and feeling angry is no reason necessarily to feel guilty.[3]

Yet there's a category of anger that we must also recognize: righteous anger. Such anger can give us courage to do what we might otherwise not be able to do, helping us to overcome the paralysis of fear. It can fuel outspokenness to rebuke evil or injustice, giving force to reproaches that otherwise we'd keep to ourselves or simply mumble in complaint.

In his classic devotional work on the emotions of Jesus, Robert Law writes, "Like all natural emotions, anger is in itself neither good nor bad. It is merely a force, a gunpowder of the soul which, according as it is directed, may blast away the obstructions of evil, or defend us from temptation as with a wall of fire, or which again may work devastating injury in our own and in other lives."[4]

In Jewish culture and writings anger plays an important role in the lives of righteous believers. Whether this emotion is good or evil depends on the object. While Jews often thought that anger toward evil or injustice was appropriate, they believed that anger against fellow humans was never justified.[5]

As seminary professor and author Walter Hansen explains, "Anger is fire. When it burns destructively, it harms and destroys life. But the anger of Jesus kindles a flame within us that warms and restores life."[6] It's no wonder that we're often confused when it comes to sorting through our emotional anger to determine when it is destructive and when it is restorative. When and how is it right to express anger? How do we respond to anger that is directed at us? How do we experience and express this emotion authentically? We look to Jesus's life and teachings to gain insight into such questions.

Jesus occasionally expresses frustration, if not fury, toward his companions, yet without ever losing control. Jesus's anger also flashes against temptation, and thunders especially against the sanctimonious and hypocritical formalism of the religious elite of his day, who, furious and indignant over his teachings and his followers, constantly rebuke Jesus; these same leaders eventually execute Jesus in their outrage over his assertion of religious authority.

Such contentiousness starts during one of the earliest experiences of his ministry, when Jesus is just beginning in his hometown to pursue his destiny.

Lighting a Fire

During a gathering in a synagogue one Sabbath in his own hometown of Nazareth, Jesus reads from the prophet Isaiah, provoking an immediate reaction from his audience (Luke 4:16–30). In what is essentially his first sermon, he boldly declares his mission. Friends and family surround him, and you'd think he would cultivate their support as he starts out on his ministry of spiritual liberation.

Not Jesus. He sets the tone for his prophetic ministry by shaming even those who have known him for years for their parochial, hypocritical, and shortsighted ways. He declares that he himself is the fulfillment of Isaiah's prophecy: God's Spirit is upon him as he has been anointed to bring good news to the poor, to release those in captivity, to heal the blind and set the oppressed free, and to proclaim the year of the Lord's favor. In response, his angry relatives and neighbors try to throw him off a cliff.

That's just the beginning, though. Time after time throughout the gospels, Jesus challenges the authorities and openly flaunts religious customs and practices and sometimes even the law of God. He drives the elite crazy by spending time with and showing favor to drunks, prostitutes, tax collectors, and other "sinners." He boldly welcomes women, who were certainly second-class citizens at the time, to follow him and engage fully in his mission. He questions assumptions and challenges the status quo, and as a result he is the target of anger and rage from those in authority.

Let's unpack the anger in the gospels and see what we can learn.

How Jesus Experiences Anger

Jesus's anger is multifaceted, just as ours can be. Sometimes he rages, particularly at religious hypocrisy and greed. Other times he is simply frustrated or miffed at his disciples, or even at his parents. He also expresses fiery wrath over evil in the world as well as over death and its impact on those he loves. The way Jesus expresses anger varies from circumstance to circumstance, from encounter to encounter. The more aware we become of his emotional expressions, the more human and accessible Jesus becomes to us. And the more Jesus reveals the character of God.

At His Parents ·

One of the few early accounts of the young Jesus is found in Luke 2:41–52. The twelve-year-old Jesus and his parents make their customary pilgrimage to Jerusalem for the Passover festival. Afterwards Mary and Joseph start to return home, but Jesus stays behind without their knowing it; they simply assume he is part of the large group of travelers with whom they are journeying. A day later when they begin looking for him among their family and friends on the road, they fail to find him anywhere.

As a parent, I can certainly imagine their panic over missing their son for so long. It takes them three long days before they find him in the temple in Jerusalem, sitting with amazed teachers, "listening to them and asking them questions." Mary and Joseph's anxious fear quickly turns to anger: "When his parents saw him they were astonished; and his mother said to him, 'Child, why have you treated us like this? Look, your father and I have been searching for you in great anxiety.'"

Jesus in frustration scolds his parents: "Why were you searching for me? Did you not know that I must be in my Father's house?" Mary and Joseph must have been hurt by Jesus's startling rebuke. Yet Jesus is honest in his response. Frustrated by his parents' interruption of his time with the teachers in the temple, Jesus felt that they should have known why he was sitting with his teachers.

Even at an early age Jesus's mission is manifest to him, and he will not be sidetracked from it, even by his parents. Yet this account in Luke 2 ends with an important comment: "And Jesus increased in wisdom and in years, and in divine and human favor." As he grew older, Jesus became even wiser. He may have astonished the synagogue teachers and his parents with his wisdom as a boy, but he kept growing, not only in age but also in wisdom and knowledge, just as we must if we are to avoid spiritual, emotional, and intellectual stagnation.

The young Jesus most likely exhibited childish behaviors and immature thoughts, perhaps even some bad attitudes, which he had to overcome as he matured. When Jesus was pummeled by the needs of the crowds, or devastated by the ignorance of his followers, or exasperated by the attacks of the authorities, especially when he was exhausted by his ministry, his patience must have been tried. He may have snapped in anger even at a loved one from time to time. Like all of us, his temper may have occasionally gotten the better of him, and he no doubt regretted some outbursts.

At Evil

As Jesus prepares to launch his ministry, God's Spirit leads him into the wilderness, where he is tempted by Satan, who is evil incarnate (Matthew 4:1–11). Anger and conflict characterize their exchange.

Jesus's purpose in the wilderness is to cleanse himself physically, emotionally, and spiritually as he begins his work. So, during his time in the desert Jesus refuses to eat any food for forty days and nights, and as a result is ravenously hungry and easy prey for temptation when the evil one appears. The "tempter" doesn't give up on his goal of derailing and distracting Jesus from his mission. Three times he suggests that Jesus prove his divine identity, even offering him all the kingdoms of the world in return for his allegiance. But Jesus responds with anger clearly in his voice: "Away with you, Satan! For it is written, 'Worship the Lord your God, and serve only him.'"

This story conveys the certainty of Jesus's authority and the gravity of his mission. It also portrays a Jesus who expresses anger in response to this skillful attempt to lure him into doing things the easy way, or by shifting his allegiance to the ways of the world. Jesus knows his mission, and he knows the source of his wisdom and strength. It is God alone whom Jesus is determined to serve, and his anger gives him strength to stand up against temptation, to carry on and fulfill his mission of love and mercy.

In another account from early in his ministry, Jesus expresses anger at demons, presumed to be the minions of Satan, who plague individuals in insidious and harmful ways (Mark 1:21–28). He comes to Capernaum and teaches in the synagogue on the Sabbath. Suddenly a man with an "unclean spirit" in their midst cries out against Jesus. Recognizing the source of Jesus's strength, these fearful demons realize that Jesus has come to set things right and send them to their ultimate doom. The demon challenges Jesus: "I know who you are, the Holy One of God."

Jesus is not happy about this demonic revelation. No doubt those around him in the synagogue assume the speaker is crazy and merely babbling, but there is truth in what he says. So Jesus rebukes him, commanding the spirit to come out of the man. The response is violent, and with a loud cry the evil spirit obeys Jesus's command.

Jesus is angry not only with the demon inhabiting the man, but also with the loss of control over his message. Jesus knows there are important people who will not like the ways that he will challenge them. Jesus is beginning a ministry of redemption and liberation for the oppressed, but talk like this, revealing his identity as the "Holy One of God," could get him in deep trouble with the establishment.

At Those Who Need Healing

We see flashes of Jesus's anger toward those with whom you'd think Jesus would be compassionate rather than angry. In Mark 1:40–45, Jesus encounters a man with a skin disease the writer calls leprosy. He must have been a hideous sight and, like others who suffered such ailments, was kept separated from the rest of the society. He no doubt lived a life of excruciating loneliness.

The man approaches Jesus, kneeling before him and begging. He tells Jesus in words tinged with faith, humility, and deference, "If you choose, you can make me clean." The writer observes that Jesus is "moved with pity," stretches out his hand, touches the man, and heals him immediately.

However, there is a textual question here to consider. While most ancient manuscripts of this gospel use a Greek word, *splanchnistheis*, which several modern translations render "moved with pity or compassion," some older manuscripts have a different Greek word, *orgistheis*, which other translations render "becoming angry." Jesus becomes angry with a man who approaches him humbly and begs for his healing touch? That doesn't quite fit with the conventional portrayal of Jesus as loving and compassionate. Thus, most English translations prefer the version that presents Jesus as compassionate, even though the earlier manuscripts portrayed Jesus as becoming angry in this instance.

Why might the leper have moved Jesus to anger? Was it a flash of annoyance at being interrupted in his schedule? After all, Mark reported in the passage prior to this one that Jesus had set out on a mission to proclaim the good news to all of Galilee. This plan was immediately interrupted by this leprous man's request. We can certainly understand the angry feelings that arise when we're on our way to an important appointment and get stuck in gridlocked traffic.

Perhaps Jesus's anger here was stirred by a more pervasive reason; maybe he was angry at the cause of the man's need. After all, the man lived in a culture without adequate health care, with a primitive understanding of diseases and no way to treat them other than to cast out of the community those who suffered. Such lepers were excluded from family life, from religious life, from all of society.

Yet Jesus not only speaks to this unclean man, he touches him. And heals him. Preacher Emily Brown shares a lesson from this encounter: "When Jesus feels anger and then acts with compassion, he reminds us that discipleship can mean loving God and our neighbor with our actions even when we are angry, or anxious, or distracted. Discipleship can mean responding faithfully to God's surprises and life's curveballs, even when it is hard."[7]

Matthew 9:27–30 offers an odd account that we might easily miss when considering Jesus's anger. Two blind men cry loudly after Jesus, "Have mercy on us, Son of David!" As they follow him into a house Jesus asks them, "Do you believe that I am able to do this?" They respond affirmatively, "Yes, Lord." He touches their eyes and says, "According to your faith let it be done to you." And their eyes are opened. It's a wonderful story of faith and healing.

Yet there's a postscript: "Then Jesus sternly ordered them, 'See that no one knows of this.'" The Greek verb *embrimaomai*, translated here as "sternly ordered," is a scarcely used word that implies anger and indignation.[8] In fact, it is a word used in classical Greek to describe a harsh, even animalistic, fury. Why does Jesus speak to the two blind men with such irate indignation? They have been polite and respectful, and clearly possess faith that he is an authentic leader and healer. Apparently Jesus assumes that, despite his stern warning, they will virally spread the news of their healing at his hands. At this early point in his ministry, this will cause his mission to become more dangerous and difficult, as the distrust and concern of his religious enemies would only increase toward him.

In the Mark 1 passage we considered before, Jesus also "sternly warns" the leprous man not to say anything to anyone about his healing—but that man also promptly ignores the warning and tells everyone what happened. The result: "Jesus could no longer go into a town openly, but stayed out in the country; and people came to him from every quarter" (Mark 1:45).

Again we see Jesus's anger at any efforts—even well-intentioned ones from those whose lives he has made whole—to thwart or jeopardize his mission of bringing God's love and mercy to those in need, particularly by revealing it prematurely.

At His Generation

You can also sense Jesus's frustrated anger in Luke 7:31–35: "To what then will I compare the people of this generation, and what are they like? They are like children sitting in the marketplace and calling to one another, 'We played the flute for you, and you did not dance; we wailed, and you did not weep.' For John the Baptist has come eating no bread and drinking no wine, and you say, 'He has a demon'; the Son of Man has come eating and drinking, and you say, 'Look, a glutton and a drunkard, a friend of tax collectors and sinners!'"

He's talking about the people milling around him—some of them curious about this provocative new preacher, others following him because they're excited by this latest celebrity, still others looking askance at him in doubt, fear, or anger. Nobody understands him, Jesus seems to say with frustration. Nobody gets what he's all about. He compares them to whining children who don't get their way. They follow John the Baptist a while and then complain about him. Then they consider Jesus and find *him* wanting as well. There's no satisfying them. You can feel the frustration, the mocking tone of Jesus's words in these verses.

But he concludes with an intriguing koan: "Nevertheless, wisdom is vindicated by all her children." In other words, those who possess and base their lives on a core of true wisdom, who are authentic and liberated followers of Jesus, are known by the fruit of their lives. They aren't blown by the winds of the culture, the whims of human nature. Their actions, their very lives, effectively reveal the wisdom that is their empowering source: the wisdom of God.

Jesus also cursed entire cities where, despite his miraculous ministry, his message was rejected (Matthew 11:20–24). The cities represent his whole generation, the mass of self-centered, shallow people. They did not turn from their ways despite his welcoming invitation to authentic life in God's reign. His anger at their stiff-necked unbelief and hard-hearted selfishness, their empty-headed refusal to accept God's love, leads him to declare woes upon them, comparing them to cities in the Hebrew Scriptures on which God delivered fiery judgment.

They had their chance. No doubt Jesus grieves over their refusal to listen to his message. And he expresses his resulting feelings boldly, with a view perhaps to shocking them into some spiritual sense. Maybe when they hear how passionate he is about their fate, they will turn to him in faith.

At the Religious Elite

One segment of society regularly raises Jesus's ire: the religious elite, those in charge of the religious establishment of his time, those who Jesus believes have warped God's message of love, justice, and spiritual liberation in order to build up their own power, prestige, and wealth on the backs of the faithful. The gospels refer to these authorities variously as Sadducees, Pharisees, scribes, or lawyers.[9]

The Sadducees in Jesus's time were the aristocracy of Judaism and included most of the leading priestly families. This religious party focused only on the Pentateuch, the first five books of the Hebrew Bible, as a guide to correct belief and ethical behavior. Because these books teach nothing regarding eternal life, the Sadducees denied the concept of resurrection, and so found Jesus's teachings incompatible with their views.

The Sadducees were in constant theological battle with the Pharisees, who seem to be the primary target of Jesus's anger. They were an unofficial yet powerful religious group led primarily by laypersons, though some priests were involved. Their goal was to purify Israel by carefully and intentionally following the Hebraic law to its last detail. To the Torah the Pharisees added their own traditions regarding the meaning of the scriptures and how they were to be applied in daily life. They might be experts on the law but sometimes the minutiae of their explanations and elaborations obscured the pure meaning of the law. By the time of Jesus's ministry, the Pharisees had evolved into two groups: those who followed Shammai's strict views, which led them to seek violent revolt against the Romans, and those who followed Hillel, who were a bit more open-minded and tolerant. It is probable that Jesus had earlier studied with the latter group.

The scribes were trained to perform various official writing functions in society, including legal contracts, and so, like the Pharisees and Sadducees, were considered experts in the law and helped promulgate the various rules and regulations they assumed the law of God required for ultimate piety.

All of these religious authorities must have felt threatened by Jesus's growing popularity. Most of them were scandalized by his mockery of their beliefs, which did tend to miss the forest of God's loving reign for all the trees of hard-and-fast rules and regulations.

An early encounter Jesus had with some of these authorities, recorded in Mark 3:1–6 and Luke 6:6–11, reveals a most subversive Jesus. One Sabbath Jesus enters a synagogue, the place of learning for the Jewish people in the community. He spots a man with a deformed hand. The authorities keep an eye on Jesus to see if he will "cure" the man on the Sabbath, so they can accuse him of breaking the law against doing any sort of work on the holy day of rest. Jesus has already performed other miracles on the Sabbath, but the leaders want to catch him in the act and may have even set up the situation by placing the unfortunate man in a prominent place so Jesus can't help but notice him.

Jesus could have avoided a confrontation here. For one thing, the man with the deformed hand doesn't even ask Jesus to heal him, so Jesus could have ignored him. Or Jesus could have waited a few hours until the Sabbath day was over and healed him then, which would have been perfectly legal. So Jesus could have avoided breaking the Sabbath law, the man could have been healed a bit later, and the religious leaders would have had nothing to pin on Jesus.

But Jesus bites the authorities' hook, perhaps willingly, and calls the man over to him. Then he addresses the leaders directly: "Is it lawful to do good or to do harm on the Sabbath, to save life or to kill?" Jesus's straightforward yet provocative question gets no response from them.

In Mark's account, the next verse is the only passage in the gospels in which Jesus is clearly said to be angry: "He looked around at them with anger." You can imagine his furious glare, his eyes blazing as he gazes around the room at the hard-hearted authorities who have refused to help those in need, who deny the plain meaning of God's law of healing love in order to uphold the legal details of the Sabbath.

There is a more forceful source of Jesus's anger, however: "He was grieved at their hardness of heart." He knew they were so far gone that they couldn't change, and this saddened him deeply. The hardness of these religious leaders' hearts is so insidious and unyielding that they will do anything to protect their power. Jesus's grief over their injustice, oppression, and apathy erupts in anger against these authorities.

He tells the man to stretch out his hand, and it is restored. The result of this act of healing love? "The Pharisees went out and immediately conspired with the Herodians against him, how to destroy him."

Jesus rebels in anger against a power system that holds hurting people hostage. He's not interested in maintaining a set of social or religious norms that thwart the dynamic work of God in the world. So here he deliberately provokes the religious leaders, intentionally initiating controversy and destabilizing the situation. He rises above the anger to offer hope and healing, despite the consequences.[10]

Jesus pulls no verbal punches when it comes to these hypocritical authorities, and throughout the gospels he angrily chastises them. He says their father is the devil himself (John 8:44), and that they follow their father in murder and falsehood. He calls them a "brood of vipers" (Matthew 12:34), just as John the Baptist had called them when they came to John in the Jordan River to be baptized, even before Jesus's ministry began—John had seen right through them as well (Matthew 3:7).

One time (Matthew 12:34–40), Jesus fumes at them even about their words: "You brood of vipers! How can you speak good things, when you are evil? For out of the abundance of the heart the mouth speaks. The good person brings good things out of a good treasure, and the evil person brings evil things out of an evil treasure."

Some of these leaders respond to him, "Teacher, we wish to see a sign from you." Either these authorities are just as shallow and faithless as their entire generation, desirous of an entertaining and dazzling miracle, or they want to measure the man, see what he's capable of so they can deal with him properly, even control him.

Jesus refuses. "An evil and adulterous generation asks for a sign, but no sign will be given to it except the sign of the prophet Jonah. For just as Jonah was three days and three nights in the belly of the sea monster, so for three days and three nights the Son of Man will be in the heart of the earth." No doubt this glimpse ahead at his own death, burial, and resurrection went right over their heads.

Jesus castigates his generation and its leaders as evil and false; they pursue pleasure, joy, and success in ways far different than what God calls them to, and he's angry about it. I wonder what he would think of our generation.

Late in his ministry, in Matthew 23:1–36, Jesus presents a long, bitter diatribe against the religious leaders. He begins by telling the crowds and disciples gathered around him what really makes him angry about their actions. No doubt the leaders are within earshot, and they get an earful.

Jesus acknowledges that the scribes and Pharisees do at least teach God's law: "Therefore, do whatever they teach you and follow it; but do not do as they do, for they do not practice what they teach." They live according to a different standard from the one they impose on their followers. "They tie up heavy burdens, hard to bear, and lay them on the shoulders of others; but they themselves are unwilling to lift a finger to move them."

Furthermore, when they do perform good deeds, it's just for show. They do all they can to appear holy just for appearance's sake. They love the adulation, the attention, the best seats at a banquet or synagogue, so that people can see them in all their splendor. However, Jesus calls for an entirely new way of thinking and acting: "The greatest among you will be your servant. All who exalt themselves will be humbled, and all who humble themselves will be exalted."

By now, the religious leaders are no doubt fuming at Jesus's teachings to the people: red-faced, stomping on the fringes of the crowd, perhaps even catcalling at Jesus. And he lets loose on them in a stream of mocking invective that seems to go on forever:

> But woe to you, scribes and Pharisees, hypocrites! For you lock people out of the kingdom of heaven. For you do not go in yourselves, and when others are going in, you stop them. Woe to you, scribes and Pharisees, hypocrites! For you cross sea and land to make a single convert, and you make the new convert twice as much a child of hell as yourselves.... Woe to you, scribes and Pharisees, hypocrites! For you tithe mint, dill, and cumin, and have neglected the weightier matters of the law: justice and mercy and faith. It is these you ought to have practiced without neglecting the others. You blind guides! You strain out a gnat but swallow a camel! Woe to you, scribes and Pharisees, hypocrites! For you clean the outside of the cup and of the plate, but inside they are full of greed and self-indulgence. You blind Pharisee! First clean the inside of the cup, so that the outside also may become clean. Woe to you, scribes and Pharisees, hypocrites! For you are like whitewashed tombs, which on the outside look beautiful, but inside they are full of the bones of the dead and of all kinds of filth. So you also on the outside look righteous to others, but inside you are full of hypocrisy and lawlessness.... You snakes, you brood of vipers! How can you escape being sentenced to hell? (Matthew 23:13–32)

You get the idea. Jesus's anger at their hard-hearted hypocrisy consumes him. He expresses it as clearly as he possibly can, essentially telling them to "go to hell!" He points to God's standard for true godliness and finds these unworthy leaders wanting for causing untold harm to the people.

Jesus's anger is raw. It upends our traditional image of Jesus as a calm, loving messenger of peace. Frankly, it makes us wonder: Would we have wanted to follow this man? Would his anger at our generation and our authorities cause us to scoff at him as a radical subversive and turn our backs on him? Or would we see these instances as Jesus's palpable frustration over false belief and empty faith, and be pulled toward him by his overarching love, his message of liberation in God's will, his challenging call to serve?

So far we've observed Jesus expressing anger at the religious elite verbally. But in one incident recorded in all four gospels Jesus puts his rage into action. In Matthew 21, Luke 19, and Mark 11, this encounter comes relatively late in Jesus's ministry as the climax of his anger against the religious authorities. In John's gospel, however, it comes almost at the very beginning, so Jesus makes clear from the outset that he intends to overturn the corrupt religious status quo.

Jesus goes up to Jerusalem to celebrate the Passover, a pilgrim feast Jewish males were expected to attend. He comes to the temple, the very heart of Jewish life and culture, to worship. But what he sees there makes his blood boil: "In the temple he found people selling cattle, sheep, and doves, and the money changers seated at their tables. Making a whip of cords, he drove all of them out of the temple, both the sheep and the cattle. He also poured out the coins of the moneychangers and overturned their tables. He told those who were selling the doves, 'Take these things out of here! Stop making my Father's house a marketplace!' His disciples remembered that it was written, 'Zeal for your house will consume me'" (John 2:14–17).

What's going on here? Why is Jesus so furious at what's happening in the temple? Perhaps it's more about what *isn't* happening at the temple: it is hardly a place of peace and serenity conducive to the reverent worship of almighty God; in fact, the scene is anything but worshipful.

The religious leaders at the temple forced the faithful to buy "unblemished" sacrificial animals, whether sheep, cattle, or birds, at grossly inflated rates, rather than allowing worshipers to bring their own animals. In addition, these leaders had mandated that Roman coins, the coin of the realm, could not be used to buy these sacrifices because they were engraved with the image of the emperor and thus were unlawful. So the faithful had to pay fees to exchange their money for coins from Tyre, which had no graven images. What God had set forth as a means to enter into the divine presence in worship and spiritual formation had been corrupted into a tawdry, moneymaking business enterprise.

When Jesus sees what is happening, he responds in whip-cracking fury. You can imagine the chaos that ensues from his passionate response. As Jesus kicks over tables and coins go flying, the sacrificial animals scramble to get away and their shocked owners run after them. More biting than Jesus's whip, however, are his words of bitter outrage and judgment.

This is the only incident recorded in the gospels when Jesus's anger gets physical. There is a measure of premeditation involved as well, because he takes the time to make a whip of cords to set the sacrificial animals free and scatter the money-changers. He is deeply angered at the ongoing hypocrisy, the cheapening of God's holy ways to make a profit.

The word *anger* hardly describes the emotion we see played out here. The disciples witness this and recall the prophecy of Psalm 69:9, that zeal for the house of God will consume God's chosen one. Zeal is more deep-seated than anger; it is indeed a "red-hot passion" that "eats him up."[11]

In Mark's account of this ferocious rejection of the ways of the religious elite, Jesus explains, "Is it not written, 'My house shall be called a house of prayer for all the nations'? But you have made it a den of robbers" (11:17). The religious authorities were thwarting God's purpose for the temple and even mocking it to its core.

Step back for a moment and look at the context of Jesus's hot-blooded action in John 2:

> In one paragraph we see Jesus at the wedding feast;
> the next shows him in the temple courts. There he is

the genial, sympathetic guest, adding brightness to the social gathering by his presence, showing forth his glory in the miracle of simple kindness. Here, with uplifted scourge, with indignation flaming in his eyes and vibrating in his voice, he drives the profane rabble of man and beast from the precincts of God's house. He who was all friendliness, all benignity, is now all fire, fierce, rigorous, unsparing, consumed and carried away by passionate intolerance of whatever violated the honor of God and the sanctity of God's worship.[12]

Jesus is revealed here as a person who feels his emotions deeply, openly, and unambiguously. You know exactly where he stands at any moment. His actions show us that what we believe and how we act matters. It matters to God. It reveals what's wrong. It fights against injustice and oppression. It causes change. It makes noise. And it may even get us in trouble. Jesus here is hardly the "gentle Jesus, meek and mild" that Charles Wesley glorified in a hymn.

At His Disciples

When it comes to his relationship with his closest companions, Jesus doesn't often exhibit the limitless patience for which he is traditionally famous. It's one thing to be angry and indignant at those who are profiting from the misery of others, who use their authority to gain power and wealth while oppressing those in need. It's another thing to get angry with those you love, those who live with you and walk with you and believe in you.

Jesus's anger at his disciples is an entirely different sort of emotion, however, than his zealous wrath toward the hypocritical religious leaders. Yet it's nevertheless an authentic emotion he expresses frequently, ranging from irritation and frustration to outright rage.

It's helpful to contrast Jesus's emotional responses to the religious authorities and his disciples in context. For instance, in

Matthew 15:1–20, he's angry with the former, and then becomes frustrated with the latter. Sounds very human, doesn't it? You get angry over an event or circumstance and then you take out your frustration on those around you at the least little provocation. Let's see how this phenomenon unfolds here.

The scribes and Pharisees come to Jesus and ask him, "Why do your disciples break the tradition of the elders? For they do not wash their hands before they eat." Mark's version of the story adds some parenthetical background for the reader: "For the Pharisees, and all the Jews, do not eat unless they thoroughly wash their hands, thus observing the tradition of the elders; and they do not eat anything from the market unless they wash it; and there are also many other traditions that they observe, the washing of cups, pots, and bronze kettles" (Mark 7:3–4).

Jesus, as is often the case, ignores their question and throws another one back at them: "And why do you break the commandment of God for the sake of your tradition?" And he gives them an example of what he's talking about, regarding God's commandment to honor father and mother, concluding, "So, for the sake of your tradition, you make void the word of God. You hypocrites! Isaiah prophesied rightly about you when he said: 'This people honors me with their lips, but their hearts are far from me; in vain do they worship me, teaching human precepts as doctrines.'"

Angry at their calculating, self-serving interpretations of Scripture, Jesus lets them have it, throwing a verse from the Hebrew prophet Isaiah at them before finally answering their question indirectly, providing a lesson to the crowd surrounding him: "Listen and understand: it is not what goes into the mouth that defiles a person, but it is what comes out of the mouth that defiles."

Afterwards, his disciples approach him, perhaps with a bit of trepidation, and Peter asks Jesus to clarify the parable to them. Although Matthew doesn't describe Jesus's state of mind, he is evidently frustrated with his thick-headed disciples; he has to explain this parable as plainly and simply as he can to them:

"Are you also still without understanding? Do you not see that whatever goes into the mouth enters the stomach, and goes out into the sewer? But what comes out of the mouth proceeds from the heart, and this is what defiles. For out of the heart come evil intentions, murder, adultery, fornication, theft, false witness, slander. These are what defile a person, but to eat with unwashed hands does not defile."

Jesus's anger at the hypocritical leaders spills over into his interchange with his disciples. He's frustrated with them, though he may have chuckled lovingly at their lack of understanding. Jesus expresses his feelings openly and directly, so that no one has any doubt about what he means or how he feels. Authentic spiritual health, he makes clear, finds its source in a loving heart.

On another occasion, Jesus takes Peter, James, and John to a mountaintop where Jesus is transfigured before them in an astounding spectacle (Mark 9:2–29). They return down the mountain to look for the other disciples—only to find them surrounded by a large crowd with some scribes arguing with them. Jesus asks his disciples, "What are you arguing about with them?" Evidently he's wondering what fine mess they've gotten themselves into while he was away. A man in the crowd explains that he had brought his demon-possessed son to find Jesus. "I asked your disciples to cast it out, but they could not do so."

Jesus's response—directly to his own ineffective disciples—is laced with angry frustration: "You faithless generation, how much longer must I be among you? How much longer must I put up with you? Bring him to me." Jesus asks the father how long the boy has suffered, and he learns it's been happening "from childhood," and that the spirit within the boy often causes him to fall into fire or water in order to destroy him. Then the father adds, "If you are able to do anything, have pity on us and help us."

"If you are able!" Jesus scoffs at the man, echoing his words with apparent disdain or incredulity. And he adds, "All things can be done for the one who believes." Jesus's words touch the man deeply. "Immediately the father of the child cried out, 'I believe; help my unbelief!'" Jesus rebukes the spirit, commanding it to come out of the boy and never enter him again. The boy screams and convulses terribly. And then suddenly he is quiet, "like a corpse," and the surrounding crowd murmurs, "He is dead." But Jesus takes the boy by the hand, and he stands before those assembled healed and whole.

The gospels reveal several other incidents in which Jesus rebukes his disciples or becomes indignant over their lack of faith, revealing his frustration yet his deep desire to instruct them fully in the ways of God.

Later, Jesus delivers a rather stinging reproach to one of his closest companions, Peter (Matthew 16:13–28), which comes right after he praises Peter for his wisdom and strength. Jesus asks his disciples, "Who do people say that the Son of Man is?" They respond with the scuttlebutt they've heard: some people are saying Jesus must be John the Baptist come back to life, or maybe Elijah or Jeremiah or another prophet. Jesus then turns the question around to them: "But who do you say that I am?" And Peter boldly answers, "You are the Messiah, the Son of the living God."

At this point Jesus has not yet revealed his identity directly, although he certainly has hinted at it, and his words and his works have unquestionably set him apart from the other prophets. Jesus praises Peter lavishly for his response: "Blessed are you, Simon son of Jonah! For flesh and blood has not revealed this to you, but my Father in heaven. And I tell you, you are Peter, and on this rock I will build my church, and the gates of Hades will not prevail against it. I will give you the keys of the kingdom of heaven, and whatever you bind on earth will be bound in heaven, and whatever you loose on earth will be loosed in heaven."

You can almost see Peter's chest swell with pride, or perhaps he blushes in humility. Jesus then "sternly"—there's that word again—orders the disciples not to tell anyone that he is the Messiah. Peter might be right, but Jesus doesn't want to release that news yet.

After this, Matthew tells us, Jesus fleshes out for his disciples what will happen and why. He "began to show his disciples that he must go to Jerusalem and undergo great suffering at the hands of the elders and chief priests and scribes, and be killed, and on the third day be raised." Yet Peter, the dear friend Jesus has just praised so gloriously, won't have it. He takes Jesus aside and begins to rebuke him: "God forbid it, Lord! This must never happen to you." Peter doesn't want to lose his rabbi and friend. He doesn't want to even think about it. So he tells Jesus to stop babbling this nonsense about being killed.

Jesus turns to Peter and says, "Get behind me, Satan! You are a stumbling block to me; for you are setting your mind not on divine things but on human things." This is no mild scolding, for Jesus is angry with Peter. He calls Peter "Satan" because he's tempting Jesus just as Satan did in the wilderness (Matthew 4:1–11). Jesus forcefully tells Peter he is missing the big picture, the divine purpose, while Peter himself is only concerned about protecting his relationship with Jesus. These biting words sting Peter, especially coming in the wake of lavish praise. But Jesus rebukes any attempt that might cause him to doubt his own destiny, whether that attempt comes from his enemy Satan or his dear friend Peter.

Jesus goes on to explain to his disciples that those who follow him must expect to live in a much more sacrificial way: "If any want to become my followers, let them deny themselves and take up their cross and follow me. For those who want to save their life will lose it, and those who lose their life for my sake will find it. For what will it profit them if they gain the whole world but forfeit their life? Or what will they give in return for their life?"

This is the reality of following Jesus. It's not easy, and Jesus works tirelessly to make sure this message is absolutely clear to his disciples. He has no time to waste, so he won't coddle them. He'll be as direct and as transparent as he possibly can be. If his teachings cause a few hurt feelings among his followers, then that's a small price to pay to let them know the harsh reality that lies in wait for them if they choose to fully embrace his teachings and follow him.

How Jesus Responds to Anger

Anger is a two-way street: we feel and express it, but we also bear the brunt of others' anger. It would be natural to justify yourself when under attack, or to pay back the ire in a tit-for-tat exchange. How do Jesus's responses to the anger of others help us form an understanding of living authentically with this emotion?

We have seen a number of encounters Jesus had with others, including the religious elite, where both parties were angry with each other. In some cases, however, Jesus turns aside anger directed toward him by responding directly to whatever is making the other party angry, and other times simply by ignoring or deflecting the charges against him.

From John's Disciples

John the Baptist prepared the way for Jesus, announcing his coming and baptizing him according to Jewish tradition in the Jordan River. Yet even after Jesus began his ministry, John still had followers who assiduously observed the various religious practices and customs of the day. Jesus and his disciples seemed to follow a different path, and their behavior troubled two very different camps: John's disciples and the Pharisees, both of whom were particular in following the complex regulations that had developed over generations.

One time (Mark 2:18–22) some people come to Jesus and ask, "Why do John's disciples and the disciples of the Pharisees fast, but your disciples do not fast?" Fasting, of course, involves withholding food to enable focused prayer and piety. You can sense the outrage in the question, and perhaps the people asking it are John's and the Pharisees' disciples. They're saying, it's not fair; we deprive ourselves while you and your followers eat and drink whatever and whenever you want. Deftly and calmly, Jesus suggests that his presence now is a time for joy and feasting for his followers. He won't be around for long, so now is the time to eat and drink in celebration. There will be time later, after his death, for sober fasting.

Jesus offers a new way of living. "No one sews a piece of unshrunk cloth on an old cloak; otherwise, the patch pulls away from it, the new from the old, and a worse tear is made. And no one puts new wine into old wineskins; otherwise, the wine will burst the skins, and the wine is lost, and so are the skins; but one puts new wine into fresh wineskins." In other words, the way of Jesus really doesn't fit into the old way with its multitude of rules and regulations. His is the way of liberated, radical love, a way that builds upon the past but offers a fresh approach to life in the steadfast, relentless love of God.

Jesus defuses what could be an angry attack on his ways with an explanation that certainly must have caused his inquisitors to ponder who Jesus is and to what kind of life he calls us.

From His Friends and Followers

In Luke 10:38–42 we encounter Jesus's friends Mary and Martha, likely at an early point in their relationship, before Lazarus is raised from the dead. This brief story reveals the closeness of these friends and their ability to speak openly and directly to each other.

The writer reports that Martha welcomes Jesus into her home; she takes the initiative in the relationship. "She had a sister named Mary, who sat at the Lord's feet and listened to what he was saying." Mary is devoted to Jesus's teaching, carefully taking in his words, sitting at his feet as a student does with a rabbi.

"But Martha was distracted by her many tasks; so she came to him and asked, 'Lord, do you not care that my sister has left me to do all the work by myself? Tell her then to help me.'" Martha has a house full of guests, including the popular new rabbi who has been creating such an uproar throughout the country, and she is working hard to fulfill her hosting duties. Meanwhile, her sister is ignoring her needs and spending time with Jesus. So, an angry Martha complains to Jesus.

Jesus calmly speaks to Martha in words that, expressed in any other way, might have caused an even angrier response in her: "Martha, Martha, you are worried and distracted by many things; there is need of only one thing. Mary has chosen the better part, which will not be taken away from her." Speaking the truth in love, he acknowledges her worry and distraction and the unfairness of the situation, yet shows that Mary's way is preferable for the moment. While he is with them, it is important that they *be with him* wholly and sincerely. The housework will take care of itself in the proper time.

In Mark 10:32–45 an angry dispute breaks out among Jesus's disciples. The band is making its way to Jerusalem while Jesus explains that there he will be mocked, spat upon, flogged, and put to death, then raised from the dead in three days. The mood must have been restrained and pensive, because Jesus's words are frightening and sorrowful.

In the midst of this, James and John approach Jesus and ask a favor of him, almost as children would beg a parent or friend: "'Teacher, we want you to do for us whatever we ask of you.' And he said to them, 'What is it you want me to do for you?' And they said to him, 'Grant us to sit, one at your right hand and one at your left, in your glory.'" In other words, having heard Jesus say he is about to be put to death and then raised, they are looking to secure their own position in heaven with him, asking him to bestow upon them the places of highest honor.

Jesus sets them straight, telling them they don't know what they're asking, alluding to the hellish treatment he must undergo as he is tortured and crucified to assume his prime position in heaven. They don't really get it, and Jesus finally tells them it's not his place to determine who gets the places of honor and authority in the realm of glory.

Of course, the other disciples are listening to this conversation about James and John's self-centered and tone-deaf request. "When the ten heard this, they began to be angry with James and John." No doubt! Rather than being upset at James and John's self-serving request, though, the ten are jealous that those two thought to ask first for the places of honor, and they hadn't.

In light of their reaction, Jesus explains that they are not to follow the example of the world's power-mad, tyrannical rulers, who seek authority and honor at any cost. Rather, in the way of Jesus, "whoever wishes to become great among you must be your servant, and whoever wishes to be first among you must be slave of all. For the Son of Man came not to be served but to serve, and to give his life a ransom for many."

Here Jesus speaks in an honest, direct, and reassuring tone. Without belittling their desire for authority, he overturns their assumptions and welcomes them into a different way of life, one marked by loving servanthood. This, he tells them, is the way to live in the reign of God.

From the Religious Authorities

Jesus's response to the anger of the religious leaders, however, is not so reassuring and illuminating. As we've seen from the examples of his own expressions of anger, he has little patience for their hypocrisy, and routinely deflects the arrows of anger they direct toward him and his revolutionary ways through his transparent teachings and unruffled responses.

Early in his ministry, Jesus calls Levi the tax collector to follow him, thereby irritating the Pharisees (Luke 5:27–32). Tax collectors were thoroughly despised by the Israelites because they collected money on behalf of their Roman oppressors. The more taxes people like Levi collected, the more they benefited personally. The religious leaders did not consider such tax collectors to be righteous because they didn't observe the law and worked in cahoots with the Roman authorities.

Even so, Levi (also known as Matthew) immediately "got up, left everything, and followed [Jesus]." As was no doubt typical for a man of Levi's position, he throws a great banquet at his house to honor his new rabbi. It must have been a rowdy affair, drawing a large crowd of unsavory types.

"The Pharisees and their scribes were complaining to his disciples, saying, 'Why do you eat and drink with tax collectors and sinners?'" You can almost hear the annoyed disgust in their voices. Jesus again deflects their anger with a simple, straightforward response: "Those who are well have no need of a physician, but those who are sick; I have come to call not the righteous but sinners to repentance." They can't argue with that: Jesus is spending time with those who need to change the direction of their lives. Yet the way Jesus invites people to experience new life in God's reign is vastly different from the ways of the religious elite. Because of Jesus's contrary behaviors, the authorities begin to persecute him. But he keeps straight on his path: "My Father is still working, and I also am working" (John 5:16–18).

As we've seen, Jesus frequently drives the religious leaders into a fury by healing on the Sabbath. God indeed calls for a Sabbath day of rest (Exodus 20:8–11), but over the generations since the writing of the Decalogue, religious leaders had developed incredibly minute regulations around the Ten Commandments that were virtually impossible to fulfill. Jesus has God's true priorities of love and restoration at heart. The Sabbath is an important spiritual goal, but when hurting people have physical needs, they shouldn't be ignored on the Sabbath. So, whenever Jesus encounters individuals in distressing physical trouble, he heals them no matter the day or the time of day.

One Sabbath day when Jesus is teaching in a synagogue, a woman crippled for eighteen years appears (Luke 13:10–17). Jesus sees her, calls her over, and tells her, "Woman, you are set free from your ailment." He lays hands on her and immediately she straightens up and begins praising God. But the head of the synagogue, "indignant because Jesus had cured on the Sabbath," rails against what Jesus has done; be healed on the other six days, he demands, not on the Sabbath.

Jesus responds harshly to this leader and his cohorts: "You hypocrites! Does not each of you on the Sabbath untie his ox or his donkey from the manger, and lead it away to give it water? And ought not this woman, a daughter of Abraham whom Satan bound for eighteen long years, be set free from this bondage on the Sabbath day?" It's difficult for the leader to argue with such a sense of love and logic. "When he said this, all his opponents were put to shame; and the entire crowd was rejoicing at all the wonderful things that he was doing." Jesus stands up to his opponents, and the crowd's response cowers them. Their shame, however, will evolve into deepening anger—even murderous rage.

In John 6:35–71, while teaching in the synagogue in Capernaum, Jesus declares that he is the "bread of life." He has come from heaven to do his Father's will, to provide a way to God for all. This does not make the religious leaders happy. They "began to complain about him because he said, 'I am the bread that came down from heaven.' They were saying, 'Is not this Jesus, the son of Joseph, whose father and mother we know? How can he now say, "I have come down from heaven"?'" They've known this Jesus since he was a boy. They knew his mother and father. And now he's claiming that God is his Parent, that he was sent from heaven? Who does he think he is?

Jesus hears them, tells them to stop grumbling and complaining, and then explains to them who he really is. You can almost see the purple veins throbbing on their foreheads and necks as he continues to claim to be God's son: "I am the bread of life," he says. "Your ancestors ate the manna in the wilderness, and they died. This is the bread that comes down from heaven, so that one may eat of it and not die. I am the living bread that came down from heaven. Whoever eats of this bread will live forever; and the bread that I will give for the life of the world is my flesh."

The religious leaders continue their dispute, arguing that Jesus is talking nonsense. "How can this man give us his flesh to eat?" It makes absolutely no sense to them. It likely made little sense to *any* of Jesus's hearers. Jesus answers with words that will form the basis of the Eucharistic feast in churches still today, as he speaks of the deeply intimate relationship between his followers and himself.

Even his disciples are confused and frustrated by his strange words. Some of those who followed him refuse to believe him after these peculiar teachings. "This teaching is difficult; who can accept it?" they murmur to one another. Jesus hears their complaints and confronts them, "Does this offend you?... The words that I have spoken to you are spirit and life. But among you there are some who do not believe." Jesus is drawing a clear distinction between himself and the religious establishment.

The writer explains: "Because of this many of his disciples turned back and no longer went about with him." Then it gets really personal: Jesus asks the Twelve, his closest followers, "Do you also wish to go away?" Peter responds, "Lord, to whom can we go? You have the words of eternal life. We have come to believe and know that you are the Holy One of God." You get the feeling that Jesus realizes his own disciples' faith is rather fragile, and such difficult teachings can shake them as well. But, except for the one who will ultimately betray him, they're not going anywhere. Where else can they go? Peter asks, as if he realizes they're in way too deep now.

This passage is illuminating because not only do Jesus's self-avowed enemies, the religious elite, challenge him angrily, but so do many of his own followers. None of this shakes Jesus. Their anger, confusion, and frustration are palpable, but Jesus continues to explain himself openly and transparently, putting himself on the line. Jesus's integrity is far more important to him than how people choose to react to him. Jesus will not let others' anger hinder his response to God's call.

Time and time again Jesus and the religious authorities wrangle. They attack his disciples for plucking grains to munch on while walking through a wheat field on the Sabbath (Matthew 12:1–8). They question Jesus's authority for saying the things he says about himself (Mark 11:27–12:12). They try to stone him for identifying himself fully with God (John 10:22–39). In each case, Jesus patiently explains his mission and authority without a trace of doubt, with the utmost transparency, supporting his explanation with illustrations out of their own scriptures. Everything he does is exemplified in God's word; his clarity only exacerbates their fury. They can't hear it; to them it is blasphemy. But Jesus does not yield. His integrity remains unshaken.

During the Passion

The religious authorities' fury toward Jesus reaches its climax during his final week. Rather than answering their charges and explaining himself during this holy week, he takes their wrath in silence. He knows what is unfolding, and it won't be pretty but it will be right.

However, after he is arrested in the Garden of Gethsemane as a result of Judas's betrayal, Jesus does state his case. The high priest asks him about his disciples and his teachings, trying to get Jesus to incriminate himself (John 18:19–24). But Jesus replies, "I have spoken openly to the world; I have always taught in synagogues and in the temple, where all the Jews come together. I have said nothing in secret. Why do you ask me? Ask those who heard what I said to them; they know what I said."

One of the guards nearby takes Jesus's response as impudence, striking Jesus on the face and angrily shouting, "Is that how you answer the high priest?" Jesus answers, "If I have spoken wrongly, testify to the wrong. But if I have spoken rightly, why do you strike me?" Jesus justifies himself, yet without really answering any of the charges. He knows the endgame has been predetermined. There is nothing he can say to change it. And so he stands firm in his integrity in the face of his opponents' fury.

Jesus's treatment at the hands of the authorities is brutal. According to Mark's account (14:53–65), the religious leaders are trying to create enough testimony against Jesus to guarantee a death sentence from the Roman political authorities. They round up the usual suspects, and "many gave false testimony against him, and their testimony did not agree."

The high priest stands before Jesus in light of all this incompatible, false testimony and asks him, "Have you no answer? What is it that they testify against you?" Jesus remains silent. So again the high priest asks, more directly this time: "Are you the Messiah, the Son of the Blessed One?" And Jesus answers, "I am"—again using the name of God for himself (Exodus 3:14)—"I am; and 'you will see the Son of Man seated at the right hand of the Power,' and 'coming with the clouds of heaven.'" Jesus couldn't be more clear: he is God's own, possessing authority and power from on high.

Jesus seals his own fate far more definitively than the loose assortment of so-called witnesses can. The high priest rips his robes—an expression of raging self-righteousness performed when a so-called holy leader finds himself in the presence of one who has insulted or blasphemed God. He cries out in anger, "Why do we still need witnesses? You have heard his blasphemy! What is your decision?" The religious authorities gathered in furious judgment all give Jesus the thumbs down: he deserves death.

Then their rage explodes violently against Jesus. Some spit on him. Others strike him. They blindfold Jesus so he can't see to protect himself from their blows, and mock him, telling him to "prophesy!"—if you're divine, tell us who's hitting you now, Jesus! And then the guards take him and beat him even more. Jesus does not fight back. He has declared who he is with utter integrity. He is prepared to take the consequences. It is the darkest and most violent of nights.

Jesus may have expressed anger toward the religious authorities throughout his ministry, mocking and attacking them verbally, even overturning their profitable cash exchange tables in the temple. But now, he remains silent. He yields to their rage. He trusts that what is happening to him is what must be.

The religious leaders finally take Jesus to Pilate, who gives in to the fury of the enraged crowds and, despite several weak attempts to do otherwise, turns Jesus over to be crucified (John 18:28–19:22).

The entire Passion narrative is shot through with anger, from the religious leaders, the crowds, even from Pilate. But not from Jesus. He does not respond to their attacks with anger, but rather with quiet forgiveness, mercy, and love. Jesus follows his own teaching to the very end: "I say to you, Love your enemies and pray for those who persecute you" (Matthew 5:44).

What Jesus Teaches about Anger

In his teachings recorded in the four gospels, Jesus never says, "Do not be angry," but he does offer insights on how to deal with anger. Most of his teachings in this regard are found within his Sermon on the Mount, in Matthew 5–7. In this collection of Jesus's wisdom, despite offering blessing to the meek, the grieving, the persecuted—that is, to all who find themselves in need of God—"there is nothing gentle, meek or mild about the driving force behind these stabbing inversions of normal expectations. They form a code of life which is a chorus of love directed to the loveless or unlovable, of painful honesty expressing itself with embarrassing directness, of joyful rejection of any counsel suggesting careful self-regard or prudence. That, apparently, is what the Kingdom of God is like."[13]

Jesus is speaking to a crowd of ordinary people gathered around him on a mountainside. These are people living under the oppressive thumb of political and religious authority, burdened by the weight of an overly complicated code of law that distracts them from a true understanding of God's loving ways. Drawn to Jesus on the hillside, these common folk are no doubt angry over the way they must live, the way they are treated, and their absolute inability to overcome their circumstances. And Jesus's teachings about anger are totally counter to the ways of their world.

In his sermon Jesus blesses "those who are persecuted for righteousness's sake, for theirs is the kingdom of heaven." Those who live as merciful, righteous, and pure peacemakers often bear the brunt of the world's scorn. Their lifestyle causes discomfort among those who are comfortable in their wealth and their power. The people who follow God's way—rather than the proud, angry, warring, lying, powerful people—will be the ones who receive God's ultimate glory and honor.

So, Jesus says, rather than becoming angry at this persecution, rather than fighting back in rage at those who oppress you, realize instead that this treatment is a sign that God is blessing you, now and always. Being caught in the world system's crosshairs should only bring us joy, because we thereby can be assured that we are living in the full will of God.

A bit later in this sermon Jesus addresses a common situation in life: anger with a family member. "You have heard that it was said to those of ancient times, 'You shall not murder'; and 'whoever murders shall be liable to judgment,'" referring to the commandment in the Decalogue, Exodus 20:13, as well as Deuteronomy 5:17. Jesus takes this well-known commandment much further: "But I say to you that if you are angry with a brother or sister, you will be liable to judgment;… and if you say, 'You fool,' you will be liable to the hell of fire."

That seems rather drastic. Yet Jesus here and elsewhere in this sermon forces us to internalize God's law wholly. He encourages us to search our hearts for hateful, even murderous, intentions of any kind, at any level. Our external actions and our right behaviors are one thing, but it's a vastly more important thing for our hearts, our inner selves, to be oriented toward love in all things, with all people, in every situation. So, if you sense anger, resentment, or alienation toward anyone, before you do anything else, you must "go; first be reconciled to your brother or sister, and then come and offer your gift." Work out your differences, and then together come back to the community to worship God with pure hearts.

Jesus is teaching a radical way of life. Jesus's way is far more than obedience to the rules; it's all about love, loving God and neighbor as oneself. Anger dissolves when we live this way. It loses its power over us.

How do Jesus's teachings about anger jibe with his own actions? It's clear that he doesn't mean to discourage oppressed and mistreated people to seek justice, even to agitate for it as he did. He was angry with those who oppressed the poor and needy, and spoke out forcefully against such treatment. Jesus's teachings reflect an ideal way of life in the reign of God, and yet times will come when we must stand up and express truth to power in constructive, meaningful, unyielding ways, even in light of the possible consequences. Jesus expressed anger with a particular purpose: to bring about justice or reveal malice or ignorance. Learning how to balance these teachings and actions is a lifelong process for those who are called to follow the way of Jesus.

Living with Anger

Our search for the ways Jesus expresses and experiences anger has revealed a human being who radically exudes integrity, strength, and vision, one who models confidence in his mission, indignation over injustice, and love in the midst of aggravation. Throughout the gospel accounts, Jesus's demonstrations of anger reveal his authenticity. He doesn't play games. He isn't passive-aggressive or obsequious. He doesn't stuff his anger, holding it in until the breaking point. Rather, he is clear and direct and utterly righteous in his anger.

We've gleaned some answers to the questions that confronted us:

Jesus demonstrates different kinds of "anger," ranging from pique and frustration to exasperation and furious righteous indignation. Anger can be destructive or constructive, harmful or holy. Jesus models a way to express anger in ways that can be illuminating as well as instructive.

Jesus expresses anger in direct, honest ways. He will not be swayed from his mission. He is bold and clear in his message. He responds to attacks directly. Sometimes he uses anger to try to shake some spiritual sense into others, though often he realizes the effort is useless, so he expresses his judgment of hypocrisy, greed, and self-aggrandizement, particularly of those who are charged with the care of the souls of the people. Jesus states his case unambiguously in spite of opposition.

He makes no personal attacks, but seeks to uncover the evil behind the actions. There is no record of Jesus being angered by a personal offense no matter how wrong, unjust, or violent it may be. He teaches that the one who is persecuting us is also created in the image of God and is loved by God, and in that reality we can love our enemy. At the same time, just as God is righteously angered over oppression and injustice, so should we be.

Jesus's mission is to liberate human souls, to draw them into the reign of God, into a loving, selfless way of life. He is after what matters to God—and so he reveals dishonesty, fights injustice and subjugation, causes change, sets thing right. Undergirding every expression of his anger is love; Jesus speaks the truth in love. In every case the anger of Jesus is the passion of love. His love of God, his zeal for the ways of God and the true worship of God, his mission to open the reign of God to all, together make him indignant at whatever dishonors God and whatever impedes others from knowing and experiencing God. He is honest with his feelings, expresses them as directly and transparently as possible, and moves on.

Jesus responds to anger in others by calmly explaining his position. He possesses an unshakable force of honesty and truth. He stands up to angry attacks without getting drawn into fierce, thoughtless encounters. He understands that one's anger is often caused by fear, and takes that into account when he is the object of a violent outburst. He is transparent in his response to every challenge, and refuses to yield his position. He explains who he is and what he is about with utter openness and outspokenness.

Jesus's teachings regarding anger overturn our assumptions. If you are persecuted, if you are the focus of others' anger for righteousness's sake, then you are blessed, he tells us, so be joyful. If you are angry with a brother or sister, deal with it and be reconciled—make that a priority even before worship. He teaches a model of peaceful nonviolence that many throughout history have attempted to follow, even today. He recognizes that there is a place for righteous anger, as he himself has shown, but he urges us to be angry without sinning, without causing harm or seeking destruction. And he tells us there can be a cost for making such a righteous stand. Nevertheless, he encourages us to live a life of pure, authentic love and integrity.

As Robert Law concludes, "God is love; Jesus is love; the anger of Jesus and all holy anger is the anger of love. For love is not wholly sympathy and sweetness; love is full of indignation and wrath."[14]

Paying Attention to Our Anger

So how do we live with anger?

We must prayerfully and honestly compare our own experiences of anger with Jesus's. If we sense a persistent anger in our hearts about our lives, about the work we do or the people we live with or are surrounded by, if we find ourselves frequently in contentious discussions with others, or fighting for our rights, we are probably missing the mark.

Despite all the examples of Jesus's anger we've examined, and there are many more, we must recognize that Jesus used the emotion of anger judiciously—always with a specific purpose, whether to correct or instruct his bemused disciples, or to fight the injustice and hypocrisy of those who should know better, or to overcome evil and death. In every case, love is the overriding factor.

So we must pay attention to our anger, be mindful of the events or situations that set us off. We must ask ourselves, what is the character of our anger? What causes it and incites it? The answers to those questions will reveal much about our true selves. The sort of explosive, mindless rage that we often see— and that I experienced in my college newspaper's newsroom—is in no way beneficial. Many of us have been the victims of such rage. You may discover that you need to process your anger or your experiences with other people's anger with a therapist or religious counselor to determine its causes and help you express and release it in healthy ways.

To simplify the matter to the extreme, we might say there are two different kinds of anger: *the anger of the world*, which is the anger of fear and selfishness, and *the anger of Jesus*, which is the anger of love and justice. When we witness wrong done to others, particularly those who do not have the strength or means to defend themselves, then as people of faith God calls us to express the anger of love—the anger that gives us boldness and outspokenness in defense of what is right.

A Holy Anger

There is much to be said for righteous indignation regarding oppression and injustice in our times. This is a holy anger, "one of the purest, loftiest emotions of which the human spirit is capable, the fiery spark which is struck by wrongdoing out of a soul that loves the right. When a person is destitute of such emotion, when there is nothing in one that flames up at the sight of injustice, cruelty, and oppression, nothing that flashes out indignation against the liar, the hypocrite, the 'grafter,' the betrayer of sacred trusts, there is much awanting to the strength and completeness of moral humanity."[15]

Righteous anger toward inequity and injustice was a hallmark of the Occupy Wall Street movement, which began on September 17, 2011, in Zuccotti Park in Manhattan and quickly spread to numerous other cities before authorities moved in months later to squelch the determined protesters. As radio commentator Roy Lloyd explained it, "At the core of the Occupy Wall Street demonstrations is the conviction that those in the tall steeples of power—huge banks, big corporations, brokerage firms, government officials—are sitting comfortably in the high bleachers, far removed from the reality most people endure. No wonder there is anger. Greed is sucking decency and neighborliness out of America. Two thousand years ago, Jesus said hypocrites were like whitewashed tombs, looking beautiful on the outside, but filled with lawlessness and filth. He could have been describing today's high bleacher hypocrites."[16]

The Rev. Elizabeth Kaeton, an Episcopal priest, said she heard a distinct message at Zuccotti Park: "People are really angry about greed.... That's what made Jesus turn over a few tables in the temple, greed and corruption. That's the moral problem that I think the church needs to speak to." She saw the movement calling Jesus's followers to become "prophetic while being pastoral" to those who are struggling and hurting. "What I found at Wall Street was the intersection of the pastoral and the prophetic ... and that's where we need to be."[17]

There are numerous ways people of faith can be involved in helping set things right and extending the reign of God to all. You might take on a particular effort that is close to your heart—whether it is helping to shelter the homeless, feeding those in poverty, visiting women or men in prison, helping to clothe children in need, serving those with special needs, or working with youth who need an adult mentor. The needs are endless, the inequities abound. How might your holy anger be channeled into righteous, loving action?

We've learned from Jesus's example and teachings that anger can personally be a troubling and even destructive emotion, but channeled and directed in the love of God, it can proclaim a better way and fuel righteous acts. We must open ourselves to the guidance of the spirit of Jesus to determine how to understand and express our own anger, how to respond to anger in others, and in all matters, how to speak and act in the love of God.

EXPLORING EMOTIONS: ANGER

When was the last time you were so angry with a friend, a family member, or a partner that you mistreated that person out of your rage toward him or her? Recall the steps you took to allay your anger and heal that rift.

Can you recall a time when you acted out of righteous anger in an attempt to overcome an unjust situation?

Repeat "Forgive us our trespasses, as we forgive those who trespass against us" ten times every morning as preparation for a day when you know you will have to ask others' forgiveness because you have personally attacked them with your words or actions. How do you think that might help?

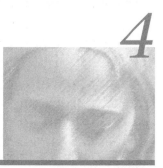

4

Fear

Energizing and Empowering a Deeper Faith

W e live in a culture of fear. The economy is in an endless collapse, a new health concern arises almost daily, international and domestic terrorists lurk around every corner waiting to pounce on us, violence erupts on our streets and even in our houses of worship, natural disasters occur more frequently and viciously as a result of our poor stewardship of the planet, our food and water are unsafe or unhealthy, all of which makes us fearful for our and our children's future.

Fear affects us in insidious ways. When we allow fear to control our lives, our health is often adversely affected. Fear can drain us of energy and confuse our perception of reality. Fear can fuel our anger, lead us to commit cowardly acts, cause us to be apathetic, prevent us from getting involved in a situation that requires strength and wisdom, and drive us to avoid our responsibilities as followers of Jesus to serve the needy and stand up for the oppressed. Fear can distract us from the joys of life. It can cause us to protect ourselves so carefully that we resist participating fully in the life around us.

As the little green Jedi philosopher Yoda told Anakin Skywalker, "Fear is the path to the Dark Side. Fear leads to anger. Anger leads to hate. Hate leads to suffering."

There are good reasons to fear; it is wise to be alert to potential dangers at the hands of other humans or nature. When we worry ourselves, however, over possible future events or situations outside our control—when we let fear strangle us—we are missing God's best intentions for us.

Our anxiety arises over a multitude of concerns: Why did my boss give me that funny look at the staff meeting about possible personnel cuts? Why haven't I heard from my daughter? What if my spouse contracts a serious illness or has a devastating accident? How am I going to pay for that unexpected car repair? We worry not only about ourselves but also about our children and grandchildren, our parents and grandparents, other family members and friends. We have more than enough reasons to be afraid.

We may try to escape the fear we feel by running away, whether through mind-altering substances, distracting pursuits, or even literally fleeing our circumstances. Even so, we often discover that our fears follow us relentlessly.

Many soldiers in Iraq and throughout the Middle East have reported their fear of a huge spider called the "camel spider." These arachnids are eight to twelve inches in length. They are speedy and aggressive. Many soldiers have claimed they were chased by a camel spider. The reason the camel spiders chase the fearful soldiers is not to attack them, however, but to *stay in their shade*. The camel spiders are nocturnal and abhor light. In fact, their scientific name is *solifugae*, Latin for "one who runs from the sun." So, during the day, they burrow into the sand to hide. But if one is disturbed and comes out into the strong sunlight, it will seek the nearest shade, which just might be a soldier's shadow. If the soldier runs, the spider will chase him down just to stay in his shadow.

We can all identify with the feeling of running from our fears only to find they can run faster than we can. Whether the threat is internal or external, what are we to do with our fears?

Do Not Be Afraid

Scholars point out that in the Bible God, or God's messenger, says, "Do not be afraid" 366 times—so that works out to one invitation not to fear for each day of the year, even in leap years. Roman Catholic priest, author, and television commentator Edward Beck explains that "perhaps God says 'Do not be afraid' so many times because God knows that we are [afraid]. What is even more perplexing than our seeming inability to embrace this injunction is the tendency of some to fear this very God who says 'Do not be afraid' 366 times. Many were raised with a severe, judgmental God who stands ready to punish even the most minor infraction. So rather than rest in the Divine bosom of one who desires to shield us from that of which we are afraid, we run from that which we perceive [is] poised to slap us down for our transgressions. Fear indeed, with no help from religion."[1]

Feeling fear is not sinful. The ways we respond to fear— whether with cowardice or with strength—reveal the authenticity of our faith.

Jesus can introduce us to the loving God who yearns for our company, who seeks to bless us with all good things, who desires that our faith should overcome our fear at every level. As we look again at his life and ministry, we'll discover how Jesus himself experiences fear, and how he deals with it. We'll see how Jesus responds to the fear of others. We'll hear what Jesus teaches about fear and how to overcome it. And, we'll learn to trust God's invitation not to fear, but rather to lean on the love and strength of God no matter what we face.

What Is Fear?

Fear is a stressful emotion aroused by a sense of impending danger, pain, evil, or other negative experience. It can be real or imagined, positive or negative. Fear can help protect us, or it can make us vulnerable. It can be intensely focused on a particular threat in the moment, or arise in anticipation of a known event in the future, or be generally experienced as a sense of anxiety or worry that may not be attributable to any particular cause.

Even reading the word *fear* can send a shiver down our spines. We worry about coming events that cause anxiety, perhaps a big test or an important meeting at work. We think of dangers, real or imagined, that our loved ones may face. We may recall times when we felt so deeply afraid that we didn't know whether we would survive our consuming fear.

Looking back I can remember many moments of fear when I faced any manner of threat to myself or my loved ones. My stomach churns, my skin prickles, and my pulse quickens at the mere memory.

As a four-year-old boy, I had to stay in a children's hospital in Pittsburgh, about eighty miles from where my family then lived in West Virginia. In those days parents rarely were allowed to spend more than an hour or two visiting their terrified children. The first time I stayed in that hospital, I remember waking up in the middle of the night in a large darkened ward lined with beds on both sides of the room. Through the windows I could see dark, menacing brick buildings with chimneys spitting out gray smoke—a child's version of hell. Boys of all ages felled by various injuries and diseases surrounded me in bed after bed. I was encompassed by pain and fear, and for days I don't recall seeing any face I knew.

Later I was moved into a semiprivate room. My mother and father would come for painfully brief visits. They were allowed to see me only once a day, in the evening. I can still feel the panic that struck me when I realized they had to depart for the night, leaving me alone in this scary, lonely place. They brought me a stuffed dog I called Taffy because of its golden color, which reminded me of the buttery pulled candy our family often made. My mother also brought me a little plastic hand mirror. As I lay in bed, I could hold the mirror up and check the window behind me; I was unable to turn around and look myself because of the surgery I'd had. In the mirror I could see when the sky began to darken, which meant visiting hours were soon to end. My heart filled with anxiety when I looked one last time only to see blackness; it was time for them to go.

I survived those experiences, and it wasn't long before I was safe and sound at home. I kept that stuffed dog; Taffy is much the worse for wear after more than five decades, but every time I see it I recall the fear I felt as an anxious child in that hospital so long ago, and I want to reach back in time and hug him. But Taffy also embodied the concerned love of my parents in those brief visits—a love that carried me through my fear.

Fear can also cause great harm in what it prevents us from doing. For instance, fear has kept me from making myself comfortable among people who are very different from me, or among those who need food to survive, clothing to keep warm, a listening ear and a comforting touch. Fear has kept me from having an honest conversation with someone who needed to be encouraged to stop a self-destructive habit. I didn't want him to be mad at me or abandon our friendship, so I never brought up this uncomfortable subject. Fear has kept me countless times from introducing myself to someone I knew would be a positive influence in my life; what if he or she rejected me?

As I look back, I realize with sorrow the profound impact fear has had on my life in so many ways. In most of these cases, however, I have eventually come to trust God and step out in faith, and I haven't regretted what happened next. What I do regret is letting my fear dampen my courage and hold me captive in so many ways for so long. Father Edward Beck writes of a time early in his ministry when he worked in an African American parish on the south side of Chicago. One year as the parish celebrated Dr. Martin Luther King's birthday, King's daughter Yolanda was the guest speaker. She told the congregation that when she was little, her father had a "play ritual" with her. He'd take her by the hand into the kitchen, lift her atop the refrigerator, then move back and open his arms and say, "Jump, Yokie, jump!" But atop the tall appliance Yolanda would cry to him to take her down, that she was afraid and it was too high. This happened time and again, and he'd always lift her back down.

One day Dr. King came home after a difficult two weeks away, during which time he had survived an assassination attempt. As he walked through the door looking exhausted, he said nothing to anyone. He simply looked at Yolanda, took her by the hand into the kitchen, and lifted her atop the refrigerator. With his voice breaking, he said to her, "Jump, Yokie, jump."

Yolanda explained that she didn't know whether it was because he'd been away so long, or looked so tired, or perhaps she'd grown up a little, but for the first time she did jump off the top of the refrigerator with abandon, landing safely in her father's arms. He held her tight and said to her, with tears brimming in his eyes, "Yokie, you've learned something very important tonight. You've learned what it means to trust someone other than yourself. You've learned what it means to jump."

We all need to learn this lesson regarding our relationship with God, Father Beck explains. "Somehow we are all that little kid sitting on top of the refrigerator afraid—afraid of intimacy, afraid of risking, afraid of failure, afraid of whatever. The outstretched arms of the power of love that casts out all fear beckons us forward to make the leap, to trust those arms will be there to catch us and embrace us in the power that perfect love generates. How long do we sit on top of that refrigerator instead?"[2]

What is fear doing to you? How is it affecting your pursuit of the career you really desire? How is it keeping you from reaching out to those you'd like to get to know? How is it hindering you from taking the holy risks you've been considering, from living the life you've yearned to lead? How is fear strangling your hopes and dreams?

Living in Hope

When Jesus walked the earth, fear was as prevalent as it is today. Civilization then required basic survival skills day after day, and physical hazards and disease were constant threats. Not only that, but the people of Israel were forced to live under a capricious and brutal Roman rule.

Through numerous scriptural exhortations, the Jewish faith encouraged individuals to trust in God and live in hope rather than in fear. Hope is a positive expectation for the future, the opposite of fear. And true, lasting hope can be found only in God. As one psalm encourages:

> *The Lord is my light and my salvation;*
> *whom shall I fear?*
> *The Lord is the stronghold of my life;*
> *of whom shall I be afraid?*
>
> *When evildoers assail me,*
> *to devour my flesh—*
> *my adversaries and foes—*
> *they shall stumble and fall.*
>
> *Though an army encamp against me,*
> *my heart shall not fear;*
> *though war rise up against me,*
> *yet I will be confident.*
>
> PSALM 27:1–3

When we are in relationship with the God who loves and cares about us utterly, when we are ordering our lives with integrity and openness to whatever God might send our way, we have nothing to fear—even in the face of overwhelming odds.

Though he, too, experienced fear, Jesus also embraced hope in the face of it. This calls our attention to some important questions we must wrestle with personally: How should we evaluate the fear we feel, and how should we deal with it? How do we best respond to fear in others? How do we understand, acknowledge, and overcome our fears honestly?

We can look to Jesus for help in overcoming our fear by seeing how he experiences fear personally, how he lets himself be afraid and yet moves steadily through his fear into faith. We can learn from the ways he responds to fear in others, and from what he teaches about fear. We can see him as a model for defeating the power of fear in our lives by resting in the everlasting presence of God.

How Jesus Experiences Fear

The gospels do not present many instances that explicitly describe Jesus experiencing fear. Even so, when you read between the lines of the stories, you'll discover Jesus feeling anxious about his ministry and whether or not people really understand his teachings, as well as palpable fear in the Garden of Gethsemane as he endures a hellish time of torment leading to his death. If he does not feel fear in these moments, then he's not human.

Fear around His Birth

Even before Jesus was born, Jesus's parents Mary and Joseph experienced some degree of fear—fear of oppression, fear of death, fear of the unknown. The gospel of Luke opens with a note of fear as the writer describes the days of King Herod of Judea, just before Jesus's birth (Luke 1:5–38).

A priest named Zechariah and his wife, Elizabeth, are righteous, devout Jews. Elizabeth is barren, so they have no children, and they are growing old, well past the time of childbearing. One day as Zechariah is going about his priestly duties in the sanctuary, an angel of the Lord appears. "When Zechariah saw him, he was terrified; and fear overwhelmed him. But the angel said to him, 'Do not be afraid, Zechariah, for your prayer has been heard. Your wife Elizabeth will bear you a son, and you will name him John.'" This son will be John the Baptist, the one who prepares the way for the coming of Jesus.

Zechariah, certainly reeling in shock not only about the presence of the angelic messenger, Gabriel, but also about the news just delivered to him, questions the angel: How could this be happening? And, because of his doubt, Zechariah loses his ability to speak.

Six months pass before God sends the angel Gabriel on another mission, to Nazareth in Galilee to Mary, a young woman engaged to Joseph, purportedly a descendant of King David. Gabriel comes to her and says, "Greetings, favored one! The Lord is with you." Notice her reaction: "But she was much perplexed by his words and pondered what sort of greeting this might be."

"Perplexed"? The word might better be translated "disturbed" or "troubled." Certainly she had to be afraid at the sudden appearance of this divine messenger, just as her relative Zechariah was. This becomes clear in the angel's next words to her: "Do not be afraid, Mary, for you have found favor with God."

But God's message to her is breathtaking: she will conceive a son who will be named Jesus. "He will be great, and will be called the Son of the Most High, and the Lord God will give to him the throne of his ancestor David. He will reign over the house of Jacob forever, and of his kingdom there will be no end."

Mary's response is not unlike Zechariah's, but the angel does not render her speechless. She says to the angel, "How can this be, since I am a virgin?" She too fails to understand how it's possible for her to be pregnant. The angel explains that God's Spirit will come upon her, and "the power of the Most High will overshadow you; therefore the child to be born will be holy; he will be called Son of God…. For nothing will be impossible with God."

Mary listens to this incredible news, accepts this astonishing promise, and responds in faith: "Here am I, the servant of the Lord; let it be with me according to your word." And the angel departs.

What about Mary's betrothed, Joseph the carpenter? Matthew 1:18–25 tells his side of the story. Before they were married, before they lived together, Mary is "found to be with child from the Holy Spirit." Despite his confused and broken heart, Joseph isn't willing to expose Mary to public disgrace, so he plans to deal with the matter and break the engagement honorably and quietly. Just then an angel of God appears to him in a dream, telling him, "Joseph, son of David, do not be afraid to take Mary as your wife, for the child conceived in her is from the Holy Spirit. She will bear a son, and you are to name him Jesus, for he will save his people from their sins."

Notice that Zechariah and Mary are encouraged by the angel not to fear. Gabriel no doubt had an awesome and glorious appearance. Joseph, however, is visited in a dream, and is told not to fear taking Mary as his wife. And he obeys. Rather than fearing public humiliation, he would help raise a son whose impact on the world would be incalculable.

"Do not be afraid." This is the message of God over and over to God's people who are faced with momentous challenges and changes. Even on the night of his birth, the baby Jesus is surrounded by people filled with amazement and fear, including lowly shepherds, who nevertheless are told by God's messengers not to fear, but to give God glory and praise.

Feeling His Fear

The gospels disclose several incidents when Jesus is afraid or troubled by fear. Yet it's clear he is never consumed by fear, at least not until his ultimate crisis in the Garden of Gethsemane.

In Mark 3:1–21, Jesus heals a man with a withered hand in the synagogue on the Sabbath, challenging the religious leaders who become angry over his action. As a result, the religious leaders begin to conspire to destroy him. Jesus knows what is happening, and that his life is at stake. Then Jesus departs with his disciples to the sea, but a "great multitude" of people follow him. Having heard about all he was doing, fascinated by this healing prodigy, "they came to him in great numbers from Judea, Jerusalem, Idumea, beyond the Jordan, and the region around Tyre and Sidon."

Jesus has a sudden attack of ochlophobia, the fear of unruly mobs. He tells his disciples to "have a boat ready for him because of the crowd, so that they would not crush him." Perhaps Jesus fears that matters are getting out of control, that people will swarm and harm him, or else proclaim him their Messiah before his time. Surrounded by the needs of hurting, diseased, abandoned people, he asks the disciples to prepare a boat for him to escape the smothering crush of the anxious crowd.

Jesus takes off up a mountain, far from the madding crowd, and there he calls to him twelve men who will be his disciples. Perhaps one of the reasons he gathers them around him is that he feels need of their protection.

Then Jesus goes home, but "the crowd came together again, so that they could not even eat." Word is moving swiftly throughout the whole land about this miracle-working teacher, and when his own family hears it, "they went out to restrain him, for people were saying, 'He has gone out of his mind.'"

This whirlwind of rising antagonism, pressing crowds, and mushrooming expectations is no doubt stressful to Jesus. Though he must have worried enough to make provisions for his security—the boat at the ready, the escape to the mountain, the appointment of twelve close companions—Jesus is never described as being emotionally out of control as a result of fear. He acknowledges his emotions, but he trusts God. He accepts the anxiety, stress, and even fear of his circumstances, but does not let those feelings overpower him. He deals with these negative feelings in practical ways, and he knows ultimately that all is well, and all will be well.

Anticipating His Terror

During his final week, from the parade of the palms to his crucifixion on a dark Friday, Jesus begins to feel deeply the fear of what is about to happen to him. He has prepared for this moment his whole life, and now it approaches. In John 12:23–36 he explains to his disciples, "The hour has come for the Son of Man to be glorified. Very truly, I tell you, unless a grain of wheat falls into the earth and dies, it remains just a single grain; but if it dies, it bears much fruit."

Jesus has stood up against the stiff-necked, hard-hearted, hypocritical religious authorities, those to whom God had given the responsibility of caring for God's people but who had turned their position into a means to acquire personal wealth and power. Moreover, Jesus has announced a new kingdom, the reign of God, raising suspicion among the secular Roman authorities. Jesus knew there would be consequences for his actions and teachings, but he also knew he had come to shake the people out of the spiritual malaise and existential fear that imprisoned them, to invite them into the commonwealth of God.

Nevertheless, it would be a brutal week for Jesus. And he feels it. "Now my soul is troubled. And what should I say— 'Father, save me from this hour'? No, it is for this reason that I have come to this hour." He is afraid, and his very soul trembles at what he is about to encounter.

A voice comes from heaven, affirming Jesus's message. Many in the crowd believe the voice to be mere thunder, but others say an angel has spoken to him. Jesus acknowledges that the voice is for their sake, not merely comforting him in his distress but verifying his word to them. "Now is the judgment of this world; now the ruler of this world will be driven out. And I, when I am lifted up from the earth, will draw all people to myself."

The people crowding around him are confused. They wonder, who is this "Son of Man" Jesus speaks of? How can he be lifted up? Jesus doesn't answer their questions, but says, "The light is with you for a little longer. Walk while you have the light, so that the darkness may not overtake you. If you walk in the darkness, you do not know where you are going. While you have the light, believe in the light, so that you may become children of light." After Jesus says this, he departs and hides from them.

This is a time of fearful darkness not only for Jesus, but also for all the people of God. Yet God's light shines on them. If they can but see the light, then the darkness, the fear and oppression, cannot defeat them. Perhaps Jesus is saying this as much to himself as he is to the anxious people gathered around him. If he can get through this dark time, he knows the way of light will be victorious.

Troubled by His Betrayer

As the story of Jesus's final week continues (John 13:1–30), we learn that "Jesus knew that his hour had come to depart from this world and go to the Father. Having loved his own who were in the world, he loved them to the end." Despite his trepidation, his love continues unshaken, undiminished. He "loved his own," and yet one of them—Judas, son of Simon Iscariot—is about to betray him to the authorities.

Certainly the authorities have enough evidence to condemn Jesus; they had interacted with him numerous times, and he had brazenly broken their laws by healing on the Sabbath and even committing blasphemy by claiming to be the Son of God. Yet apparently Judas, for whatever reason—disappointment that Jesus was not the earthly king he had hoped for, a desire for more influence, or simply a character flaw—offers to turn Jesus in for a price.

Jesus, in a small upper room with his closest followers, knows he will be turned over to the furious authorities, and one of his closest companions is about to make that happen. Yet still he lovingly serves. He rises from the table, removes his robe, pours water into a basin, and begins to wash the disciples' feet—even Judas's—and wipe them dry with a towel. They had walked long roads with him, traveled many miles in his service. Jesus loves them to the end.

Jesus dons his robe again, returns to the table with them, and asks if they understand why he washed their feet. "I have set you an example, that you also should do as I have done to you. Very truly, I tell you, servants are not greater than their master, nor are messengers greater than the one who sent them. If you know these things, you are blessed if you do them." This is Jesus's message, the heart of the good news. No matter who you are, no matter your position, no matter how you feel or what you fear, you are to serve one another freely and sacrificially.

Jesus continues to teach his disciples, but finally he can no longer contain his anxiety: "After saying this Jesus was troubled in spirit, and declared, 'Very truly, I tell you, one of you will betray me.'" This is the second time in this account that Jesus is described as "troubled"—the Greek word *etarachthe* means to be disturbed, terrified, confused, stirred up, or agitated. Jesus is anxious and alarmed, shaken to the core of his being over what is about to unfold. This dark night is filled with betrayal, confusion, and fear.

The Climax of Fear

When Jesus finishes teaching and praying, he and the disciples cross the Kidron Valley and find their way into an olive garden called Gethsemane. As they gather on this dark night, Jesus asks his disciples to sit with him while he prays. Mark's account (14:32–42) says he takes Peter, James, and John with him a little farther to a place in the garden where he could pray, and he "began to be distressed and agitated. And he said to them, 'I am deeply grieved, even to death; remain here, and keep awake.'" He is greatly troubled; in another translation Jesus says, "My soul is overwhelmed with sorrow to the point of death."

Jesus, clearly overcome by fear over what looms ahead, asks his closest disciples—those who had seen him transfigured on the mountaintop not long before—simply to stay awake, to watch out for him, while he went further into the garden to pray alone, to let his feelings out before his holy Parent. His palpable fear weighs on him like a heavy cloak. He must be shivering both from the cold of the night air and from the fear that grips him.

"And going a little farther, he threw himself on the ground and prayed that, if it were possible, the hour might pass from him." Jesus is desperate, consumed by his emotions and physically distraught. We have never seen him in this place in the gospels, throwing himself down in agony, groveling before God to take this moment of desperate fear away from him.

Mark says Jesus addresses God as "Abba, Father." *Abba* is the familiar, affectionate Aramaic form of the word for father. He is begging his "daddy" to hear him. He acknowledges that with God "all things are possible" and pleads for God to "remove this cup from me"—the cup of suffering and death. And yet he asks for "not what I want, but what you want." Jesus is willing to let go of his fear, his terror over the betrayal, suffering, and death that await him, for the greater glory of the will of God.

Perhaps this act of surrender calms his heart and pacifies his troubled soul. Jesus returns to his closest companions and finds them not awake and alert on his behalf, but sleeping. They no doubt have fallen into a disturbed doze of exhausted grief and fear, huddling together for warmth in the cold reality of their desperate situation. To Peter Jesus complains, "Simon, are you asleep? Could you not keep awake one hour? Keep awake and pray that you may not come into the time of trial; the spirit indeed is willing, but the flesh is weak." He is disappointed in his friend, asking him again to stay awake and pray. In doing so, he likely is trying to encourage himself: Jesus's spirit is willing—he knows his suffering and death will benefit all humanity—but his flesh is filled with anxious, agitated terror.

Again Jesus leaves his three disciples and goes to cry out in prayer. He asks God to spare him, and yet again surrenders to the inevitable. In Matthew's account (26:42) this second prayer is, "My Father, if this cannot pass unless I drink it, your will be done." If there is no other way, then he is willing to die.

A third time Jesus comes and complains to his sleeping disciples, "Are you still sleeping and taking your rest? Enough! The hour has come; the Son of Man is betrayed into the hands of sinners. Get up, let us be going. See, my betrayer is at hand." It is time.

Jesus has wrestled with his terror—the ultimate matters of torture and brutal death—and surrenders to God's will. As a fully human being he has embraced his feelings, acknowledged them, prayed over them, and turned them over to God. He confronts his deepest fears, his ambivalence about what is to happen, so that, out of his deep anguish, he can say yes to God: "Your will be done."

Fear of Abandonment

Jesus goes through a number of "trials" in a subdued state. He has surrendered to the inevitability of what is unfolding, so we don't witness specific examples of his fear. He endures the questioning of the religious and political authorities without any emotional outbursts.

Ultimately he is nailed to a cross and left to die over several excruciating hours (Matthew 27:45–50). "From noon on, darkness came over the whole land until three in the afternoon. And about three o'clock Jesus cried with a loud voice, *'Eli, Eli, lema sabachthani?'* that is, 'My God, my God, why have you forsaken me?'"

On the cross Jesus feels utterly abandoned and forsaken. Unitarian pastor Forrest Church once said in a sermon: "We know that Jesus struggled with fear as he hung dying on the cross. It is written all over his last words.... Here we find him, at the hour of his death, quoting not the comforting 23rd Psalm but the starker 22nd—not 'I shall walk through the valley of the shadow of death and fear no evil for thou are with me' but 'My God, my God, why hast thou forsaken me?' Instead of the comforting words that usher in the close of the 23rd Psalm, 'My cup runneth over,' Jesus moans, 'I thirst.'"[3]

As Jesus struggles for his final breath on the cross, in the pit of painful abandonment, we discover that "the fear of Jesus is just like our fear. He worries. He wonders if he has done all he could to accomplish his mission, and at the end of his life, for one dramatic moment, he fears that he has failed, that everything was for naught."[4]

Yet even in the midst of this fear and failure, Jesus answers with love. On the cross, mocked and insulted by the crowd, tortured by the Roman guards, he gazes upon them all, sweat and blood no doubt blurring his vision, and prays, "Father, forgive them; for they do not know what they are doing" (Luke 23:34).

As he hangs there dying, Jesus considers not his own hideous situation and fate; rather, he is concerned about the fate of others. He forgives and he offers love. This is the very essence of the gospel, seeping out of his broken, weary body: Love God, love your neighbor as yourself. Finally, "Jesus cried again with a loud voice and breathed his last." It is finished. Yet despite the violence of his death, on the cross Jesus's fear is transformed by love, and both bear witness to the reconciling power of God.

Trust in the Darkest Moments

At the end, Jesus had been imprisoned, tortured, beaten, stripped, and emptied of all life. It was for him a time of utter darkness, aloneness, emptiness. He knew this fate was coming; he did not want to face it, he even feared it—and yet he surrendered to it, showing us the way to loving sacrifice even unto death.

Jesus was as human as we are, and like us he experienced fear. He let himself feel it, but he didn't let his fear consume him or keep him stuck in powerlessness. He prayed to God for peace and freedom, for wisdom to deal with the situations in which he found himself. His trust in God and his love for God sustained him in the darkest moments of his life, and his understanding of his mission in life kept him moving forward through his fear.

Jesus's fears were well grounded. He was, after all, tortured to death. His teachings and actions, as he well knew, caused such consternation and panic among the religious and secular authorities that they believed they had no choice but to silence him in what they assumed would be a permanent manner.

How Jesus Responds to Fear

Paradoxically, Jesus himself often struck fear in the hearts of his own disciples, causing them to be concerned for their safety and even for their lives. His miraculous actions repeatedly sent them to their knees, cowering in the realization that this man was imbued by a holy power far beyond mortal understanding.

Early in his ministry, Jesus stands on the shore of Lake Gennesaret teaching a swelling crowd of listeners who press in on him so they can better hear him (Luke 5:1–11). Jesus notices a couple of fishing boats nearby, so he gets into one and asks its owner, who happens to be Simon Peter, to put it out a little way from the shore. From this floating lectern Jesus continues to teach the crowds.

After finishing his teaching, Jesus tells Simon to go out to deeper water to catch some fish. Biting his tongue and perhaps with a frustrated sigh, Simon explains to Jesus, "Master, we have worked all night long but have caught nothing. Yet if you say so, I will let down the nets." When he and his partner do so, they end up catching so many fish that their nets begin to break from the strain and nearly sink the boat. Overcome by fearful awe, Simon Peter falls to his knees, astonished by this simple gesture of Jesus, stricken by a sense of unworthiness.

Simon is frightened by the power he has witnessed, for Jesus tells him, "Do not be afraid; from now on you will be catching people." Simon and his companions bring their boats back to shore and leave everything to follow this astonishing rabbi. In response to their fear of his power, an unflappable Jesus offers both a comforting word and a calling to serve. He's asking these simple men to recognize who he is and become part of what he is doing.

Trust in a Loving Power

A community in the land of the Gerasenes had been gripped by fear because of a man living among the tombs who was possessed by a legion of demons (Mark 5:1–20). His violent outbursts caused all sorts of mayhem, to the point that people would try to restrain him with chains so he would not attack them. Yet he wrenched the chains apart and broke his shackles into pieces. "No one had the strength to subdue him."

Jesus comes to this stressed-out community by boat, and as soon as he steps onto the shore the disturbed man runs to Jesus and bows down before him, and Jesus commands the unclean spirit to come out. The man cries out at the top of his lungs, "What have you to do with me, Jesus, Son of the Most High God? I adjure you by God, do not torment me."

Nearby a herd of pigs is feeding on a hillside. The spirits within the man beg Jesus to send them into the pigs. Immediately the herd of some two thousand pigs rushes down the bank into the sea, where they drown. It must have been a fearsome sight; the swineherds run off and spread the news about what has happened, drawing crowds of people to see Jesus and the man, whom they now find, Mark reports, "clothed and in his right mind, the very man who had had the legion; and they were afraid."

"They were afraid." This is the community that has had to deal with this terrorizing man for some time, trying and failing to contain his violent outbursts, fearing what he might do next. But now that man is whole, and Jesus is the reason why. Their fear shifts from the legion of evil spirits to this powerful stranger who can command them. As a result, they implore Jesus to leave their neighborhood.

Jesus gets into the boat to leave, and the healed man begs to go with him. But Jesus refuses, telling him, "'Go home to your friends, and tell them how much the Lord has done for you, and what mercy he has shown you.' And he went away and began to proclaim in the Decapolis how much Jesus had done for him; and everyone was amazed." Jesus wants the healed man to demonstrate to his family and friends, to his whole community, what the mercy of God looks like in the flesh. As a result, the people's fear of Jesus is transformed into amazement.

Jesus doesn't tell these people explicitly not to be afraid. Instead he demonstrates that their fear is pointless and harmful. They, too, need to trust in the loving power of God, a force that wipes fear away.

Accept God's Peace in the Storm

The gospels include several stories in which terrified disciples face a stormy sea. Matthew, Mark, and Luke all record a time when Jesus suggests that they all go in a boat to the other side of the lake, leaving the crowd behind. It is evening, and as they sail across the sea while Jesus sleeps in peaceful exhaustion on a cushion, a horrendous storm arises (Mark 4:35–41). The storm is strong enough to create panic and fear among these hardened fishermen, but not enough to disturb Jesus's sleep.

The disciples wake him, shouting, "Teacher, do you not care that we are perishing?" Of course he cares, but in their panic they blame him for not being concerned about their survival. He wakes up, rebukes the wind and says to the sea, "Peace! Be still!" The storm stops to a dead calm.

Jesus turns to his friends, who are still panting in their panic, and says, perhaps rubbing the sleep from his eyes, "Why are you afraid? Have you still no faith?" These men had been with him for some time by now, had seen him work miracles, and yet still didn't get it. Jesus suggests once again that fear can be overcome by faith, faith in the one who has the power to calm the storm of life's chaotic circumstances. The disciples are frightened—not only by the storm, but also by this astonishing man Jesus. They say to one another, "Who then is this, that even the wind and the sea obey him?"

As my friend Edward Beck points out, "Maybe that's the way it feels sometimes—like Jesus (or God) is asleep in the boat while we are perishing. *Don't you see that we are drowning?* becomes the cry of our hearts. *Don't you see that my husband is abusive? Don't you see that my son is drug addicted? Don't you see that my best friend is being sent to prison? Are you asleep?* We fear that we are being left to deal with these vagaries of life alone. But the words echo back, 'Why are you afraid, you people of little faith?'"[5]

Later, the disciples again are in a boat at sea (Matthew 14:22–27). Having just fed thousands of people with a few loaves of bread and two fish, Jesus tells the disciples to get into the boat and go on ahead of him to the other side of the sea while he dismisses the crowd. But before joining them, Jesus goes "up into the hills by himself to pray," staying there alone until evening. By this time the disciples' boat is far from land, and the winds and rough seas begin to batter it. The disciples fight the elements once more into the night. It is early morning when Jesus comes walking toward them—on the water.

The disciples can't believe their eyes: they are terrified, screaming, "It is a ghost!" Jesus speaks reassuringly to them: "Take heart, it is I; do not be afraid." Again, he offers words of comfort. No need to be frightened; it's just me! The disciples fear not only the apparition they see but also the incredible power Jesus displays by walking on the water.

Unlike the similar account in the gospels of Mark and John, Matthew appends an interesting story about Peter here (14:28–33). Just a moment ago Peter was one of the terrified, screaming disciples, but now, realizing his friend and rabbi Jesus is with him, he responds to Jesus's call to take courage and fear not. Peter answers Jesus, "Lord, if it is you, command me to come to you on the water." Is he testing Jesus, or himself? Jesus simply says, "Come." So, Peter climbs over the side of the boat, dips his foot in the water, and starts walking on the water toward Jesus, who still stands on the surface. How must Peter have felt in this brief moment of grace, moving into the unknown, moving through his fear toward his beloved rabbi?

Yet the waves are still rough enough to cause concern. When Peter notices this, he becomes frightened again and starts to sink, crying out, "Lord, save me!" Jesus immediately reaches out and catches him, saying no doubt with a teasing smile, "You of little faith, why did you doubt?"

Again Jesus challenges us to overcome fear with faith, because fear only limits us while faithful risk taking opens us up to possibilities beyond our imagining. When we trust that Jesus's loving grasp will hold us up, we can move ahead fearlessly.

Stand Up, Fear Not

After climbing a mountain with Peter, James, and John, Jesus offers them a word of comfort in the midst of their fear (Matthew 17:2–7). Jesus is "transfigured" before them there: "his face shone like the sun, and his clothes became dazzling white. Suddenly there appeared to them Moses and Elijah, talking with him." Moved by this awe-inspiring sight, Peter babbles in excitement about building three dwellings so Jesus, Moses, and Elijah can stay there. As he does, a bright cloud passes over them and a voice booms, "This is my Son, the Beloved; with him I am well pleased; listen to him!"

That sends the disciples right over the edge: when they hear this, they fall to the ground, "overcome by fear." Notice Jesus's response: "But Jesus came and touched them, saying, 'Get up and do not be afraid.'" From their prostrate positions they look up and see no one but Jesus; the other figures have vanished.

Jesus comes to them as they lie on the ground in a quivering pile, terrified by what they have seen and heard. He reaches out to them with a healing touch. But then he commands them to stand up and fear not. There is both comfort and challenge in his response to his closest disciples here. He is present with them in their fear, so they can trust him despite their fear.

Fear at the Resurrection

The religious and secular authorities' fear of Jesus's authority and popularity ensnares him, just as he had predicted, and they eventually put Jesus to death. His broken body is buried in a tomb, though the story does not end there. Yet even amid the power and glory of Jesus's resurrection, there is still fear. Fear is the characteristic reaction to the resurrection, an event that inspires confusion and awe even today.

After the dark weekend as the first day of the week dawns, a great earthquake suddenly shakes the land, "for an angel of the Lord, descending from heaven, came and rolled back the stone and sat on it. His appearance was like lightning, and his clothing white as snow. For fear of him the guards shook and became like dead men" (Matthew 28:1–10).

Meanwhile in Mark's account, Mary Magdalene, Mary the mother of James, and Salome go to the tomb after the Sabbath to bring spices to anoint Jesus's body for permanent burial. When they arrive, they realize to their consternation that the tomb is open; the stone covering the opening has been rolled back. Fearing that Jesus's body has been stolen, they enter the sepulcher to find a "young man, dressed in a white robe, sitting on the right side; and they were alarmed" (Mark 16:5).

Who is this? What has happened to Jesus's body? In their grief-fueled terror, they must have been deeply agitated. But, just as the angel told Zechariah, Mary, and Joseph before Jesus was born, now God's messenger assures the women, "Do not be afraid." Then the angel explains, "I know that you are looking for Jesus who was crucified. He is not here; for he has been raised, as he said. Come, see the place where he lay. Then go quickly and tell his disciples, 'He has been raised from the dead, and indeed he is going ahead of you to Galilee; there you will see him. This is my message for you.' So they left the tomb quickly with fear and great joy, and ran to tell his disciples." The women are as terrified as the guards had been, but their fear is overcome by joy.

While the women are on their way, suddenly Jesus himself meets them with a cheerful word, "Greetings!" Imagine the emotions racing through them at this moment: from profound grief to a mixture of fear, astonishment, shock, joy, and love. They approach him and embrace his feet, worshiping him. And Jesus says to them, "Do not be afraid; go and tell my brothers to go to Galilee; there they will see me."

In Mark's account, the women "went out and fled from the tomb, for terror and amazement had seized them; and they said nothing to anyone, for they were afraid" (16:8). According to most scholars, this is how the gospel of Mark originally concluded. Two other endings—one short, one longer—apparently were appended to give the story a much more inspiring and positive ending. The later editors might have felt uncomfortable that, even in the midst of resurrection, Mark's gospel ends in fear. Yet the story of the resurrected Jesus is one of conquering fear, of facing utter darkness and isolation and moving through it to a glorious reality.

The gospels recount a number of times the resurrected Jesus appears to his disciples, provoking awe and even fear among them. Luke 24:36–49 tells of one time the disciples gather after the resurrection talking about all they had experienced, when Jesus suddenly stands in their midst and says, "Peace be with you." The disciples are "startled and terrified," assuming they are seeing a ghost.

Jesus says to them, "Why are you frightened, and why do doubts arise in your hearts? Look at my hands and my feet; see that it is I myself. Touch me and see; for a ghost does not have flesh and bones as you see that I have." It all comes down to their faith. Doubt and fear have shaken the disciples, and Jesus wonders why. All that he had told them has come about. He is not a ghost; he is a resurrected human. They have all the proof for their faith that they need if they would simply trust in it. Faith can overcome fear and doubt.

Jesus spends time with his dear companions, eating broiled fish with them and unfolding for them all that was written about him in the Law of Moses, the Prophets, and the Psalms. Everything that has happened, he tells them, is part of God's way. Now it is up to them to proclaim the loving message to all nations.

The disciples' fear is understandable. They have witnessed and experienced events no human being ever had before. They are given a challenging call to change the world with God's love. Their faith in their friend Jesus will enable them to overcome their fear and share his love with everyone.

What Jesus Teaches about Fear

In his teaching about worry in the Sermon on the Mount, Jesus says, "So do not worry about tomorrow, for tomorrow will bring worries of its own. Today's trouble is enough for today" (Matthew 6:34).

Jesus is realistic. He understands that life can be troubling, that our worrisome concerns can occupy us in a visceral way. Getting through this day requires wisdom, skill, and fortitude. We must be prudent and resourceful; we must plan carefully, because the troubles we must deal with today require our full attention. Yet today also brings opportunities for spiritual clarity, for unfettered joy, for meaningful interaction with others, for nurturing love. If we spend our time worrying about the details of our days, we lose the gifts of the present moment. Jesus is encouraging us to live in the now, to deal with what we must while availing ourselves of the resources of our loving God. When we do, our worries fade away.

Trust in God's Care

In Matthew 10:24–31 Jesus explains that those who follow him should expect persecution, as it is the natural result of upsetting the status quo. Even so, there is no need to fear; God will provide all we need in the face of opposition. Jesus nevertheless challenges us to boldly and fearlessly proclaim the way of God's reign in spite of fearful circumstances.

The overarching truth Jesus offers here is that God is concerned about every facet of our lives. After all, "Are not two sparrows sold for a penny? Yet not one of them will fall to the ground apart from your Father. And even the hairs of your head are all counted. So do not be afraid; you are of more value than many sparrows." Jesus assures us that we are of infinite worth to God, so we have no reason to fear.

But then Jesus goes further: "Do not be afraid, little flock, for it is your Father's good pleasure to give you the kingdom. Sell your possessions, and give alms. Make purses for yourselves that do not wear out, an unfailing treasure in heaven, where no thief comes near and no moth destroys. For where your treasure is, there your heart will be also" (Luke 12:32–34). If our hearts are in the right place, there is no room within them for the fear that damages our will and inhibits fullness of life. If our strivings are in pursuit of the eternal values of God, then God promises to supply what we need to enjoy a full life on earth— which will no doubt be far less than what most people assume.

The Way, the Truth, and the Life

In the upper room with the disciples, as they dine on the Passover meal together one last time, Jesus has washed their feet, revealed the betrayer, and begun to share his final words about their relationship and the future that awaits them. Jesus knows the disciples need to be reassured regarding his love. Yet knowing what awaits him, he is likely feeling intense fear as well.

He begins this time of teaching, recorded in John 14:1–20, with a word of encouragement for his uneasy, distressed friends: "Do not let your hearts be troubled. Believe in God, believe also in me." Jesus assures them that God knows what God is doing, and that Jesus can be trusted because he and God are one. Again, we hear his mantra that faith can overcome fear. And he promises that his disciples will be together with him again in God's realm, adding, "you know the way to the place where I am going."

Mired in confusion and fear, Thomas interjects: "Lord, we do not know where you are going. How can we know the way?" You can hear his frustration and concern, which the other disciples likely share in this moment. Jesus responds, "I am the way, and the truth, and the life." They do know the way, because they know Jesus.

If we accept and follow this radical way of trust in God, our hearts will not be troubled. And we will have divine help in this, Jesus promises: "I will ask the Father, and he will give you another Advocate, to be with you forever. This is the Spirit of truth, whom the world cannot receive, because it neither sees him nor knows him. You know him, because he abides with you, and he will be in you." In their fear of imminent loss and abandonment, Jesus promises his disciples—and those of us who follow him still—that we will not be orphaned and alone. Jesus's Spirit comes and takes up residence within us.

Jesus assures his friends, "In a little while the world will no longer see me, but you will see me; because I live, you also will live. On that day you will know that I am in my Father, and you in me, and I in you." *You in me, and I in you.* This is as intimate a relationship as a human being can possibly experience. The Spirit of Jesus is within us, comforting us, keeping us whole, empowering us, encouraging us. In the light of this loving relationship, fear flees. It is banished.

Overcoming Fear

Living in fear is no way to live. Dealing with our fear requires great inner strength and faith. As theologian Scott Bader-Saye writes, "We cannot command ourselves to feel less fear. Quite the contrary, our overwhelming fears need, themselves, to be overwhelmed by bigger and better things, by a sense of adventure and fullness of life that comes from locating our fears and vulnerabilities within a larger story that is ultimately hopeful and not tragic."[6]

We can learn much about how to overwhelm our fear with "bigger and better things" from Jesus's own experiences of fear, his responses to fear, and his teachings about fear. By doing so we can overcome the paralyzing fear that keeps us from experiencing a life of abundant, liberating love.

So, we need to be wise about fear and reflect seriously about its impact on our lives. Let us recognize our feelings of fear without letting them control us. Let us withstand fear's influence without expecting that we can or should be indomitable. Let us learn to consider the possibility of fear as a gift of God—because it can protect us, teach us, make us stronger. As Episcopal Bishop J. Neil Alexander put it, we live at the intersection of terror and promise; it's up to us to determine which way to go.[7] But first we must understand the role fear plays in our relationship with God.

Experiencing the Fear of God

Jesus was able to persevere in the face of bone-shaking fear because of his utterly trusting relationship with and faith in God. Yet according to Jewish teaching, faith like this arises from a kind of fear—fear not of the future, not of dangers of any kind, but *fear of God*.

The Hebrew Scriptures Jesus studied were full of encouragements to fear God, such as this one: "The fear of the Lord is the beginning of wisdom; all those who practice it have a good understanding. His praise endures forever" (Psalm 111:10). And the writer of Ecclesiastes offers this conclusion to his trenchant evaluation of life on earth: "Fear God, and keep his commandments; for that is the whole duty of everyone" (12:13).

It was the "fear of God"—the reverent, loving awe in the presence of the all-powerful, all-knowing, all-present Father/Mother—that kept Jesus's life on mission and his priorities in order. The fear of God is the beginning and the end of our faith.

This is quite a different sort of fear from the anxiety-filled state of mind we usually associate with fear, though it is not entirely unrelated. The fear of God is an awe of God's unfathomable power and wisdom, a reverent faith that has its source in the holiness and otherness of God. In fact, according to one noted rabbi, the "fear of God" is the "Hebrew equivalent of 'religion.' It is the mainspring of religion, morality, and wisdom." The fear of God doesn't make us shrink from God as one would from a wild beast or an evil dictator; rather, it draws us nearer to God and fills us with reverential awe. This fear, the rabbi suggests, is "identical with love and service." It implies a hatred of evil and "makes for righteousness and peace."[8]

In the Bible, the fear of God is a gift. It is the source and beginning of wisdom, of life fulfilled. Although many find the concept of fearing God abhorrent, we should remember that this fear is not the kind that keeps us tied up in unhealthy knots. This fear is a proper understanding of our relationship with the loving God of the universe, the God of grace who is able to calm our anxieties and give us the strength to persevere.

So, it is healthy to develop a pure, reverent fear of God, with its source in God's limitless love, and to let that faithful fear of God overcome the fears of this life. This fear of God builds hope and enables us to overcome the emotional fears we have in and of this world. In his sojourn on earth, Jesus clearly displays both kinds of fear: emotional anxiety and reverence for God.

Scripture reminds us time and again that God's presence is a refuge, and so there is no reason to fear if we dwell in it. The reason we need not fear what the future holds or what the world may throw at us is that we have a proper relationship with and understanding of God: we fear God.

Moses expressed this paradox to the Israelites after God gave him the Ten Commandments on Mount Sinai in the midst of a terrifying, thunderous cloud: "When all the people witnessed the thunder and lightning, the sound of the trumpet, and the mountain smoking, they were afraid and trembled and stood at a distance, and said to Moses, 'You speak to us, and we will listen;

but do not let God speak to us, or we will die.' Moses said to the people, *'Do not be afraid*; for God has come only to test you and to put the *fear of [God]* upon you so that you do not sin'" (Exodus 20:18–20; italics added).

Jesus taught the same balanced approach to fear to his disciples: "*Do not fear those* who kill the body but cannot kill the soul; *rather fear [God]* who can destroy both soul and body in hell" (Matthew 10:28; italics added).

These two kinds of fear are not synonymous. We don't replace our fear of the world or of the future with a terror of God. Many teachers suggest replacing the concept of "fear of God" with "reverence for God," a sense of awe over God's supreme power and majesty. Reverence and awe are certainly part of this fear of God, but as theologian and professor Ellen Davis explains: "The writers are speaking first of all of our proper gut response to God. Fear is the unmistakable feeling in our bodies, in our stomachs and our scalp, when we run up hard against the power of God. From a biblical perspective, there is nothing neurotic about fearing God. The neurotic thing is *not* to be afraid, or to be afraid of the wrong thing. That is why God chooses to be known to us, so that we may stop being afraid of the wrong thing. When God is fully revealed to us and we 'get it,' then we experience the conversion of our fear."[9]

The healthy fear of God acknowledges that God is utterly holy and almighty; God is love indeed, and God cares intimately about each of us. It is healthy to maintain our pure fear of God, a fear with its source in limitless love, and let that faithful fear of God overwhelm our fears and anxieties in this life. The healthy fear of God urges us to yearn for God, to seek the face of the Lord, as the psalmist put it (Psalm 27:8), to bask in the welcoming yet challenging presence of God.

God's awesome presence reveals the worldly fears that hinder and entangle us, and they shrink away in the heat of holy love. The God of unlimited power and love, who never threatens our truest good but is at work purely to sustain it, wants only to turn our fear away from the worldly forces that seek to manipulate, control, and coerce us, and redirect it to a healthy relationship with our loving God.[10]

In this light, an early incident in Mark's gospel (Mark 1:21–28) reveals an insight into our relationship with Jesus as well. Mark reports that the people are "astounded" at Jesus's teaching. And then Jesus heals a man in their midst with an unclean spirit, and the people are "amazed." Notice those words *astounded* and *amazed*. Both of these verbs imply fear. For instance, the Greek verb *ethambethesan* translated as "amazed" here means to astonish *to the point of fright*.

Time and again throughout Mark's gospel the writer describes something Jesus says or does that leaves the witnesses astonished, afraid, amazed, or fearful. So if those witnesses had been open to God's redemptive work in their lives, their fear of Jesus would have become the same sort as the reverent fear of God. It was their choice, and it is ours: Do we run *from* Jesus, afraid of who he is and what he will do? Or do we run *to* him in reverent trust and fearless faith?

A Positive, Energizing Fear

Healthy fear can energize us to act in ways far beyond what we might imagine is possible for us. If we respond to our fearful circumstances with clarity of mind, in faith and wisdom, we can be safe and empowered. If we let fear continually fester within us, then we are only opening ourselves to a painful paralysis.

As one expert in anxiety disorders puts it, "Worry is supposed to be Step 1 of problem solving, but it can be problem-generating instead. If it gets going too long, it actually overrides your ability to problem-solve."[11] So, when fear or anxiety creeps into your life, embrace it and let it empower your positive, active, prayerful response.

As we remind ourselves that Jesus felt the very same feelings of fear, anxiety, and dread that we sometimes do, we can also see that *he acted in love even amid those feelings*. He didn't let his fear hinder his love and service to others. He moved through his emotions to fulfill his calling.

Even as he faced death on the cross, he offered the hope of paradise to one of the thieves hanging on a cross next to him. Despite his feelings of abandonment by God, he put his beloved mother Mary and his dearest friend John together in a new relationship of care and trust. He did not let his fearful emotions strangle the overarching love that he ceaselessly expressed.

As Forrest Church preached, "When we feel that we are alone, that God is not with us—when our heart is filled with dread about life or about death—we can take to heart not the fear of God, but the saving fear of Jesus, his own sense of abandonment by God, his all-too-human thirst. We can reach out as he did, not only *for* help—though that is a very fine thing to do—but *to* help as well. Letting go, Jesus recalled his own saving truth: love your neighbor; love your enemy; God is love; and love casts out all fear."[12]

Following Jesus's Example

Jesus offers tangible help in overcoming our fear through his example in moments of fear, stress, and utter anxiety:

Jesus lets himself feel his fear. He doesn't repress his anxiety or deny that he is deeply troubled at times; he is completely open and transparent about how he feels.

Jesus prays honestly about his fear, crying out to God in his pain. He knows his loving Abba/Ima will hear him.

Jesus trusts the love of God to give him the wisdom and strength he needs to overcome his fear-filled circumstances.

Jesus shares his fearful feelings with his companions, and asks for their support. Even though his disciples are of little help in their sleepy stupor when Jesus is experiencing the terror of his impending doom in the Garden of Gethsemane, he nevertheless asks for their encouragement.

Jesus keeps the bigger picture in mind as he faces his fears. He knows he is to be a martyr for the way of life God has called him to live and share; it is inevitable. He acknowledges that his death will have ramifications for all of humanity. He trusts God that life will continue beyond this world in resurrection. When he brings these truths to mind, he gains courage to press on despite his fear of the torture and death that he anticipates.

Jesus helps us see that a loving faith in God—based on a proper fear of God—allows no room for the earthly fears that cripple us from living as God invites us to live. Even so, many times we feel alone, powerless, and wholly vulnerable in our anxiety and fear. We cannot embrace God as we could a human lover; we cannot crawl into God's lap and feel the protective warmth of hope incarnate. So God's consolation may at times seem to be a fickle promise. But sometimes that promise is all we have to hold on to. In faith we can believe that it will be enough.

In those times of fearful loneliness we need to keep in mind what matters to God, and Jesus makes it very clear that *we* matter to God. God knows us and loves us—knows us so well that God is aware of the number of hairs on our head. God knows when even a sparrow falls, so God certainly is aware of and concerned about our needs.

So, we must carefully examine the fears that paralyze and limit us, and acknowledge that they are rooted in our lack of faith. Only then can we move from fear into faithfulness, defeating the power of fear in our lives through love. Only then, like Jesus, can we respond to fear calmly and clearly.

But, this type of courageous faith in the face of fear is possible only when we capture a true understanding of what it means to follow Jesus in living in the way of God, because that is not without risk. It requires courage. It will lead us into risky behaviors such as reaching out to those in need, feeding the hungry, clothing the naked, visiting the prisoner, welcoming the stranger (Matthew 25:31–46). Following Jesus means walking in the way of self-sacrificial love.

Imagine your life without the fear that can strangle and weaken. Imagine being empowered by the courage that comes from knowing and trusting your loving heavenly Father/Mother in every aspect of your life. If that were your reality, what might you be doing differently today? To whom would you reach out? What would you work to set right? What ministry might you finally take up? What righteous risks would you pursue?

When we are in relationship with the God who loves and cares about us infinitely, when we are ordering our lives with integrity and openness to whatever God might send our way, we have nothing to fear as we wrestle with these questions—even in the face of overwhelming odds.

Living fully and meaningfully requires that we acknowledge the power that unhealthy fear has on our behavior, on our attitudes, on our whole life. Without the courage of faith in the face of fear, we may miss out on some immense blessing, gift, or calling of God. Let us ask God to shine the light of the limitless and lively divine love onto the dark, fearful areas of our hearts. When we do, we'll find we can't wait to see where God takes us next.

Exploring Emotions: Fear

Picture a time when you worried about things over which you had no control—such as the sudden loss of a job, the disruption of the natural world, the collapse of the economy, the end of the world. Think about the steps you took to overcome that anxiety. How effective were these steps?

Many times we awake in the middle of the night with irrational, though sometimes quite real, fears. Can you think of ways that God helps us overcomes those fears?

What are the three most fearful situations in your life today? How many of them are truly important to you? How can you separate authentic fears from those that paralyze and limit us even though they are simply the minor worries of our days?

5

Grief

Being Present to the Process in Hope

G rief can be an uninvited yet unrelenting companion on our life's journey.

Grief has been a part of my life in varying degrees since childhood. My first experience of grief at age nine walloped me unexpectedly. I'd experienced sadness often enough, of course—over losing a favorite comic book, over a childish insult from a friend, over losing a hard-fought game of softball in the backyard. Never before, however, had I felt the heavy, shocking assault of grief that massive loss causes.

One late October afternoon I walked home from elementary school, casually entered the front door of our dark-red brick parsonage in Huntington, West Virginia, and yelled, "Mom, I'm home!" I wanted to get my homework done and go outside to play with my buddies or maybe watch *Soupy Sales* on channel three. But that wasn't to be. Coming down the stairs, my mother, dressed as if she were going to church, was crying. Alarmed at seeing my mother in tears, an uneasy fear crept through my body. Sensing my panic, she came to me and explained through her sobs that my dear great aunt Maude had died in a car accident.

I was stunned; my childhood world was rocked by the news. Aunt Maude was my mother's father's sister, a retired schoolteacher from another town who remained single all her life. Aunt Maude often came to stay with us and seemed to take particular delight in me, or at least that's how it felt to me. She would hold me in her lap and read me books with great expression. She would bring me little gifts—a toy, a book. She was a dear heart, and I loved her deeply. Now Aunt Maude was dead. My young mind churned with the confused realization that she was gone forever.

The next few days of funeral and burial preparations are mostly lost to my memory. But, I do vividly remember approaching the open casket with my family during the funeral service to say goodbye to Aunt Maude. I could barely peer over the edge of the casket to look in. When I did, I was shocked.

It wasn't Aunt Maude! It didn't look anything like her. This waxy body was wearing lipstick and orange rouge; I never saw Aunt Maude wearing makeup. I was so confused, and that bewilderment only compounded my grief.

This was just the first of my experiences of grief: broken hearts, lost opportunities, the deaths of many other dear family members, a best friend moving away, a loved one nearly broken by addiction. Even so, I consider my life blessed with many rich experiences and wonderful people. And I believe grief is in some unfathomable way a part of that blessing.

Rising above Grief

Some people seem to attract a spirit of grief; it clings to them like a static-charged sock. Their whole orientation in life is toward what is going wrong, what they have lost, what they have never possessed. So, they are mired in the sludge of grief and woe. Others seem to have suffered far more than the average human in manifold ways, and yet maintain a crystalline hope, an easy freedom from the clutches of depression. They are able to rise above their grief—not because they have ignored it or repressed it, but because they have reckoned with it and embraced it. They have understood the place of grief in the richness of life. And they are blessed.

What makes the difference? How have you encountered grief, and how have you responded to it? How can we learn to embrace grief, learn from it, and move on?

Once again we turn to the example of Jesus, who felt grief just as deeply and wholly as we do. The gospels tell of several times when Jesus is grieved by a variety of matters; yet he never lets his grief hinder his mission to love and serve.

What Is Grief?

Any definition of grief makes it shallower than our experience of it. We all know feelings of sadness, sorrow, and mourning; we experience them to various degrees every day.

Grief is an emotion caused by the loss of something good and important to us or to those we love. When we lose something of great value—whether a person, place, possession, or opportunity—our hearts express sorrow and grief.

In the Hebrew Scriptures and ancient Jewish culture, sorrow is encouraged in a variety of circumstances; for instance, it is right to feel grief over trouble, death, and destruction. Such grief is often exhibited very visibly, even physically.[1]

The ancient Greeks and early church leaders often taught that godliness or propriety should vanquish grief and sorrow; however, the writers of the Christian Bible generally considered grief and sorrow to be deeply meaningful human emotions that enable us to wrestle meaningfully with the tragedy in our lives.[2]

As we'll see, sorrow and grief can have a redemptive impact on us, as Jesus will illuminate. Cynthia Bourgeault writes, "I have often suspected that the most profound product of this world is tears. I don't mean that to be morbid. Rather, I mean that tears express that vulnerability in which we can endure having our heart broken and go right on loving. In the tears flows a sweetness not of our own making, which has been known in our tradition as the Divine Mercy. Our jagged and hard-edged earth plane is the realm in which this mercy is the most deeply, excruciatingly, and beautifully released. That's our business down here. That's what we're here for."[3]

Offering Solace with a Broken Heart

Many years ago when I was a seminary student, I was required to do a thirteen-week internship in a local church. However, the megachurch I belonged to then was crawling with seminarians so there were few opportunities to get a true taste of local parish ministry, and I wanted to immerse myself as best I could to discern the call of God I was attempting to follow.

In my search for the best ministry setting for me, I happened to spot a three-by-five card posted on a service opportunities bulletin board in the student center. The seminary was theologically conservative, so I was surprised that the card offered an opportunity to serve at a United Church of Christ congregation in South Dallas. For months my fellow seminarians had ignored that card on the bulletin board, no doubt because the UCC was considered so liberal. But I called the phone number listed, talked with Pastor Jerry, and ended up serving there as the unpaid "student assistant pastor," not for thirteen weeks but for a whole year.

They were a precious flock, and they put up with my youthful inexperience. The pastor made me part of everything he did. So, on top of a regular load of seminary classes and several part-time jobs, I preached once a month; taught a junior high Sunday school class (with three members on a good Sunday); helped print and fold the church newsletters; and sat in on premarital counseling sessions, church board meetings, and Bible studies. The experience stretched me far beyond my expectations. Serving at the Church of the Master taught me volumes about hospitality and love, as well as about being part of a caring community of faith.

Jessie, a widow with a heart as big as her neatly kept ranch house in South Dallas, was a member of this small congregation that met in a strip-mall storefront. Her daughters, Millie and

Martha, both in their fifties, had inherited the gene of generous hospitality from their mother. That year they made my little family and me, so far away from home and feeling orphaned, part of their family. On every special day—Easter, Thanksgiving, July Fourth—we joined them and their extended family for an abundant homemade meal and loving, often laugh-filled, fellowship. When my son was born that year, all three of them were as giddy as grandmothers.

Toward the end of that internship year, Millie suffered a heart attack. I got the call that she had been rushed to intensive care at a nearby hospital and made my way there as soon as I could. I still remember seeing Millie in a coma, her little round body at the mercy of a ventilator that caused her lungs to inhale and exhale noisily at a shockingly harsh pace. I was grief-stricken. I felt so helpless. Millie had become one of my loving surrogate aunts, and she was in crisis.

Millie passed away quickly. Jessie and Martha were devastated by the unexpected loss; Millie was the youngest, after all. One of the most difficult tasks I ever had to do was to help the pastor lead the funeral service, while grieving along with Millie's family and friends. It was the first time I had to offer pastoral solace to those who were grieving, and it was an even more difficult effort because of my own grief. Yet in that newly made family we all supported one another, blessing the tears we all shed, laughing at the memories, binding each other's wounds, and recalling for ourselves and one another the eternal love of God for us all.

In times like these we can find help from Jesus's life and teachings. Jesus offers true joy and peace amid our grief and sorrow, and we'll discover how by grappling with some deep questions, enabling us to make sense of and embrace this emotion authentically.

We can look to Jesus for help in learning how to feel our grief and allow it to heal us and empower us, by seeing how he experiences grief personally and how he lets himself be sorrowful without hindering his mission of love. We can observe the ways he responds to grief in others, and hear what he teaches about grief. We can consider him a model for authentically feeling grief, working through it, and waiting in faith for the clouds to part once again.

How Jesus Experiences Grief

The gospel accounts reveal Jesus's personal grief in several situations and imply it in others. Other than in the Garden of Gethsemane when facing his certain doom, Jesus does not often feel grief over his own loss, but rather feels sorrow over the plight of others.

For example, in Matthew 9, as Jesus travels about the cities and villages teaching in the synagogues, he proclaims his good news of God's reign and cures diseases among the people. "When he saw the crowds, he had compassion for them, because they were harassed and helpless, like sheep without a shepherd" (Matthew 9:36).

The word *compassion* in the original Greek encompasses love and tender concern, but also grief. Jesus recognizes that these people are oppressed and powerless; their hope has been deeply wounded. He is grieved on account of their pain and their dismal condition in life. It's natural to feel sorrow and pity for those who are suffering, but Jesus's grief for them grows out of his sincere love for them. This compassionate grief will drive Jesus in his mission of loving service to his death on behalf of those who suffer.

Grief over Hardened Hearts

Jesus experiences grief over the religious leaders and their attitudes as well, but this grief is fueled by anger rather than by compassion. We have contemplated Jesus's anger with the religious leaders over their hardness of heart toward those who suffer, and now we witness the way in which grief and anger are commingled.

Jesus has entered the synagogue and notices a man with a withered hand (Mark 3:1–6). The callous authorities watch

Jesus to see if he will break the Sabbath law and heal the man: "He looked around at them with anger; he was grieved at their hardness of heart." Jesus tells the man to stretch out his hand; the man follows Jesus's command and is healed. The leaders judge Jesus for breaking the law and healing the man, yet they themselves plot Jesus's murder; this maddening, hypocritical injustice provokes both sadness and anger in Jesus's heart.

Jesus is grieved by those who have been entrusted with the care of God's people. They have ignored true human needs and striven to maintain their power to determine what is right and wrong in every situation. Jesus's heart is saddened by their mixed-up priorities. They are missing the heart of God in their pursuit of the black-and-white letter of the law, and in their attempts to ensure control over it.

We, too, should be grieved when our leaders in religion or government strive to uphold their own power and position at the cost of those who are truly hurting. Following God's heart in passionate faith means that we seek to fulfill the needs of the brothers and sisters in our midst, rather than ignoring them or casting them out for the sake of our own sense of propriety.

The Sighing Jesus

In Mark's gospel Jesus sighs more than once. These sighs are signs of his sorrow over the needs or pain of those who are ill or oppressed, as well as over the religious leaders and the entire shallow and self-absorbed generation in which he lives. Jesus's sigh blends anger and grief.

Jesus's compassionate grief over the ill and the hurting is poignant and human. Mark 7:34 captures the sigh Jesus expresses over a deaf man, whom he heals. In sadness and frustration he sighs in Mark 8:12 because of Pharisaical intransigence and the shallowness of the whole culture.

In John 11, however, when Jesus joins his friends Mary and Martha at the tomb of their beloved Lazarus, there is no sigh; there is rather the unrestrained weeping of a broken heart.

Some commentators assume Jesus would never grieve because he knew he was able to restore Lazarus to life, but it cannot be clearer that Jesus experiences a rush of grief so deep here that he bursts into tears. Here, outside the tomb, Jesus feels his grief fully, and enters into and embraces the grief of those around him. His fury at death is strangled and overwhelmed by his sorrow over death's catastrophic impact on the human family.

As this moving story reveals to us in all its emotional aspects of love, anger, and grief, Jesus was fully human. He experienced and expressed real emotions just as we do. He loved his friends Lazarus, Mary, and Martha. The message of this account in John, however, and indeed of the entire gospel of John, goes much deeper than that, as leading New Testament scholar N. T. Wright points out:

> When we look at Jesus, *not least when we look at Jesus in tears*, we are seeing not just a flesh-and-blood human being but the Word made flesh (1.1–14). The Word, through whom the worlds were made, weeps like a baby at the grave of his friend. Only when we stop and ponder this will we understand the full mystery of John's gospel. Only when we put away our high-and-dry pictures of who God is and replace them with pictures in which the Word who is God can cry with the world's crying will we discover what the word "God" really means.[4]

A Heart Broken by Rejection

Jesus's grief extends outside his circle of friends to all the people of Jerusalem and beyond. His heart breaks as he laments over the city of God that he loves: "Jerusalem, Jerusalem, the city that kills the prophets and stones those who are sent to it! How often have I desired to gather your children together as a hen gathers her brood under her wings, and you were not willing!" (Luke 13:34). With maternal imagery he reveals his deep love for and grief over the fickle, unbelieving religious capital. His love compels his grief.

In the week before his arrest and crucifixion, Jesus returns to the city to enter in triumph, but, "As he came near and saw the city, he wept over it, saying, 'If you, even you, had only recognized on this day the things that make for peace! But now they are hidden from your eyes. Indeed, the days will come upon you, when your enemies will set up ramparts around you and surround you, and hem you in on every side. They will crush you to the ground, you and your children within you, and they will not leave within you one stone upon another; because you did not recognize the time of your visitation from God'" (Luke 19:41–44).

Jesus is heartbroken over the city's certain rejection of his message of love and justice. *If only...!* Jesus laments, anticipating the disastrous consequences of the inhabitants' self-absorption and indifference to God's ways. *If only* they had understood and accepted Jesus's teachings and his identity, *if only* they had accepted God's call to live in peace and love, the future would have been far different. His sorrow is much like the laments of the Hebrew prophets over Israel hundreds of years earlier in the face of the people's rejection of God's ways. Jesus expresses genuine grief over the loss of what could have been.

Deeply Grieved, Even to Death

At the end of his final week we find Jesus with his disciples in the Garden of Gethsemane awaiting certain betrayal and arrest. As we saw in the chapter on fear, Jesus is mired in anxiety over the violent torture and death that awaits him. Yet he is also grief-stricken. In fact, Matthew's account says when he took Peter, James, and John further into the garden with him, Jesus "began to be grieved and agitated." He says to them, "I am deeply grieved, even to death" (Matthew 26:37–38). Jesus is profoundly sorrowful—not because he fears an uncertain destiny, nor even because of the excruciating physical suffering he is about to face. Rather, his grief arises from the reality that he has always lived wholly for the will of God, yet he anticipates alienation from his heavenly Parent in death.

Does Jesus really know what will unfold in the next hours and beyond? Even if he does, he is nevertheless fearful and sorrowful. He shares his feelings openly with his close friends and seeks their support, simply through their presence with him. Then "Jesus offered up prayers and supplications, with loud cries and tears" (Hebrews 5:7). In prayer Jesus confesses to his loving Father/Mother, "Now my soul is troubled" (John 12:27).

Once again we see Jesus honestly recognizing his emotions, expressing his grief clearly, and asking for what he needs in the moment. In this time of great emotional upheaval, he remains authentic and transparent.

Grief through the Passion

In all four gospels, strong and emotionally intense language dominates the Passion narratives. This is to be expected, because the archetypal story of an innocent person abused and ultimately destroyed by powerful and self-serving authorities draws out our deepest sense of sympathy and sorrow, and forces us to consider the role we may have played in the injustice.

In this final week of his life, Jesus allows himself to experience a whole range of emotions while continuing to move forward toward the cross with unshakable determination. As Matthew Elliott observes, "our emotions can be changed by what we choose to dwell upon, or what thoughts we choose not to dwell upon. However, even Jesus must allow the thoughts of the future suffering to be at the forefront of his mind for a time. He does not deny these thoughts but gives himself the freedom to experience a time of deep emotional pain.... As we all have experienced with great grief, there are times we choose to dwell on other things and go on with life, and times we must just let it flow out of our hearts."[5]

Jesus "gives himself the freedom" to experience his grief. Allowing ourselves to openly experience grief fully is a key aspect to working through our own sorrow-stricken state of mind.

Over time preachers and writers have applied the words of the prophet Isaiah to Jesus, calling him a "man of sorrows":

"He was despised and rejected by others; a man of suffering and acquainted with infirmity; and as one from whom others hide their faces he was despised, and we held him of no account. Surely he has borne our infirmities and carried our diseases; yet we accounted him stricken, struck down by God, and afflicted. But he was wounded for our transgressions, crushed for our iniquities; upon him was the punishment that made us whole, and by his bruises we are healed" (Isaiah 53:1–5).

Jesus was an authentic human who felt his grief, sought comfort, and refused to let his sorrow hinder his mission of love.

How Jesus Responds to Grief

During his sojourn on earth Jesus encounters numerous people who are mourning, hurting, and oppressed, who seem to be ground down by the somber burdens life has placed onto their backs. Time and again in the gospels we see him respond with compassion—healing their physical and emotional problems, offering them a new way of life by following him. Jesus is swarmed by needs wherever he goes and seeks to offer the solace and wholeness only God can provide.

When we look at a few particular instances in which people are clearly grieving, we can see a fuller picture of Jesus's response to grief. Does he ignore the need in light of his greater mission? Does he simply offer platitudes in an effort to soothe others' misery? Or does he respond genuinely, directly, and clearly to those whose hearts have been broken?

By Offering Promises of Hope

One time Jesus and his disciples, along with a large crowd, make their way back to the hill country of Galilee, arriving in the town of Nain. As they approach the town gate, Jesus notices a dead man being carried out for burial. He learns that this man was his mother's only son, and she was already a widow. A large crowd of mourners surrounds her as they trudge to the tomb (Luke 7:11–17).

This woman faces a life not only of utter loneliness but also of poverty, now lacking any breadwinner, and Jesus realizes it. "When the Lord saw her, he had compassion for her and said to her, 'Do not weep.'" Jesus's heart goes out to her, but his words must have been shocking to her and the mourners. *Don't weep?* Doesn't he understand what has happened? Doesn't he realize her bottomless grief over her loss?

Yet Jesus offers not a mere platitude; he offers a promise of real hope. Without any recorded request for help from the woman, with no evidence of her faith in him, Jesus is driven by compassion to touch the bier on which the son's body lies. Once again Jesus ignores the laws against ritual defilement that occurs in that touch, just as he has ignored the ramifications of touching the lepers he has healed.

As he touches the shroud Jesus says, "Young man, I say to you, rise!" Immediately the man sits up and begins to speak, and Jesus guides him down from the bier and takes him to his astonished mother. The mourners are seized by fear—but it's the fear of God, for they praise God and recognize Jesus as a great prophet. "God has looked favorably on his people!" they shout, and the news about Jesus spreads like wildfire.

This particular story of healing occurs only in Luke, and only here in this gospel is the emotion of compassion attributed to Jesus. Jesus's compassion in the face of deep grief drives him to do all he can to provide comfort through the restoration of the son to his mother.

Jesus possesses the power and authority to heal the dead son, a power we ourselves of course do not have. But we, like him, can be present to those in our midst who are in grief, and we can offer our love and concern in God's name. We can have faith that God is present in their loss. And, we can share this faith with others.

By Encouraging Faith in Something Bigger

Amid a crowd surrounding Jesus appears a man named Jairus, who is described as "a leader of the synagogue" (Luke 8:40–56).

He's part of the religious elite whom Jesus normally would castigate. However, Jairus is dealing with a heartbreaking problem and comes to Jesus in desperation. He falls at Jesus's feet and begs him to come with him. His only daughter, about twelve, is dying.

Jesus immediately starts off with Jairus toward his house but is soon surrounded by a pressing crowd. In that crowd there is a woman who has suffered internal bleeding for twelve years, and who has sought help from physicians without any relief. In her desperate grief, she reaches out to Jesus and touches the edge of his cloak. Immediately, she is healed. Jesus senses it and asks, "Who touched me?" Everyone denies it. Peter thinks Jesus is crazy to even ask: "Master, the crowds surround you and press in on you." But Jesus knows someone has purposefully touched him, because he felt that "power had gone out from me." The healed woman, trembling perhaps both in fear and in joy over her healing, comes to him and falls down before him, explaining what has happened. Jesus blesses her with comforting words: "Daughter, your faith has made you well; go in peace."

This slight delay, despite its grace, has been costly. Just as they turn to continue on, someone comes from Jairus's house to report, "Your daughter is dead; do not trouble the teacher any longer." Imagine the sharp pain of dashed hopes in Jairus's heart when he hears this news. Yet Jesus urges Jairus, "Do not fear. Only believe, and she will be saved." Jesus's words, though comforting, must have been utterly confusing as well. The word has come that the daughter has died. What can Jesus do about it now?

Even so, Jesus encourages the faith of those who grieve. If they trust that Jesus is who he says he is, they can believe that God can heal and restore. It is not all about Jesus's divine power; the implication is that without their faith, the healings would not have happened.

They arrive with a crowd in tow at Jairus's house. Jesus, Peter, John, James, and Jairus and his wife enter and find the girl lying there dead, surrounded by weeping and wailing mourners. Jesus says, "Do not weep; for she is not dead but sleeping." In Mark's account (5:38–40), Jesus chides the loudly wailing mourners: "Why do you make a commotion and weep? The child is not dead but sleeping." Their response is derisive laughter; they are shocked silly either at Jesus's insensitivity or his breathtaking foolishness.

Jesus ignores their reaction, takes the beloved daughter by the hand, and says, "Child, get up!" Immediately her spirit returns and she wakes up. Jesus directs her parents to give her food, a moving detail that reflects Jesus's care and concern. Despite their faith, Jairus and his wife are astounded at this, and Jesus orders them to tell no one what has happened.

Jesus acknowledges Jairus's emotional state, and certainly understands it, but urges him to open his mind and his heart to something bigger: the reality of God's loving and healing power. He commands the man, in a sense, to channel his grief into a limitless faith in God, and to trust what happens as a result. If he can do that, sadness will not only be dissolved, but it will also be transformed into joy.

Unremittingly surrounded by grief and distress, Jesus responds to acts of faith with healing and restoration, and with his calming presence. Immediately, he offers a comforting touch, a healing word, an assurance of faith in spite of the odds. We can do the same with those who grieve.

By Revealing Himself

The resurrected Jesus encounters the grief of others on the road to Emmaus. Two followers of Jesus are journeying to a village about seven miles from Jerusalem, talking about everything that has happened in their lives over the past few weeks. They are surely frightened and saddened by the day's reports of the disappearance of Jesus's body from the tomb and confused about the accounts of his resurrection. They are getting out of town for their own protection (Luke 24:13–35).

As they walk and talk, Jesus himself comes near and joins them; however, "their eyes were kept from recognizing him," perhaps because they were in shock, or because tears still filled their eyes over the loss. They pitied themselves and longed for earlier days. Jesus casually asks them what they're talking about. "They stood still, looking sad." Who is this stranger who is so oblivious?

One of them, Cleopas, finally answers him: "Are you the only stranger in Jerusalem who does not know the things that have taken place in these days?" Jesus plays along. "What things?" he asks. They then recount the teachings and activities of Jesus, a prophet of God who has been crucified, the one so many had hoped would redeem Israel. Now, on this third day after his death, there are astounding reports from some of the women of their group that his body is gone from the tomb, that angels have told them he is alive. They explain that others went to the tomb and also found it empty.

Jesus, perhaps chuckling with delight, must have shocked them with his next words: "Oh, how foolish you are, and how slow of heart to believe all that the prophets have declared! Was it not necessary that the Messiah should suffer these things and then enter into his glory?" Then Jesus unfolds the meaning of the scriptures, starting with the books of Moses and the prophets, interpreting to this astonished and confused pair how these texts reveal Jesus's identity and purpose.

Cynthia Bourgeault observes, "Clearly they are stuck in their story, and their stuckness is what makes them unable to see the person standing right before their faces. They are trapped in the past, filled with self-pity and doubt, and no one can recognize anything in this state. What Jesus does in this case is a delightful exercise of 'skillful means': he rewrites their story for them. Verse by verse he leads them through the pertinent [Hebrew] scriptures, reinterpreting their meaning in the light of himself and leading them to the inevitable conclusion that death can't be the end."[6]

As they approach Emmaus together, this strange man walks ahead of the couple as if he were traveling on. They urge him to stay with them, as evening has fallen. So he does. At supper, dining with them, Jesus takes the bread, blesses it, breaks it, and gives it to them. Only in the moment of the broken loaf are their eyes opened: they recognize that this is Jesus himself—and he vanishes from their sight.

In that moment their grief has certainly been broken, their confusion cleared as they acknowledge what has happened: "Were not our hearts burning within us while he was talking to us on the road, while he was opening the scriptures to us?"

This account on the road to Emmaus is a beautiful and emotionally rich story of hope overcoming grief, of the presence of Jesus enabling others to turn their focus away from their sorrowful circumstances and toward God. The breakthrough experienced by Cleopas and his unnamed companion is not so much about *what* they see as it is about *how* they see: "They have come to understand that their attuned hearts are the instruments of recognition and that these same attuned hearts will bind them to their risen Lord moment by moment and forever. They have finally located their inner homing beacon."[7]

Through all these accounts and many others, we see that Jesus responds proactively to grief. He is a man of sorrows, and he knows how it feels to suffer loss, to weep, to have his heart broken. And so he is able to offer solace to others who grieve, to reach out to those who weep with a healing word and comforting touch. He offers good reasons not to be troubled through faith in God. He doesn't exhort those who mourn never to grieve, but rather offers comfort appropriate to the circumstances.[8] In his love and authenticity he offers hope, and he shows a way forward.

What Jesus Teaches about Grief

As a human being Jesus knows what it feels like to grieve. He understands the normal and natural process of grieving, and through his teachings he offers words of comfort and inspiration to those who mourn.

In his Sermon on the Mount early in Matthew's gospel, he specifically proclaims God's blessing on those who grieve. These are the first words out of his mouth: "Blessed are the poor in spirit, for theirs is the kingdom of heaven. Blessed are those who mourn, for they will be comforted" (Matthew 5:1–4). Whereas Luke's account simply says that "the poor"—those who live in abject poverty—are blessed, Matthew broadens this blessed group to include those who are depleted of all their spiritual resources, whose grief has devastated them both physically and emotionally.

Jesus offers solace, declaring that, whether these poor people realize it or not, they are within the realm of God's care. Theirs *is*—present tense—the kingdom of heaven. This is the reality of the way of God; though it might not feel real to the spiritually impoverished, it is true. Catching a glimpse of this reality can be the first step toward moving through a meaningful process of grieving.

Jesus expands what he is teaching by saying, "Blessed are those who mourn, for they will be comforted." Of the nine Greek words used for grief in the Christian Scriptures, the word used here is the harshest emotionally. This is the heart-wrecking, soul-rattling sort of mourning for those who are dead, a grief over the most intense losses. Jesus promises blessing and comfort, even happiness, to those who suffer this depth of grief. As those who mourn enter into the reign of God now, they can be assured of God's comforting fullness—perhaps not in the present moment, but surely in time. Acknowledging this reality is the starting point to fullness and authenticity even in the midst of grief.

Grief Gives Birth to Joy

To the disciples in the upper room, as they await the awful events of Jesus's arrest and crucifixion, Jesus also offers hope (John 16:12–24). He has spelled out what is to happen, and it is a devastating denouement for his friends to contemplate. Jesus knows that what is about to unfold will cause profound grief for his closest followers: "Because I have said these things to you, sorrow has filled your hearts."

Jesus isn't trying to stop his disciples from feeling this grief; he doesn't seek to protect them or forbid them from feeling these devastating emotions. Rather, he understands that these emotions are a natural response to the events that will unfold.

Jesus explains to his confused and grieving disciples, "A little while, and you will no longer see me, and again a little while, and you will see me." The disciples are baffled by what he means, and murmur among themselves until he tells them more plainly, "Very truly, I tell you, you will weep and mourn, but the world will rejoice; you will have pain, but your pain will turn into joy. When a woman is in labor, she has pain, because her hour has come. But when her child is born, she no longer remembers the anguish because of the joy of having brought a human being into the world. So you have pain now; but I will see you again, and your hearts will rejoice, and no one will take your joy from you."

Jesus uses the analogy of childbirth to help calm the disciples' fears and grief. While there is pain and sorrow in what is to come, ultimately the joy of resurrection and of new life will be such that they will completely forget the grief they feel now. Bourgeault writes of this evocative image, "In a real way the disciples are about to become the midwives for such a birth as the world had never seen before: the revelation of the Kingdom of Heaven in its fullness and the inauguration of a whole new level of intimacy between the human and the divine."[9] This is the hope Jesus offers to all who grieve.

Freedom from Grief

One of the last acts Jesus does in this life is to offer hope to someone who is grieving. As he hangs in excruciating pain on the cross, Jesus responds to the repentant grief of one being crucified next to him. "One of the criminals who were hanged there kept deriding him and saying, 'Are you not the Messiah? Save yourself and us!' But the other rebuked him, saying, 'Do you not fear God, since you are under the same sentence of condemnation? And we indeed have been condemned justly, for we are getting what we deserve for our deeds, but this man has done nothing wrong.' Then he said, 'Jesus, remember me when you come into your kingdom.' He replied, 'Truly I tell you, today you will be with me in Paradise'" (Luke 23:39–43).

In this dark moment, this admitted malefactor humbly asks that Jesus keep him in his mind and heart. He acknowledges Jesus as a servant of God, and Jesus—his own life ebbing away—knows this man's heart.

In a way, the two criminals being crucified on either side of Jesus represent every sort of person Jesus encountered during his sojourn on earth. He was either mocked or acknowledged, ignored or followed, his simple way of life rejected or accepted. Jesus offers freedom from our grief—whether over the loss of something dear or over our own failures. It is the freedom that comes from trusting in God's ways and walking in the path of love.

Jesus is utterly realistic about grief in this world and its devastating impact on our lives. He has experienced it himself. But he knows God's love shines forever even on the dark places of our soul, guiding us as we move through the process of grief into the dawn of a new day.

Living with Grief

Jesus experienced grief; he was a man of sorrows. Indeed, he expressed his grief openly in diverse ways. We have observed Jesus in his grief, watched as he responded to those in grief, and listened to his teachings on dealing with grief. Jesus encourages us to feel our grief, to enter into the process of mourning, with the faith and hope that God will heal us and restore us ultimately. We can look to him as a model for how we can authentically own and process our grief, work through it, and trust God as we wait for the darkness to lift. We can remember that while Jesus let himself grieve, he never allowed his sadness to hinder his mission of loving service.

How does Jesus serve as a model for us in terms of grief? Here are some thoughts arising from our study:

Jesus is fully human and experiences true grief. Jesus has compassion—a combination of love, pity, and grief—for the
oppressed people of Israel whose leaders were not the caring
shepherds God intended them to be. Jesus feels an angry sorrow
over the religious authorities' utter disregard of the people's
needs while they themselves worked to strengthen their own
wealth, position, and power. Their mixed-up priorities resulted
in oppression and sorrow among God's people, and this breaks
Jesus's heart.

Jesus experiences full-blown grief at the tomb of his friend
Lazarus, and is sorrowful over death's devastating impact on the
human family. We see his heart breaking over his beloved but
fickle Jerusalem, a city that will praise and honor him one day
and put him to death days later, purposely rejecting God's ways.
In the Garden of Gethsemane we witness his grief over the violent and lonely death he faces.

Through it all we see Jesus acknowledging and expressing his
grief openly and honestly, asking his friends for what he needs,
getting rest and time alone, seeking God's healing presence in
prayer. Yet he never lets his emotion hinder his mission.

Jesus responds proactively to those who grieve. He reacts in compassionate action to those who approach him in their grief, asking for his help. He listens to them and offers solace and healing.
He doesn't try to stifle their emotions; rather, he opens their
eyes to the larger reality of God's love and care. With a calming
presence Jesus offers a healing touch and a hopeful word. He
refuses to extend false hope, but occasionally does share ways to
overcome the grief.

Jesus's presence offers the hope that eventually we can overcome grief, a hope that enables those who grieve to move forward
in faith in their own way and time. We can follow in Jesus's foot-
steps, being present to those in our midst who grieve, serving as
a calming companion, offering our love and help in God's name.

A pediatric nurse once wrote to advice columnist Ann Landers
about her experiences offering support to grieving parents. She
explained that she wouldn't say "I know how you feel," because

she doesn't. Or, "You'll get over it," because even though life will go on, you won't. "So what will I say? I will say, 'I'm here. I care. Anytime. Anywhere.' I will talk about your loved one. We'll laugh about the good memories. I won't mind how long you grieve. I won't tell you to pull yourself together. No, I don't know how you feel—but with sharing, perhaps I will learn a little of what you are going through. And perhaps you'll feel comfortable with me and find your burden eased. Try me."[10] I think that's exactly the attitude Jesus would ask of us toward those who are grieving.

Jesus knows what it means to grieve, so his teachings are marked by authentic hope. Jesus began his Sermon on the Mount acknowledging and blessing those who mourn, promising ultimate comfort. Those who are poor in spirit can mourn in the consoling fullness of God's presence—if they open themselves to that graceful offer and allow themselves time to come to that place. Jesus offers hope in his teaching, a present hope that though we grieve, we understand that we are always in the presence of God's love and know in our weary bones that joy will eventually overcome our pain.

If we are grieving our own failure and loss, whether in our work, in our relationships, or in our moral lives, we must allow the grief and pain to work its way through our being for as long as it takes. We should seek to understand what has caused this grief and let it be present fully in our consciousness. When we do, God can graciously open space in our hearts, a place where God already is present, and minister to us where we are. This is what leads to repentance, changing our minds and moving in a new direction toward God. We can trust that God will welcome us with joyful celebration, as in the story of the prodigal son (Luke 15:11–32).

By the same token, it is easy to fall into the trap of offering easy answers and hopeful platitudes to those in need. Jesus rather offered his very presence, his listening ears, and his healing touch. We can in the same way encourage those in sorrow to move through the process at their pace and pray for God to work within their broken souls.

Wrestling with the Ramifications

As we have studied Jesus's ways and words, we have no doubt wrestled personally with important questions related to grief and sorrow:

How should we evaluate the grief within us? Are we moving through the grieving process intentionally, allowing ourselves to feel our feelings, but keeping our hearts open a crack for the hope God offers?

How might we best respond to the grief of others? Are we as quick to be present to those who suffer in calming love as Jesus was? Do we resist trying to fix the situation, but offer as much hope as the mourner can bear in the moment?

What should we ponder in our minds and hearts about grief? How can we prepare ourselves physically, emotionally, and spiritually for those times in our lives when sorrow strikes us? How can we keep Jesus's example in mind as we move in our world surrounded by those who grieve?

How do we make sense of and embrace this emotion authentically? Can we accept the fact that we will never understand all the whys of grief, that we can only trust in a loving God whose ultimate purpose for us is a greater glory?

Life is a long process of struggling with questions like these, and we will never fully answer them. Yet this is the beauty and challenge of living authentically in the reign of God.

Following the Way of Jesus

Life indeed brims with grief. We allow ourselves to be consumed with "what ifs" regarding missed opportunities; we recite the losses in life we've borne in our hearts until their brittle edges are smoothed out only by our soul's exhaustion. We get stuck in the miserable morass of our mourning and refuse to look up toward the light.

But we can watch Jesus as he lets himself grieve and then keeps moving. We can see how he is lovingly present with those who grieve, offering a healing touch and a compassionate word. We can listen to his words of hope.

We may never understand the *why* of our losses. We may fail to ever see what God is working out through us and in us in gracious redemption. One writer tells the story of a parishioner in his church whose very young son had died. She had lived with the pain of his death her whole life. She explained that as soon as she saw God in heaven, she would ask why God took her son from her at such a young age. What was the point of it?

He writes, "I couldn't tell her the point of it all either, but I could see one significant sign of redemption: This woman who had suffered such a loss was one of the most understanding, forgiving, and empathetic people I've known. She was the type of person into whose eyes you could look and see she had suffered, and because of that, she knew how to love; you felt you could tell her anything and that you wouldn't be judged."[11]

Sometimes our grief is so overwhelming that we simply are unable to see the redemptive healing that God is performing within us. Even without realizing it, as a result of our own painful, sorrowful experience, we have become a blessing to others.

That is the way of Jesus in this world of grief.

EXPLORING EMOTIONS: GRIEF

Remember a time when your life was shattered by the death of a loved one. How did you respond? Was your grief redemptive? Did you discover a way to embrace your grief in order to learn to trust in a loving God?

We spend much of our waking life grieving the loss of one aspect or another of our lives: our health, our relationships, our communities when we move from one place to another, our loved ones through separation or death, and sometimes our religion. What are some ways that you can productively live with these moments of loss so that they define your life in a positive rather than a negative way?

Recall a time when you sat with a grieving friend. Were you able to help that individual embrace the sorrow of the moment, and help him or her embrace the deep and lasting love of God? What might you have done differently?

6

Joy

Savoring God's Gifts

J oy. Think of joy. Feel it.

Joyful memories like gossamer caress my heart; they flow over me like a gentle stream. Images cascade over one another:

The birth of my daughter, hearing her natal cry over a hospital telephone at a time when fathers were restricted from delivery rooms....

The birth of my son three years later, when I could be present despite the need for a cesarean section, as he fought to overcome some initial physical difficulties....

The births of my grandson and granddaughter, launching a whole new phase of life....

Starting a new relationship by getting to know each other over Sunday brunch....

Experiencing the sublime support of a colleague's listening ear and caring heart....

Walking with my loved one in a sun-drenched garden on a crystalline spring day....

Reaching a major milestone in a long process of self-improvement....

On and on the joyful images and memories flow, and I realize just how blessed by joy my life has been.

How about you? What joyful memories come to your mind? What remembered experiences stir the effervescent thrill of joy in your heart?

Sometimes joy erupts suddenly, bursting through the mundane character of our everyday lives. Other times joy wafts gently through our very core, and we float on a calm and delightful breeze.

Recently I have experienced a sense of deep joy in my daily routine, simply sitting with my loved one in our tiny living room listening to the Gabriel Fauré, Liquid Mind, or French Cafe channels on Pandora, sharing news tidbits and experiences of the day, reading an elegantly written book, making plans for tomorrow and next weekend, enjoying all that life has given us. I simply sit there, realizing I am touched by joy.

Yet joy eludes many individuals. The burdens and difficulties of life, perhaps involving ongoing ill health, financial reversals, relationship woes, and fears of a worse future, can distract us from the simple joys that are already ours. Just when we think dawn is about to break for us on a hopeful, more blissful new day, another storm arises, drowning our glimpse of joy.

We know Jesus as a man of sorrows, and yet he was able to squeeze moments of joy out of a difficult and demanding life. We may miss marvelous moments of humor and joy in the gospels simply because we don't expect to see them. In fact, as one commentator observes, there is a "widespread theological aberration" that "misconceives God as a humorless taskmaster.... Somber expectations of holy writ take much away from the good fun in the Gospels."[1]

We all know people who live blissfully and who are able to find joy deep within the folds of a heavy, dismal burden. Sometimes such people drive us crazy. It is wise, after all, to be realistic about life and its needs and problems. Perhaps, though, we miss too many opportunities to experience the joy, and not only to experience it, but also to share it with others, enabling them to see the happy light slicing the dark horizon.

The Joyful Jesus

Jesus again provides an example of someone who lets himself feel the whole range of human emotions, including joy. As we have made our journey through the array of emotions, we've learned that love is Jesus's foundation. We've navigated the difficult and demanding emotions of anger, fear, and grief. Now we find hope in the more positive, uplifting emotion of joy.

Though we may never have realized it, Jesus was a human being who experienced and shared joy. Jesus entered this world in joy, but it was a dark and mean world. As Matthew Elliott puts it, "The gospel of joy was born into a world that was difficult, sullen and without purpose. The prevalent philosophies of the day did not aim at producing a joyful life. The joy of Christianity was a radical departure from the spirit of the age. The gospels radiate joy as the story of salvation is good news, a reason to rejoice."[2]

A careful reading of the scriptures reveals that joy was a natural part of Jesus's personality, his thinking, his way of life. Joy offered him a release from the constant barrage of human need surrounding him, as well as from the awful destiny that awaited him. We'll encounter some unexpected moments of lightness in the gospel accounts of Jesus's experiences, as well as in his teachings. If we weren't so jaded by our familiarity with them, we'd realize that many of his parables are laugh-out-loud funny.

Historian Diarmaid MacCulloch observes, "Jesus was convinced of his special mission to preach a message from God which centered on an imminent transformation of the world, yet he spoke of himself with deliberate irony and ambiguity, and used a delicate humor that is revealed in the content of some of his sayings.... He made crowds laugh."[3]

In fact, Jesus was frequently criticized by John the Baptist's ascetic followers, as well as by the uptight religious aristocracy, for being such a fun seeker, hanging out and even partying with prostitutes, drunkards, and other undesirables. You can almost see them seething at the raucous laughter emanating from a tavern or lower-class home in which they've spotted this radical rabbi.

In Jesus, joy is an infectious force ringing in his voice and gleaming in his eyes. Yet as Quaker writer Elton Trueblood writes,

> The widespread failure to recognize and to appreciate the humor of Christ is one of the most amazing aspects of the era named for Him. Anyone who reads the Synoptic Gospels with a relative freedom from presuppositions might be expected to see that Christ laughed, and that He expected others to laugh, but our capacity to miss this aspect of His life is phenomenal. We are so sure that He was always deadly serious that we often twist His words in order to try to make them conform to our preconceived mold. A misguided piety has made us fear that acceptance of His obvious wit and humor would somehow be idly blasphemous or sacrilegious. Religion, we think, is serious business, and serious business is incompatible with banter.[4]

So, we continue our journey through the emotions of this passionate Jesus to dig deeper into the meaning of joy, how Jesus lived in it, what he taught about it, how he held it out as a gift of God for our life. We'll discover what joy truly is, what brought Jesus joy and how he shared it. We'll find ways to enhance the joy in our own lives, appreciating God as its source and finding ways to share it with others in authentic and meaningful ways.

We need joy in our lives, and God, as always, is ready to share it with us freely and lavishly.

What Is Joy?

We know joy when we feel it. We know when the sublime and authentic emotion washes over us, sometimes unexpectedly, filling us to overflowing. We know how elusive and short-lived joy can be, as delicate as the petals of a fragile lotus flower. Yet joy can also be deep, coursing through our innermost being like a river.

Dr. Matthew A. Elliott offers a helpful description: "The joy we desire is full of life and vitality. Joy is not confidence, it is emotion, it is a bounce in our step and a smile. As we grow to understand the worldview of the gospel we will increase our joy.... We affirm that the most basic definition of joy is the feeling that comes from something good happening to an object you love."[5]

Jesus can help us to understand that the deepest, most lasting, and most authentic joy is rooted in faith. Jesus possessed an absolute and invincible faith in God, and this was the foundation for his joy. He shows us that true bliss comes when we live our lives recognizing that eternal reality beyond the outward existence of this moment-by-moment world.

In our consideration of joy, we can distinguish between physical and spiritual pleasures. Physical pleasures are sensation, possessing a location in one or another body part: the pleasure of a good back massage, of eating an exquisite meal, of good sex (although the best sex involves much more than just the physical).

Many human pleasures are not physical pleasures of sensation, however; rather, they are spiritual or psychological in character. Such spiritual pleasures are pleasures of meaning. When you receive good news about the health of your newborn or achieve a significant milestone, you feel joy in your heart, in your gut—a delight or satisfaction in the moment that all is right in the world. We can also take spiritual pleasure in physical activities, such as playing the piano or a good game of tennis, as well as in enjoying music or good humor. This is joy, and it is one sort of spiritual pleasure.

Jesus was raised in the joy-infused Jewish culture. The Hebrew Scriptures proclaim frequently that praise and celebration flow out of a heart filled with joy, and that one who seeks to *love* God will also *enjoy* God. Spiritual separation from God, the scriptures say, results in a lack of joy, while honest and wholehearted relationship with God brings true joy. And the psalmists offer a number of reasons to express joy—see for example Psalms 1; 16:7–11; 47; 81:1–4; 95:1–3; 98; and 100, among many others. Undeniably, joy is at the very heart and center of the Jewish faith, and of all faith.

We see joy breaking through in Jesus's teachings as well as in his daily way of life. No matter what our circumstances, no matter what heavy burdens weigh us down, Jesus points to the God of joy for hope, showing us how we can discover the joy already within us, how we can hold on to and appreciate the joys that come our way, helping us embrace the emotion of joy as richly and fully as we can.

And it can be a rather raucous joy, as author and scholar Louie Crew points out: "To enjoy the Jesus of scripture, we need to appreciate sarcasm, puns, enigmas, and paradoxes—all part of Jesus' arsenal." When we consider the gospels through the lens of joy, we find scenes that are "richly humorous, full of high spirits, acceptance, and welcome. They show Jesus as warm, personal, and sensual."[6]

Jesus once again points the way to joyful light in the midst of darkness. The simple pleasures of life may come and go, he tells us, but the joy of our God can sustain us and strengthen us all the days of our lives.

How Jesus Experiences Joy

Few experiences are more joyful than the birth of a child. At the birth of Jesus, the very in-breaking of the incarnate Word into human existence, joy abounded. From the accounts in Matthew and Luke we see that Mary and Joseph, the angels, the shepherds, the Magi—all were infused with holy joy at the birth of Jesus, proclaiming the glad tidings and singing glory to God in the highest heaven. The angel announced to the shepherds, "Do not be afraid; for see—I am bringing you good news of great joy for all the people: to you is born this day in the city of David a Savior, who is the Messiah, the Lord" (Luke 2:10–11).

Later, the devout Simeon and the prophetess Anna greet the eight-day-old baby at the temple and are thrilled by the fulfilled promise of God. Jesus's presence on earth provides them magnificent reason to rejoice.

Yet in the midst of all this joy the new family faces many difficulties: having to escape with their lives to Egypt to avoid King Herod's alarming decree issued in response to the perceived threat against his rule (Matthew 2), making a living in a difficult time under foreign occupation, making sense of what all of this meant to them and their son.

Perhaps the incomparable joy surrounding Jesus's birth faded quickly in the stark light of this world. Most likely this family's existence took on a far bleaker cast as they carried many of the same burdens that other families in this region carried. Yet one can nevertheless sense in the pages of the gospels a sustaining joy that particularly filled the heart of Jesus's mother, who so willingly yielded to God's astonishing will.

In the joy that filled his mother's heart, Jesus surely found a basis for approaching life in the real world of grit, pain, and opposition and ultimately of death. Mary knew Jesus faced a difficult path, and he no doubt came to understand that as well. Yet she also endowed him with a sense of hopeful joy that would carry him through the dark times into the light of resurrection.

With His Disciples and "Sinners"

Early in his ministry we catch glimpses of Jesus's joy and his attitude toward it. The disciples of John the Baptist and some of the Pharisees carefully observe the sober fasts of their faith. In stark contrast to their piety, they notice that Jesus's disciples do not fast; in fact, they are notorious for their eating and drinking (Luke 5:30).

Jesus responds to their attack: "The wedding guests cannot fast while the bridegroom is with them, can they?" (Mark 2:19). He likens his time with his disciples to a wedding party. It is right to celebrate and enjoy the company of the groom. Mourning and fasting will come later, but now it's party time. Jesus is bringing the reign of God to the people, after all. His joy overflows into his friends' hearts as fasting is turned into feasting.

Jesus was so well known for gaiety that he emphasizes this in one of his most sarcastic responses to his critics: "John the Baptist has come eating no bread and drinking no wine, and you say, 'He has a demon'; the Son of Man has come eating and drinking, and you say, 'Look, a glutton and a drunkard, a friend of tax collectors and sinners!'" (Luke 7:33–34). His critics simply could not be satisfied. If they didn't like the harsh purity of John, and also didn't appreciate the wine-imbibing gaiety of Jesus, what exactly did they want? You can't have it both ways, Jesus tells them with tongue in cheek.

With Children

Jesus's joy can be glimpsed between the lines in a brief account of his teaching and ministering among the crowds. "People were bringing little children to him in order that he might touch them; and the disciples spoke sternly to them" (Mark 10:13–16). The disciples are trying to protect their rabbi from the joyous and rambunctious presence of little children; after all, he has serious business to attend to and the youngsters are distracting, so the disciples bark at the parents and their children to leave Jesus alone.

"But when Jesus saw this, he was indignant and said to them, 'Let the little children come to me; do not stop them; for it is to such as these that the kingdom of God belongs. Truly I tell you, whoever does not receive the kingdom of God as a little child will never enter it.' And he took them up in his arms, laid his hands on them, and blessed them."

What does childhood represent if not the fun, carefree life of joyful humility? Children tend to be loud and happy and energetic. Yes, they can also be quiet and pensive, but there is no mistaking the joy that fills the hearts of most small children, who have yet to be bruised and burned by the troubles of the world.

I can certainly understand the irritated concern of the disciples. For the past decade or so, our Day1 offices and recording studio have been housed on the third floor of the children's center at All Saints' Episcopal Church in Midtown Atlanta. During the week a daycare facility thrives on the first floor, and often offers day camps and other boisterous activities for children of all ages on the second floor just below us. Occasionally the frantic energy and noise emanating from below us can be a bit bothersome, particularly when we're trying to concentrate on our work or record a radio program.

But Jesus celebrates the joyful heart of a child, and so should we. He says the way of the child is the approach to life that those who want to enter into the reign of God should take: children are cheerful, free, open, creative, positive, and playful. No doubt with a big smile on his face, Jesus warmly embraces several children and blesses them. And he encourages us to be like children, not only in simple humility but also in playful joy.

In His Mission

An incident in Luke 10:1–24 contains surprising moments of joy. Jesus, managing the ever-growing impact of his popular ministry, appoints seventy of his followers to go ahead of him in pairs to every town to prepare the way for his visits. He instructs them carefully, explaining that he is sending them out into the world "like lambs into the midst of wolves." He tells them to take nothing with them—no money, no extra clothing or other items—and offers explicit directions regarding what they are to do and say. Their purpose is to minister in the name of Jesus, healing the sick, preaching his message of hope in the coming of God's reign. He acknowledges that some towns will accept their ministry in his name, but others will reject them.

These seventy followers do as he says, and return "with joy," reporting amazing responses among the people as they healed and taught them. They are bursting with happy excitement over their spiritual successes. Jesus encourages them by saying he has given them the authority to overcome the power of the enemy. "Nevertheless, do not rejoice at this, that the spirits submit to you, but rejoice that your names are written in heaven." Jesus explains that the source of their joy should not be in their authoritative empowerment to serve in exhilarating ways. They have nothing to do with that; it is the work of God within them. So, their joy should arise wholly out of the reality that they belong to God, who gives them their healing mission and the power to fulfill it.

Luke goes on to explain that Jesus's heart is filled with joy as a result of what has happened. "At that same hour Jesus rejoiced in the Holy Spirit and said, 'I thank you, Father, Lord of heaven and earth, because you have hidden these things from the wise and the intelligent and have revealed them to infants; yes, Father, for such was your gracious will....'" His joy springs forth from his wonderfully intimate relationship with his holy Parent.

Then Jesus turns to his disciples and says to them privately, "Blessed are the eyes that see what you see! For I tell you that many prophets and kings desired to see what you see, but did not see it, and to hear what you hear, but did not hear it." Their joy in fulfilling his ministry is unmatched in human history. Even the famous prophets and powerful kings had yearned for this reality, but the disciples have seen it with their own eyes.

Jesus's joy is palpable. As scholar Stephen Voorwinde describes it, his joy is "far more intense and exuberant than that of his followers. They return 'with joy' (10.17) and 'rejoice' (10.20), but Jesus can be described as 'full of joy' (10.21). While Jesus and the [seventy] share the common denominator of joy, his joy is of a different class.... His disciples are happy, Jesus is thrilled. They are glad, he is overjoyed. They are excited, he is exuberant. He is a man on a mission, and now he is beginning to see that mission fulfilled. A task that is close to his heart is being carried out. Others have caught his vision and are beginning to run with it. The mere thought of it gives him a deep sense of satisfaction."[7]

Jesus sees God at work among the people, realizes his message is making headway, and encourages his disciples to be happy because of their amazing experiences. They are finally fulfilling the will of God on this earth, satisfying a yearning that has existed among God's people for centuries. The time has come, and their joy is real. Although dark opposition looms, ultimately all will be well.

Surrounding the Resurrection

In earlier chapters we considered the darker emotions swirling around the resurrection of Jesus. The disciples, like Jesus himself, were fearful and grief stricken. As Jesus's broken body had collapsed on the cross, so had their whole world. Yet as we move from the seemingly endless hours of grief and abandonment of Holy Saturday to the shimmering dawn of Resurrection Sunday, the realization of Jesus's defeat of death grows and takes hold of his followers, and joy breaks out. Love has proven victorious.

In the account in Luke 24, the women come to the tomb to prepare Jesus's body but find it missing. Two men in dazzling array tell them Jesus has risen from the dead, and they recall his teachings about the resurrection. Filled now with joyful amazement, they leave to tell the others what has happened. The male disciples scoff at their report and go to see for themselves. They, too, become "amazed" at what has happened.

Meanwhile, Luke 24 also tells the story of the two disciples walking to Emmaus, whom we met in the chapter on grief. When Jesus breaks the bread in their presence as they share a meal, they realize, finally, who he is, and race back to Jerusalem with the news, their hearts burning with joy. As these two breathlessly share what they've experienced with the disciples, Jesus suddenly stands in their presence. They are "startled and terrified," assuming they are seeing a ghost. Jesus extends his hands and feet, revealing his crucifixion wounds. Luke observes that "in their joy they were disbelieving and still wondering"— joyful but confused.

In the midst of this emotional maelstrom, Jesus asks them for something to eat, and they offer broiled fish. As he eats it, he explains again everything written in the Hebrew Scriptures—the Law of Moses, the Prophets, and the Psalms—that is fulfilled in him. "He opened their minds to understand the scriptures."

Jesus explains that he is sending them out to be his witnesses to all nations, from Jerusalem and beyond, and they will be "clothed with power from on high." As he blesses them, he is carried up into heaven. "And they worshiped him, and returned to Jerusalem with great joy; and they were continually in the temple blessing God."

Luke's account ends in joy, although his story of the nascent church would continue in the book of Acts, colored by much pain, suffering, opposition, and death. Even so, the disciples' mission is one of joy to the end.

What Jesus Teaches about Joy

Many of us have become so familiar with Jesus's teachings that we miss how often he uses playful, even sarcastic, humor. Jesus is no stand-up comedian, but the twinkle in his eyes is apparent as he upends cultural and religious norms and reveals the radical ways of God's reign in the world.

Historian Elton Trueblood discovered this reality as he and his wife were reading perfunctorily from Matthew 7 to their four-year-old son. Suddenly, the little boy began to laugh: "He laughed because he saw how preposterous it would be for a man to be so deeply concerned about a speck in another person's eye, that he was unconscious of the fact that his own eye had a beam in it ... the very idea struck him as ludicrous. His gay laughter was a rebuke to his parents for their failure to respond to humor in an unexpected place."[8]

Trueblood points to thirty passages in the synoptic gospels that he finds humorous,[9] and if we open our minds to seeing them that way, we can appreciate the humor in them as well. Many of Jesus's parables convey this joyful absurdity, including the amusing images he shared of casting pearls before swine, straining out a gnat from a cup but swallowing a camel, keeping a burning lamp under a bed, and watching the blind leading the blind.

One time Jesus jests about the wealthy, saying, "It is easier for a camel to go through the eye of a needle than for someone who is rich to enter the kingdom of God" (Matthew 19:24). The vast majority of the people around Jesus were poor, and here he takes their rich "superiors" down a notch or two. His listeners must have laughed their heads off.

Beyond his use of humor, however, Jesus reveals a joyful way of life for those who enter God's reign. He urges his followers not to draw their happiness from the things of this world, but instead to be happy about the values of God.

Jesus's teaching is imbued also with a genuine hope for eternal joy. In Luke's sermon on the plain, for instance, Jesus says, "Blessed are you when people hate you, and when they exclude you, revile you, and defame you on account of the Son of Man. Rejoice in that day and leap for joy, for surely your reward is great in heaven; for that is what their ancestors did to the prophets" (Luke 6:22–23; cf. Matthew 5:11).

Jesus proclaims a reversal of all human, worldly values. Within God's reign the humble, weak, and poor are the happy ones. Contentment and joy are found only in following the ways of God rather than the selfish and greedy ways of the world. How fully we enjoy our lives relates directly to how fully we give ourselves to God.

Joy in the Parables

The stories Jesus told are filled not only with playfulness but also with true joy. In Luke 15 Jesus tells a series of parables about the joy of finding a lost sheep and a lost coin, with the implication that God is just as joyful when a soul finds its way into God's embrace. Jesus offers the coup de grâce in the moving story of the prodigal son who, upon his humiliated return, hears his father tell his offended older brother, "We had to celebrate and rejoice, because this brother of yours was dead and has come to life; he was lost and has been found."

God can't help it. God is a joyous God, a loving and forgiving God. God can't stop until all the lost and wounded are gathered up in a divine embrace. And then it's time for a party.

Living within God's commonwealth is a reality to rejoice in. Jesus tells a dramatic story about a man who, leaving for a long journey, calls his servants together and entrusts his property to them (Matthew 25:14–30). Those who invested the master's gifts wisely and earned great profit hear the master tell them, "Well done, good and trustworthy [servant]; you have been trustworthy in a few things, I will put you in charge of many things; enter into the joy of your master."

What a lovely invitation: *"Enter into the joy of God."* If we hear it as God speaking to us, whom God has gifted and empowered and entrusted with responsibility in the divine reign, it is empowering. God wants us to share in the joy of God's reign. True joy comes from experiencing the celebration of living fully, sharing with one another in a feast of self-offering.

The Joy of Discipleship

In his lengthy farewell discourse with his disciples in the upper room, Jesus explains, "I have said these things to you so that my joy may be in you, and that your joy may be complete" (John 15:9–12).

Later, in John 16:16–28, which we considered in the chapter on grief, Jesus again promises joy, even though he and his disciples are about to endure the most difficult hours of their lives. "Very truly, I tell you, you will weep and mourn, but the world will rejoice; you will have pain, but your pain will turn into joy." He uses the imagery of a pregnant woman to explain his point. "When a woman is in labor, she has pain, because her hour has come. But when her child is born, she no longer remembers the anguish because of the joy of having brought a human being into the world. So you have pain now; but I will see you again, and your hearts will rejoice, and no one will take your joy from you."

Any parent can identify with what Jesus is saying here. We can all recall times when we were in the darkest, most frightening pain, but everything worked out, sometimes even better than we expected; the pain dissipates in fresh joy that we can never lose.

This is the way living in the reign of God works: fully exercising our gifts, experiencing the pleasure of wholly engaging with our loving God in the world, and realizing the unending joy that redounds to us all.

Living in Joy

The gospels make it evident that Jesus was a charismatic figure who aroused the interest of immense crowds of ordinary people and encouraged many to follow him. No doubt a prominent reason for his charisma was the unbounded joy that fueled his life and ministry. Jesus offers this same empowering joy to his followers today (John 15:11).

Yes, we have seen Jesus as the "man of sorrows." It is because his life was so shaded by grief that his joy stands out so starkly. It is a precious joy. Jesus "is no 'sky-blue' optimist. This man of joy has dwelt in the heart of blackest night. He has seen hell, here on earth, in men's hearts, flaming in their eyes, triumphing in their deeds. Yet his joy is unconquered."[10]

Jesus's joy gives us an anchor for our troubled souls. In his classic devotional work, *The Emotions of Jesus*, Robert Law sublimely captures how joyful the faith of Jesus was—and how joyful faith in Jesus can be for us:

> We seldom realize, and never adequately, what a stupendous thing it is just to believe in God, in a God who is really God.... Such belief, if sincere and vital, must colour all life. God must be its strength and joy, or its terror and despair. And Jesus Christ believed in such a God as no other has believed. To no other has God been a reality at once so universal and so immediately near.... And to Jesus this was joy, perfect and ineffable; because God was to Him not only the Supreme Potentate—the Omnipotent, Omniscient, Omnipresent; [God] was all this, but [God] was the Father, who is Love.... [Jesus's] joy is reflected in the Gospels exactly as it must have been ordinarily present in His life. He does not pause in His work to speak of His joy. It does not so much appear in bursts of sudden splendour as it is the light that shines in the face of common day and colours all the landscape.... Joy in the absolute, all-embracing goodness, wisdom,

and sovereign power of the Father, joy in imparting this
joy to others—this was the joy of Jesus.[11]

As we unite with our loving God in faith, Jesus promises that we,
too, can possess this limitless joy, not only here and now in the
darkness of this world, but also forever and ever in the presence
of God. But we must choose to live this way. We can respond to
our circumstances in fear, sadness, or apathy, or we can stretch
ourselves forward into the joyful embrace of God, squeezing
every drop of holy merriment out of life. This approach is not an
empty, idiotic optimism; it is based on the promises of the God
of the universe, validated and modeled by our loving rabbi Jesus.

Knowing the Joy of Jesus

Spirituality author Marianne Williamson has said, "Joy is what happens to us when we allow ourselves to recognize how good things
really are." As we see how Jesus himself experienced joy and hear
what he taught about it, both to the crowds and to his most intimate
friends, we may realize the joy of which he speaks has been within
us all along, and yet has been smothered by our worries and our
frustrations, our sadness, emptiness, and loneliness. Jesus invites us
to tap into the ever-coursing joy of God that is readily available to
flow through us, and to let it bubble up into our conscious reality.

We have gained a better sense of what joy really means: it's
not silly frivolity; rather, it is a holy hilarity, a deep exhilaration,
a rich bliss, a solid gladness, a merry wholeness.

We've seen that Jesus experienced joy in the presence of his
friends over meals and at parties, as well as in the company of
playful children. He shared his joy with his disciples, and with
the crowds, through his teachings. We've discovered God's
promises of joy to those who live fully within their divine calling.

Along the way, we have come to know the joy of Jesus in
fresh ways:

*Jesus is free with his joy in the presence of his disciples and fol-
lowers*—including those the elite would have dismissed with a

thoughtless wave. Jesus doesn't hold back. He gives himself to enjoying life, celebrating it in the company of his friends.

Jesus invites us to come to God with childlike hearts—full of wonder, curiosity, playfulness, and exuberance.

Jesus tells us that the deepest joy comes in helping to fulfill God's will on earth—by happily serving others in word and deed despite any opposition that might arise.

Jesus finds meaningful joy in the everyday events of human life—as he illustrates again and again in his parables that communicate how to live as a child of God.

Jesus's joy climaxes in the resurrection—the promise of new life that can empower us day by day as we follow in his way.

Jesus promises complete joy to those who take up his challenge to follow him—a joy that can fill us with overflowing hope in these days and usher us into the glorious presence of God forever.

Weeping Tears of Joy

Many years ago during the season of Lent, I found myself awash in apathy about my life, stuck in an interesting but unchallenging job, yearning for fresh purpose. I wanted to get away by myself—a new experience for me at the time, and a practice I've continued over the years since. I wanted to meet with God to get a revived sense of direction for my life.

I arranged to stay in a cabin at Camp Mikell, the Episcopal camp in North Georgia. On the porch overlooking a rocky, rambunctious creek, alone in a rocking chair on a cool mid-March evening, I cataloged my feelings. I felt frazzled after a long, hard, nonstop day at the advertising agency where I worked at the time. I also felt some unsettled fear; even though I'd been to this camp several times, this time I'd gotten lost driving here in the dark. But now I was feeling safer, and a little hopeful, though I had no idea what I would do or what might happen.

After I read Evening Prayer in the *Book of Common Prayer*, I wrote a while in my journal, and found the process moving and refreshing. Maybe this would work after all, I thought.

Saturday morning, after a restful night's sleep, I began with Morning Prayer, another part of "praying the hours" in the liturgical tradition. In the prayer of confession, the phrase "and what we have left undone" jumped out at me. I was struck by the sense that my life was full of *left undones*.

A series of verses came to me as I read the prayer book:

> "For he is our God, and we are the people of his pasture, and the sheep of his hand. O that today you would listen to his voice!" (Psalm 95:7).
> "Oh! Teach us to live well! Teach us to live wisely and well!" (Psalm 90:12, *The Message*).
> "And let the loveliness of our Lord, our God, rest on us, confirming the work that we do. Oh, yes. Affirm the work that we do!" (Psalm 90:17, *The Message*).

As verse tumbled upon verse, I began weeping. Sobs burst out from deep within me. How I wanted to experience these promises personally! Then I remember almost literally feeling the embrace of Jesus. It was so real, so pure, a moment filled with ineffable joy.

My scribbled journal notes, hardly able to capture the depth of the renewal I felt, record it this way: "Overcome by the love and presence of Jesus! Weeping tears of joy—not sadness. Feel accepted and loved and cherished like a friend and lover."

Finally, another verse came to me:

> *God can do anything, you know—far more than you could ever imagine or guess or request in your wildest dreams! He does it not by pushing us around but by working within us, his Spirit deeply and gently within us.*
> *Glory to God in the church!*
> *Glory to God in the Messiah, in Jesus!*
> *Glory down all the generations!*
> *Glory through all millennia! Oh, yes!*
>
> EPHESIANS 3:20–21, *THE MESSAGE*

This blissful experience carried on through the rest of my retreat weekend, and I believe it was the starting point of a rich journey over many years during which I was finally able to begin opening my eyes and my heart to God's wider, more challenging adventure for me—an adventure that would start by moving into a fulfilling new ministry and ultimately enable me to come to grips with accepting myself and my whole identity, which then set me free to be open even more to following Jesus in living fully, and joyfully, in God's realm.

The Joy of Fulfillment

So what does it mean to live in the joy of Jesus? It means we carry out the obligations of our life—our career, our family relationships, our commitments to serve—heartily. We perform our obligations and efforts with joyful love, thereby fulfilling the unique call of God upon us. It means we savor with gratitude everything God gives us to enjoy—the pleasures of a good life that refresh us in body, mind, and spirit. It means we do all this mindfully, so that we avoid harming others or entering into self-indulgent or unhealthy activities.

What if joy is elusive? What if we don't feel it? Sometimes we need to acknowledge that and take inventory of our emotions and their causes. Often we are simply tired or stressed out, and our zest for life has drained away. Jesus encourages us to be honest about how we feel. Perhaps we can remind ourselves of the reality of joy, and our emotions will follow.

Theologian Paul Tillich puts our search for joy into context: "Only the fulfillment of what we really are can give us joy. Joy is nothing else than the awareness of our being fulfilled in our true being, in our personal center. And this fulfillment is possible only if we unite ourselves with what others really are. It is reality that gives joy, and reality alone. The Bible speaks so often of joy because it is the most realistic of all books.... Joy is born out of union with reality itself."[12]

Living in the joy of Jesus, more than anything, means having so much of Jesus within us, so much of God's love filling us, that we cannot help but share it with others. No matter what emotions we may encounter, within ourselves or in others, we can experience those emotions fully and authentically, and yet know that underneath them is divine joy that sustains us forever.

EXPLORING EMOTIONS: JOY

Do you make time for joy in your life? Do you make it a part of your daily schedule? If not, how can you make it more of a priority in your life?

Do you think God laughs at our mistakes and our shortcomings? Can you laugh at yourself and allow yourself to approach God with a childlike joy of heart?

When was the last time you laughed uncontrollably until you cried, danced with abandon in the brilliant sunshine, sang with gusto in the middle of a crowded city street? When was the last time you embraced the deep joy life brings? Why has it been so long, and what is stopping you now?

CONCLUSION

Living Authentically

Thich Nhat Hanh tells us that in Buddhism, the energy that helps us "touch life deeply" is known as *smrti*, the energy of mindfulness.[1]

Jesus is full of *smrti*. Jesus knows himself. He is mindful of his feelings and expresses them clearly and directly. He allows his emotions to empower his life positively. And he invites us to join him in this authentic way of living.

Jesus began his teaching ministry on a hill surrounded by hungry, wounded people who yearned for meaning and fullness in their impoverished lives. They may have misunderstood why he came and what he was about to do; they may not have had even a glimmer of an understanding of what he was all about. Yet they were drawn to him, and he connected directly and intimately with them as he shared the blessings of God. These blessings, the Beatitudes (Matthew 5), focus on our emotional life—our mourning, our passion, our fear, our suffering.

Roman Catholic priest and author Richard Rohr writes, "Suffering is the necessary deep feeling of the human situation. If we don't feel pain, suffering, human failure, and weakness, we stand antiseptically apart from it, and remain numb and small."

Jesus, however, refuses to numb himself from human emotions. "The irony is not that God should feel so fiercely; it's that his creatures feel so feebly," Rohr says. "If there is nothing in your life to cry about, if there is nothing in your life to yell about, you must be out of touch. We must all feel and know the immense pain of this global humanity. Then we are no longer isolated, but a true member of the universal Body of Christ. Then we know God not only from the outside but from the inside."[2]

One in Whom There Is No Deceit

Jesus brings light to our understanding of who we are and how we feel, and why that understanding is so vital for a deeply meaningful and genuine life. Early in his ministry, while in Galilee, Jesus meets a man named Nathanael (John 1:43–51). His brother Philip has invited Nathanael to "come and see" the man he and his friends have met, a man who has already stirred their faith and hope. Nathanael scoffs, but goes with them. As Nathanael approaches, Jesus says of him, "Here is truly an Israelite in whom there is no deceit!"

Jesus is engaging in some clever wordplay—these men would have known that their ancestor Israel, formerly Jacob, was known as the "Deceiver" because of the ways he tricked his brother, Esau, and his father, Isaac. But Jesus is also commenting on the observed character of Nathanael, declaring him to be a man in whom there is nothing false. Nathanael is honest and direct; he says what he thinks ("Can anything good come out of Nazareth?"). He responds with openness to his brother's invitation to explore a fresh opportunity for growth by meeting this new rabbi. And Jesus praises Nathanael for this.

"Where did you get to know me?" Nathanael asks Jesus in surprised confusion. Jesus's answer causes him to fall down in awe and proclaim, "Rabbi, you are the Son of God! You are the King of Israel!" What could have caused such an enthusiastic response? Jesus simply tells him, "I saw you under the fig tree before Philip called you." In some way Nathanael must have revealed himself under that fig tree as an honest human being. Jesus then says to Nathanael, "Do you believe because I told you that I saw you under the fig tree? You will see greater things than these." Nathanael is stunned by this praise of his authenticity, and this invitation to new life.

Jesus deeply values living without deceit, without falsehood, without timidity. He yearns for us to be integrated and whole, utterly transparent and emotionally clean, filled with *smrti* just as he was. Not only does a life marked by honesty and wholeness open us up to the richness of our spiritual relationship with God, but it also empowers us to live as meaningfully and lovingly in this world as we possibly can.

An Integrated Spirit

We see the significance of authenticity in Jesus's interaction with the Samaritan woman, who comes in the hot midday sun to draw water from the well (John 4:5–42). This woman has a sordid history, and Jesus apparently knows it. Even so, Jesus offers her not the brackish well water she has come for, but "living water … a spring of water gushing up to eternal life."

She responds almost desperately: "Sir, give me this water, so that I may never be thirsty or have to keep coming here to draw water." She doesn't quite get it, but she wants whatever it is he's selling. Jesus, perhaps testing her honesty, says, "Go, call your husband, and come back." How will she respond to that? Will she cover up her self-destructive ways, or be truthful?

She is honest with Jesus, up to a certain point. "I have no husband," she replies, no doubt sheepishly, and Jesus teasingly agrees with her: "You are right in saying, 'I have no husband'; for you have had five husbands, and the one you have now is not your husband. What you have said is true!"

She's starting to catch a glimpse of who this Jesus really is. "Sir, I see that you are a prophet," she says, and immediately attempts to change the subject to ask a theological question concerning the practices of the Jews and the Samaritans. Brushing aside her technical question, Jesus boldly replies, "The hour is coming, and is now here, when the true worshipers will worship the Father in spirit and truth, for the Father seeks such as these to worship him. God is spirit, and those who worship him must worship in spirit and truth."

God seeks a spirit of truth within us, a spirit that can only be realized when our *emotional* life is integrated with our *spiritual* life, when we are the same person on the outside as we are on the inside. Jesus makes it clear that emotional authenticity is the basis on which we build our spiritual relationship with God, because God knows our true identity inside and out. Jesus invites this spiritually thirsty woman, and each of us, to enter into this kind of integrated life.

In his teaching on the mountain, which he started by offering blessings upon our emotional authenticity, Jesus warns of false prophets: "You will know them by their fruits…. Every good tree bears good fruit, but the bad tree bears bad fruit. A good tree cannot bear bad fruit, nor can a bad tree bear good fruit…. Thus you will know them by their fruits" (Matthew 7:15–20).

"You will know them by their fruits." Relating spiritually to God in honesty and wholeness rather than in hypocrisy and deceit produces "good fruit" in our lives—love and compassion, peace and joy, meaning and purpose. If our lives are not yielding this good fruit, it isn't God's fault.

Jesus follows this by warning against hypocrisy and dishonesty. "Not everyone who says to me, 'Lord, Lord,' will enter the kingdom of heaven, but only the one who does the will of my Father in heaven" (Matthew 7:21)—a will that Jesus has made plain involves heartfelt genuineness in approaching God in faith.

So it isn't God's responsibility to make sure we are living a well-adjusted religious life—it is ours, and our expectations help shape that life. Jesus didn't say he came to give us happiness, but blessedness. He didn't promise that we'd have an easy life, but an abundant life, one that focuses primarily not on religion or even spirituality, but on loving God and loving others.

It is only this sort of authentic spiritual approach to life that enables us to endure and even flourish in this world. "Everyone then who hears these words of mine and acts on them will be like a wise man who built his house on rock. The rain fell, the floods came, and the winds blew and beat on that house, but it did not fall, because it had been founded on rock" (Matthew 7:24–25).

Living with passionate authenticity, as honestly and fully as Jesus did, is the rock on which we can build meaningful lives, the foundation that brings us security and strength.

Rivers of Living Water

Jesus's emotional life was intense and honest. He let himself feel his feelings wholly and expressed them directly. While Jesus's emotional life resembles a roaring mountain river, with clear water flowing in uninhibited torrents, we may feel as though our emotional lives resemble a stagnant, scum-covered pond, decaying, subdued, and murky. Jesus invites us to open ourselves to him and drink deeply of his life: "Let anyone who is thirsty come to me, and let the one who believes in me drink. As the scripture has said, 'Out of the believer's heart shall flow rivers of living water'" (John 7:37–38).

By accepting this invitation we fulfill the ancient Hebrew prayer, the *Shema*, which calls us to "love the Lord your God with all your heart, and with all your soul, and with all your might." Such a love has as its goal not emotional ecstasy nor spiritual detachment, but rather the experience and expression of a full range of healthy, passionate emotions, which are the natural overflow of our spiritual life.

Jesus offers us liberation from emotional wounding. The way to fullness and well-being can be difficult, and may require the help of a spiritual director, counselor, or therapist. Even so, Jesus offers the promise of a pure and whole emotional authenticity if we will seek it.

And when we do, this is what God does: God shatters the oppressive, hypercontrolled order that we have so carefully constructed to protect ourselves from the pain and difficulty of life and of all our relationships in this world. God forces us to choose whether to hold tight to a stifling, unfulfilling emotional life, or to let go in the liberation of genuine wholeness.

When we choose to live authentically, important implications arise for our relationships with others. Just as Jesus built relationships of love, honesty, and trust, we, too, are called to do the same, enjoying the company of one another in a fellowship of love. In doing so we are better prepared and engaged to carry one another's problems and burdens, as well as all of life's difficulties that threaten to overwhelm us.

Jesus is not so much interested that we become "nice, well-adjusted people," but rather that we thrive as individuals who in healthy, transparent ways are able to forgive and love.[3] In order to help us become what we truly yearn to be, we will have to deal with a little chaos in our lives, but that can only help crack apart our self-protective barriers and yield the blessing of a fulfilling, fruitful life as a human being.

Fully Realized Human Beings

Jesus was the fully realized human being, and he can fill us with a passion for becoming truly, wholly, utterly human as well.

Theologian Walter Wink has written elegantly on Jesus as the "Son of Man," the "human being." He reveals that Jesus did not intend to be the only such utterly human being. "I would prefer to say, Jesus incarnated God in his own person in order to show all of us how to incarnate God. And to incarnate God is what it means to be fully human."[4]

When we consider Jesus to be the only incarnate Son of God, we are diminishing ourselves by assuming that the same wholeness and realness are not possible within us. Wink explains: "The implications of these reflections are profound. It means that we are free to go on the journey that Jesus charted rather than to worship the journey of Jesus. This means we are to be cocreators of God. It means that we can, if we have the courage, recover the healing ministry of Jesus and his very Jewish kind of persistent prayer. It ... makes him as available to Jews or Muslims as to Christians, indeed, available to anyone seeking the Human Being within."[5]

Jesus invites us into the reign of God that encourages and provokes authenticity, that calls us to become fully human beings before the face of God. The quest for this kind of life arises from a yearning hunger to become a uniquely individual human who, like Jesus, possesses the personal characteristics of God, including emotions. The goal is that we may love and cherish others in a way that celebrates each person's unique and precious realities.

We are called to be God's daughters and sons, authentic human beings who follow Jesus's model of wholeness and sincerity in every area of life. In light of this, we can rethink the goal of life: it is "not to become something we are not—divine—but to become what we truly are—human," Wink writes. "We are not required to become divine: flawless, perfect, without blemish. We are invited simply to become human, which means growing through our sins and mistakes, learning by trial and error, being redeemed over and over from compulsive behavior—become ourselves, scars and all. It means embracing and transforming those elements in us that we find unacceptable. It means giving up pretending to be good and, instead, becoming real."[6]

Jesus models realness and beckons us to follow him. The journey starts by understanding our own feelings and why we feel them, and by seeing how Jesus lived a life of passionate emotional authenticity so that we can follow him into wholeness.

Now What?

When I entered into the process of discernment regarding whether I should pursue ordination as an Episcopal priest, I was hoping it could be handled as easily and quickly as possible. After all, I was already ordained—couldn't I simply transfer my ordination to the church of which I'd been a member for more than two decades? Why must I go through the intense, time-consuming, and exhausting process of discernment, spending several weeks at a different local parish than I was used to, getting involved in a demanding reflection group of mentors and peers, spending several days and a night on the streets of downtown Atlanta to engage the homeless, and successfully completing all the tests and examinations required to get to the place of ordination?

However, my bishop saw the wisdom in pushing me into the process. Once I understood and accepted that, I decided to go for it, to go all in, to express a radical availability to learn and to serve and to live into the process as fully and fervently as I could.

It hasn't been easy. On top of all the other responsibilities and relationships in my life, this process has added layers of new activities and demanded intense thought and reflection. Yet it has been truly life changing. I have tried to put into practice what I have been learning through this study of Jesus's emotions, living as fully and authentically and as spiritually empowered as I can.

I am still in this life-shaping process, and regardless of where it leads me I believe that, finally, in some small way, I am starting to get it, starting to catch a glimpse of what Jesus wants for each of us regarding the way we live. I also understand that Jesus can be for me, and for all of us, a revolutionary model of one who knows and loves God so thoroughly that we can't help but grow toward emotionally wholeness and authenticity.

I once heard about this Jesus in a sermon: "Jesus knew what it meant to say, 'Here I am.' At the temptation, he said, 'Here I am, torn with ambition.' At the tomb of Lazarus, he said, 'Here I am, broken and weeping.' At the Mount of Olives, he said, 'Here I am, wanting this cup to pass from me.' Even his last night, tossing and turning unable to sleep, he prays for God's guidance. Even on the cross during the worst nightmare of all—he was torn, 'My God, my God, why hast thou forsaken me?' But at the very end he was at one with the Father, at peace. Picture him there praying the old Jewish prayer that a child would say the last thing before dropping off to sleep, 'Into thy hands I commit my spirit.' 'Here I am, Lord. I am yours completely and fully.'"[7]

This passionate Jesus calls you to follow him into the most meaningful, enjoyable, and loving life you could ever imagine. A life like this starts by saying honestly to God something like this:

Here I am. This is me, God, just as I am, just as you have created me, with all my emotions, with all my unique personality traits and strange quirks, with all the talents and gifts you have instilled within me.

Here I am, with the peculiar calling and purpose to love and serve with which you have blessed and energized me.

Here I am, possessing a spirit of wholeness and honesty through which you empower me, just as you did Jesus.

Here I am. This is who I am, this is my God-imprinted, Spirit-caressed identity.

Here I am. Now what?

EXPLORING AUTHENTIC LIVING

Buddhism teaches us that *smrti* is the energy of mindfulness that helps us touch life deeply. How has your study enabled you to increase in *smrti*?

How honestly do you think you have lived your life with those in your closest circles? Was there a time in your life when you lived in deceit? How did that feel? How will you seek to live a more authentic life in the days ahead?

Jesus is the utterly human being, and he invites us all to live as fully realized persons as well. Do you think that is truly possible? How will you live in light of this aspiration?

Now what?

Notes

A Personal Word of Introduction

1. Beverley Elliott, "The Wheat and the Weeds—Let Them Be," sermon delivered at St. Bartholomew's Episcopal Church, Atlanta, Ga., July 17, 2011.
2. Bourgeault, *Wisdom Jesus*, 4.
3. Ibid., 91.
4. Nhat Hanh, *Living Buddha, Living Christ*, 52–53.

1. Understanding Our Emotions

1. See Oakley, *Morality and the Emotions*, 139.
2. See M.P. Morrissey, "Reason and Emotion: Modern and Classical Views," *Horizons* 16 (1986): 275.
3. Elliott, *Faithful Feelings*, 248.
4. Roberts, *Spiritual Emotions*, 18.
5. Helminski, *Living Presence*, 157.
6. See Elliott, *Faithful Feelings*, 130.
7. Ibid., 264–65.
8. Marcus J. Borg, interview on the *Today Show*, NBC, April 14, 1995, quoted in Borg, *Jesus: Uncovering the Life, Teachings, and Relevance of a Religious Revolutionary*, 164.
9. Borg, *Meeting Jesus Again*, 22.
10. Elliott, *Faithful Feelings*, 111.
11. MacCulloch, *Christianity*, 2.
12. Andrew Sullivan, "When Not Seeing Is Believing," *Time*, October 2, 2006, www.time.com/time/magazine/article/0,9171,1541466,00.html.
13. G. Walter Hansen, "The Emotions of Jesus and Why We Need to Experience Them," *Christianity Today* 41/2 (1997): 42ff.

14. For more on this, see Marcus J. Borg's *Meeting Jesus Again for the First Time* and *Jesus: Uncovering the Life, Teachings, and Relevance of a Religious Revolutionary*, and John Dominic Crossan's *Jesus: A Revolutionary Biography*, among many others.
15. Trueblood, *Humor of Christ*, 20.
16. Dorothy L. Sayers, *Letters to a Diminished Church: Passionate Arguments for the Relevance of Christian Doctrine* (Nashville, TN: Thomas Nelson Publishers, 2004), 4.
17. See Voorwinde, *Jesus' Emotions*, 2.
18. Law, *Emotions of Jesus*, 53–54.
19. Bourgeault, *Wisdom Jesus*, 103.

2. Love: The Centerpiece of Life

1. Elliott, *Faithful Feelings*, 135.
2. Ibid., 164.
3. Martin Luther King Jr., "The Power of Non-Violence" (speech), June 4, 1957, TeachingAmericanHistory.org, http://teachingamericanhistory. org/library/index.asp?document=1131.
4. Templeton, *Agape Love*, 1–3.
5. Borg, *Meeting Jesus Again*, 47.
6. Roberts, *Spiritual Emotions*, 179–80.
7. Nouwen, *Making All Things New*, 49–50.
8. Manning, *Rabbi's Heartbeat*, 96–97.
9. See Voorwinde, *Jesus' Emotions*, 138.
10. Bourgeault, *Wisdom Jesus*, 108.

3. Anger: In Defense of Justice

1. Aaron Ben-Ze'ev, "Anger and Hate," *Journal of Social Philosophy* 23 (1992): 85–86.
2. Law, *Emotions of Jesus*, 90–91.
3. See Elliott, *Faithful Feelings*, 212.
4. Law, *Emotions of Jesus*, 91–92.
5. See Elliott, *Faithful Feelings*, 98.
6. Hansen, "Emotions of Jesus," 42ff.
7. Emily M. Brown, "Jesus Interrupted" (sermon), *Day1* radio program, February 12, 2012, http://day1.org/3548-jesus_interrupted.
8. Voorwinde, *Jesus' Emotions*, 23.
9. Information on the description of these religious leaders is based on definitions found in Wright, *John for Everyone, Part 2*, 181–85.
10. Some of these ideas come from Sayers, *Letters to a Diminished Church*.

11. Voorwinde, *Jesus' Emotions*, 163.
12. Law, *Emotions of Jesus*, 94.
13. MacCulloch, *Christianity*, 88.
14. Law, *Emotions of Jesus*, 100–101.
15. Ibid., 97.
16. Roy Lloyd, "Greed, Hypocrisy, and Occupy Wall Street," a commentary delivered on 1010 WINS, New York, NY, in October 2011, http://day1.org/3367-roy_lloyd_greed_hypocrisy_and_occupy_wall_street.
17. Sharon Sheridan, "Clergy, Laity Support Nonviolent Protests at Occupy Wall Street," Episcopal News Service, October 25, 2011, www.ecusa.anglican.org/79425_130309_ENG_HTM.htm.

4. Fear: Energizing and Empowering a Deeper Faith

1. Beck, *Soul Provider*, 195–196.
2. Ibid., 199–201.
3. Forrest Church, "The Fear of Jesus" (sermon), April 11, 2004, www.forrestchurch.com/writings/sermons/easter-2004.html.
4. Ibid.
5. Beck, *Soul Provider*, 196 (italics in original).
6. Bader-Saye, *Following Jesus*, 60.
7. J. Neil Alexander, sermon delivered at St. Bartholomew's Episcopal Church, Atlanta, Ga., December 11, 2011.
8. Adolf Guttmacher, "Fear of God," in *The Jewish Encyclopedia*, eds. Cyrus Adler, et al. (New York: Funk & Wagnalls, 1906).
9. Davis, *Getting Involved with God*, 102.
10. See Bader-Saye, *Following Jesus*, 43.
11. Reid Wilson, quoted in Alice Parker, "The Two Faces of Anxiety," *Time*, December 5, 2011, 60, www.time.com/time/magazine/article/0,9171,2100106,00.html.
12. Church, "Fear of Jesus."

5. Grief: Being Present to the Process in Hope

1. See Elliott, *Faithful Feelings*, 98.
2. Ibid., 205.
3. Bourgeault, *Wisdom Jesus*, 100.
4. Wright, *John for Everyone, Part 2*, 10–11 (italics in original).
5. Elliott, *Faithful Feelings*, 206.
6. Bourgeault, *Wisdom Jesus*, 129–30.
7. Ibid., 130.
8. See Elliott, *Faithful Feelings*, 206.

9. Bourgeault, *Wisdom Jesus*, 109.

10. Canfield and Hansen, eds., *Chicken Soup*, 46–47.

11. Sayers, *Letters to a Diminished Church*.

6. Joy: Savoring God's Gifts

1. Louie Crew, "Did Jesus Laugh?" *Lutheran Forum* 7.2 (1973): 22–24, www.whosoever.org/v8i3/louielaugh.shtml.

2. Elliott, *Faithful Feelings*, 172.

3. MacCulloch, *Christianity*, 90. British spellings changed.

4. Trueblood, *Humor of Christ*, 15.

5. Elliott, *Faithful Feelings*, 166.

6. Crew, "Did Jesus Laugh?"

7. Voorwinde, *Jesus' Emotions*, 130–31.

8. Trueblood, *Humor of Christ*, 9.

9. Ibid., 127.

10. Law, *Emotions of Jesus*, 5.

11. Ibid., 6–9.

12. Tillich, *New Being*, 146.

Conclusion: Living Authentically

1. Nhat Hanh, *True Love*, 17.

2. Richard Rohr, Daily Meditation: "Suffering," March 27, 2012. Adapted from Rohr, *Radical Grace*, 209.

3. See Galli, "Good News."

4. Walter Wink, quoted in Frederic Brussat and Mary Ann Brussat, review of *The Human Being: Jesus and the Enigma of the Son of the Man*, by Walter Wink, Spirituality & Practice, www.spiritualityandpractice.com/books/books.php?id=3602.

5. Wink, *Human Being*, 139.

6. Ibid., 29.

7. William J. Carl III, "Having Trouble Sleeping Through the Night?" (sermon), *Day1*, November 16, 2008, http://day1.org/1119-having_trouble_sleeping_through_the_night.

Suggestions for
Further Reading

Bader-Saye, Scott. *Following Jesus in a Culture of Fear.* Grand Rapids, MI: Brazos Press, 2007.

Beck, Edward L. *Soul Provider: Spiritual Steps to Limitless Love.* New York: Doubleday, 2007.

Borg, Marcus J. *Jesus: Uncovering the Life, Teachings, and Relevance of a Religious Revolutionary.* San Francisco: HarperOne, 2006.

———. *Meeting Jesus Again for the First Time.* San Francisco: HarperSanFrancisco, 1994.

Bourgeault, Cynthia. *The Wisdom Jesus: Transforming Heart and Mind—a New Perspective on Christ and His Message.* Boston: Shambhala, 2008.

Canfield, Jack, and Mark Victor Hansen, eds. *Chicken Soup for the Grieving Soul.* Deerfield Beach, FL: Health Communications, 2003.

Crossan, John Dominic. *Jesus: A Revolutionary Biography.* San Francisco: HarperSanFrancisco, 1994.

Davis, Ellen F. *Getting Involved with God: Rediscovering the Old Testament.* Cambridge, MA: Cowley Press, 2001.

Elliott, Matthew A. *Faithful Feelings: Rethinking Emotion in the New Testament.* Grand Rapids, MI: Kregel Publications, 2006.

Godsey, R. Kirby. *Is God a Christian?* Macon, GA: Mercer University Press, 2011.

Helminski, Kabir. *Living Presence: A Sufi Way to Mindfulness and the Essential Self.* New York: Jeremy Tarcher, 1992.

Law, Robert. *The Emotions of Jesus.* New York: Charles Scribner's Sons, 1915.

MacCulloch, Diarmaid. *Christianity: The First Three Thousand Years.* New York: Penguin Books, 2009.

Manning, Brennan. *The Rabbi's Heartbeat.* Colorado Springs, CO: NavPress, 2003.

Nhat Hanh, Thich. *Living Buddha, Living Christ.* New York: Riverhead Books, 1995.

———. *True Love: A Practice for Awakening the Heart.* Boston: Shambhala, 2004.

Nouwen, Henri. *Making All Things New.* New York: Harper & Row, 1981.

Oakley, Justin. *Morality and the Emotions.* London: Routledge, 1992.

O'Day, Gail R., and David Peterson, eds. *The Access Bible: New Revised Standard Version.* New York: Oxford University Press, 1999.

Roberts, Robert C. *Spiritual Emotions: A Psychology of Christian Virtues.* Grand Rapids, MI: William B. Eerdmans, 2007.

Rohr, Richard. *Radical Grace: Daily Meditations by Richard Rohr.* Cincinnati: St. Anthony Messenger Press, 1993.

Templeton, John. *Agape Love: A Tradition Found in Eight World Religions.* Radnor, PA: Templeton Foundation Press, 1999.

Tillich, Paul. *The New Being.* New York: Charles Scribner, 1955.

Trueblood, Elton. *The Humor of Christ.* New York: Harper & Row, 1964.

Turner, Nigel. *Christian Words.* Nashville: Thomas Nelson, 1981.

Voorwinde, Stephen. *Jesus' Emotions in the Gospels.* London: T&T Clark, 2011.

Wink, Walter. *The Human Being: Jesus and the Enigma of the Son of the Man.* Chicago: Fortress Press, 2001.

Wright, N. T. *John for Everyone: Part 2, Chapters 11–21.* London: SPCK, 2002.

Scripture Index

Inspiration

Finding Time for the Timeless: Spirituality in the Workweek
By John McQuiston II

Offers refreshing stories of everyday spiritual practices people use to free themselves from the work and worry mindset of our culture.
5⅛ x 6½, 208 pp, Quality PB, 978-1-59473-383-3 **$9.99**

God the *What?*: What Our Metaphors for God Reveal about Our Beliefs in God by Carolyn Jane Bohler

Inspires you to consider a wide range of images of God in order to refine how you imagine God. 6 x 9, 192 pp, Quality PB, 978-1-59473-251-5 **$16.99**

How Did I Get to Be 70 When I'm 35 Inside?: Spiritual Surprises of Later Life by Linda Douty

Encourages you to focus on the inner changes of aging to help you greet your later years as the grand adventure they can be. 6 x 9, 208 pp, Quality PB, 978-1-59473-297-3 **$16.99**

Restoring Life's Missing Pieces: The Spiritual Power of Remembering & Reuniting with People, Places, Things & Self by Caren Goldman

A powerful and thought-provoking look at reunions of all kinds as roads to remembering and re-membering ourselves.
6 x 9, 208 pp, Quality PB, 978-1-59473-295-9 **$16.99**

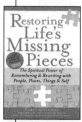

Saving Civility: 52 Ways to Tame Rude, Crude & Attitude for a Polite Planet
By Sara Hacala

Provides fifty-two practical ways you can reverse the course of incivility and make the world a more enriching, pleasant place to live.
6 x 9, 240 pp, Quality PB 978-1-59473-314-7 **$16.99**

Spiritually Healthy Divorce: Navigating Disruption with Insight & Hope
by Carolyne Call

A spiritual map to help you move through the twists and turns of divorce.
6 x 9, 224 pp, Quality PB, 978-1-59473-288-1 **$16.99**

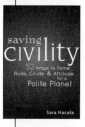

Who Is My God? 2nd Edition
An Innovative Guide to Finding Your Spiritual Identity
by the Editors at SkyLight Paths

Provides the Spiritual Identity Self-Test™ to uncover the components of your unique spirituality. 6 x 9, 160 pp, Quality PB, 978-1-59473-014-6 **$15.99**

Journeys of Simplicity
Traveling Light with Thomas Merton, Bashō,
Edward Abbey, Annie Dillard & Others
by Philip Harnden
Invites you to consider a more graceful way of traveling through life.
PB includes journal pages to help you get started on
your own spiritual journey.
5 x 7¼, 144 pp, Quality PB, 978-1-59473-181-5 **$12.99**
5 x 7¼, 128 pp, HC, 978-1-893361-76-8 **$16.95**

Or phone, fax, mail or e-mail to: SKYLIGHT PATHS Publishing
Sunset Farm Offices, Route 4 • P.O. Box 237 • Woodstock, Vermont 05091
Tel: (802) 457-4000 • Fax: (802) 457-4004 • www.skylightpaths.com
Credit card orders: (800) 962-4544 (8:30AM–5:30PM EST Monday–Friday)
Generous discounts on quantity orders. SATISFACTION GUARANTEED. Prices subject to change.

Children's Spirituality

Adam & Eve's First Sunset: God's New Day
by Sandy Eisenberg Sasso; Full-color illus. by Joani Keller Rothenberg 9 x 12, 32 pp, Full-color illus.,
HC, 978-1-58023-177-0 **$17.95*** *For ages 4 & up*

Because Nothing Looks Like God
by Lawrence Kushner and Karen Kushner; Full-color illus. by Dawn W. Majewski
Invites parents and children to explore the questions we all have about God.
11 x 8½, 32 pp, Full-color illus., HC, 978-1-58023-092-6 **$17.99*** *For ages 4 & up*

Also available: **Teacher's Guide** 8½ x 11, 22 pp, PB, 978-1-58023-140-4 **$6.95**

But God Remembered: Stories of Women from Creation to the
Promised Land *by Sandy Eisenberg Sasso; Full-color illus. by Bethanne Andersen*
A fascinating collection of four different stories of women only briefly men-
tioned in biblical tradition and religious texts.
9 x 12, 32 pp, Full-color illus., Quality PB, 978-1-58023-372-9 **$8.99*** *For ages 8 & up*

Cain & Abel: Finding the Fruits of Peace
by Sandy Eisenberg Sasso; Full-color illus. by Joani Keller Rothenberg
A sensitive recasting of the ancient tale shows we have the power to deal with anger
in positive ways. "Editor's Choice." —American Library Association's *Booklist*
9 x 12, 32 pp, Full-color illus., HC, 978-1-58023-123-7 **$16.95*** *For ages 5 & up*

Does God Hear My Prayer?
by August Gold; Full-color photos by Diane Hardy Waller
Introduces preschoolers and young readers to prayer and how it helps them
express their own emotions.
10 x 8½, 32 pp, Full-color photo illus., Quality PB, 978-1-59473-102-0 **$8.99** *For ages 3–6*

The 11th Commandment: Wisdom from Our Children *by The Children of America*
"If there were an Eleventh Commandment, what would it be?" Children of many
religious denominations across America answer this question—in their own draw-
ings and words. "A rare book of spiritual celebration for all people, of all ages,
for all time." —*Bookviews* 8 x 10, 48 pp, Full-color illus., HC, 978-1-879045-46-0 **$16.95***
For all ages

For Heaven's Sake *by Sandy Eisenberg Sasso; Full-color illus. by Kathryn Kunz Finney*
Heaven is often found where you least expect it.
9 x 12, 32 pp, Full-color illus., HC, 978-1-58023-054-4 **$16.95*** *For ages 4 & up*

God in Between *by Sandy Eisenberg Sasso; Full-color illus. by Sally Sweetland*
A magical, mythical tale that teaches that God can be found where we are.
9 x 12, 32 pp, Full-color illus., HC, 978-1-879045-86-6 **$16.95*** *For ages 4 & up*

God's Paintbrush: Special 10th Anniversary Edition
by Sandy Eisenberg Sasso; Full-color illus. by Annette Compton
Invites children of all faiths and backgrounds to encounter God through moments
in their own lives. 11 x 8½, 32 pp, Full-color illus., HC, 978-1-58023-195-4 **$17.95*** *For ages 4 & up*

Also available: **God's Paintbrush Teacher's Guide**
8½ x 11, 32 pp, PB, 978-1-879045-57-6 **$8.95**

God's Paintbrush Celebration Kit: A Spiritual Activity Kit for Teachers and
Students of All Faiths, All Backgrounds 9½ x 12, 40 Full-color Activity Sheets & Teacher
Folder w/ complete instructions, HC, 978-1-58023-050-6 **$21.95**
Additional activity sheets available:
8-Student Activity Sheet Pack (40 sheets/5 sessions), 978-1-58023-058-2 **$19.95**
Single-Student Activity Sheet Pack (5 sessions), 978-1-58023-059-9 **$3.95**

I Am God's Paintbrush (A Board Book)
by Sandy Eisenberg Sasso; Full-color illus. by Annette Compton
5 x 5, 24 pp, Full-color illus., Board Book, 978-1-59473-265-2 **$7.99** *For ages 0–4*

* A book from Jewish Lights, SkyLight Paths' sister imprint

Judaism / Christianity / Islam / Interfaith

All Politics Is Religious: Speaking Faith to the Media, Policy Makers and Community *By Rabbi Dennis S. Ross; Foreword by Rev. Barry W. Lynn*
Provides ideas and strategies for expressing a clear, forceful and progressive religious point of view that is all too often overlooked and under-represented in public discourse. 6 x 9, 192 pp, Quality PB, 978-1-59473-374-1 **$18.99**

Religion Gone Astray: What We Found at the Heart of Interfaith
By Pastor Don Mackenzie, Rabbi Ted Falcon and Imam Jamal Rahman
Welcome to the deeper dimensions of interfaith dialogue—exploring that which divides us personally, spiritually and institutionally.
6 x 9, 192 pp, Quality PB, 978-1-59473-317-8 **$16.99**

Getting to the Heart of Interfaith: The Eye-Opening, Hope-Filled Friendship of a Pastor, a Rabbi & an Imam *by Pastor Don Mackenzie, Rabbi Ted Falcon and Imam Jamal Rahman*
6 x 9, 192 pp, Quality PB, 978-1-59473-263-8 **$16.99**

Hearing the Call across Traditions: Readings on Faith and Service
Edited by Adam Davis; Foreword by Eboo Patel
6 x 9, 352 pp, Quality PB, 978-1-59473-303-1 **$18.99**; HC, 978-1-59473-264-5 **$29.99**

How to Do Good & Avoid Evil: A Global Ethic from the Sources of Judaism
by Hans Küng and Rabbi Walter Homolka; Translated by Rev. Dr. John Bowden
6 x 9, 224 pp, HC, 978-1-59473-255-3 **$19.99**

Blessed Relief: What Christians Can Learn from Buddhists about Suffering
by Gordon Peerman 6 x 9, 208 pp, Quality PB, 978-1-59473-252-2 **$16.99**

Christians & Jews—Faith to Faith: Tragic History, Promising Present, Fragile Future *by Rabbi James Rudin* 6 x 9, 288 pp, HC, 978-1-58023-432-0 **$24.99***

Christians & Jews in Dialogue: Learning in the Presence of the Other *by Mary C. Boys and Sara S. Lee; Foreword by Dorothy C. Bass* 6 x 9, 240 pp, Quality PB, 978-1-59473-254-6 **$18.99**

InterActive Faith: The Essential Interreligious Community-Building Handbook
Edited by Rev. Bud Heckman with Rori Picker Neiss; Foreword by Rev. Dirk Ficca
6 x 9, 304 pp, Quality PB, 978-1-59473-273-7 **$16.99**; HC, 978-1-59473-237-9 **$29.99**

The Jewish Approach to God: A Brief Introduction for Christians
by Rabbi Neil Gillman, PhD 5½ x 8½, 192 pp, Quality PB, 978-1-58023-190-9 **$16.95***

The Jewish Approach to Repairing the World (Tikkun Olam): A Brief Introduction for Christians *by Rabbi Elliot N. Dorff, PhD, with Rev. Cory Willson*
5½ x 8½, 256 pp, Quality PB, 978-1-58023-349-1 **$16.99***

The Jewish Connection to Israel, the Promised Land: A Brief Introduction for Christians *by Rabbi Eugene Korn, PhD* 5½ x 8½, 192 pp, Quality PB, 978-1-58023-318-7 **$14.99***

Jewish Holidays: A Brief Introduction for Christians *by Rabbi Kerry M. Olitzky and Rabbi Daniel Judson* 5½ x 8½, 176 pp, Quality PB, 978-1-58023-302-6 **$16.99***

Jewish Ritual: A Brief Introduction for Christians
by Rabbi Kerry M. Olitzky and Rabbi Daniel Judson 5½ x 8½, 144 pp, Quality PB, 978-1-58023-210-4 **$14.99***

Jewish Spirituality: A Brief Introduction for Christians *by Rabbi Lawrence Kushner*
5½ x 8½, 112 pp, Quality PB, 978-1-58023-150-3 **$12.95***

A Jewish Understanding of the New Testament *by Rabbi Samuel Sandmel;*
New preface by Rabbi David Sandmel 5½ x 8½, 368 pp, Quality PB, 978-1-59473-048-1 **$19.99***

Modern Jews Engage the New Testament: Enhancing Jewish Well-Being in a Christian Environment *by Rabbi Michael J. Cook, PhD* 6 x 9, 416 pp, HC, 978-1-58023-313-2 **$29.99***

Talking about God: Exploring the Meaning of Religious Life with Kierkegaard, Buber, Tillich and Heschel *by Daniel F. Polish, PhD* 6 x 9, 160 pp, Quality PB, 978-1-59473-272-0 **$16.99**

We Jews and Jesus: Exploring Theological Differences for Mutual Understanding
by Rabbi Samuel Sandmel; New preface by Rabbi David Sandmel
6 x 9, 192 pp, Quality PB, 978-1-59473-208-9 **$16.99**

Who Are the Real Chosen People? The Meaning of Chosenness in Judaism, Christianity and Islam *by Reuven Firestone, PhD*
6 x 9, 176 pp, Quality PB, 978-1-59473-290-4 **$16.99**; HC, 978-1-59473-248-5 **$21.99**

* A book from Jewish Lights, SkyLight Paths' sister imprint

Bible Stories / Folktales

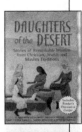

Abraham's Bind & Other Bible Tales of Trickery, Folly, Mercy and Love *by Michael J. Caduto*

New retellings of episodes in the lives of familiar biblical characters explore relevant life lessons. 6 x 9, 224 pp, HC, 978-1-59473-186-0 **$19.99**

Daughters of the Desert: Stories of Remarkable Women from Christian, Jewish and Muslim Traditions *by Claire Rudolf Murphy,*

Meghan Nuttall Sayres, Mary Cronk Farrell, Sarah Conover and Betsy Wharton

Breathes new life into the old tales of our female ancestors in faith. Uses traditional scriptural passages as starting points, then with vivid detail fills in historical context and place. Chapters reveal the voices of Sarah, Hagar, Huldah, Esther, Salome, Mary Magdalene, Lydia, Khadija, Fatima and many more. Historical fiction ideal for readers of all ages.

5½ x 8½, 192 pp, Quality PB, 978-1-59473-106-8 **$14.99** Inc. reader's discussion guide
HC, 978-1-893361-72-0 **$19.95**

The Triumph of Eve & Other Subversive Bible Tales
by Matt Biers-Ariel

These engaging retellings of familiar Bible stories are witty, often hilarious and always profound. They invite you to grapple with questions and issues that are often hidden in the original texts.

5½ x 8½, 192 pp, Quality PB, 978-1-59473-176-1 **$14.99**

Also available: **The Triumph of Eve Teacher's Guide**
8½ x 11, 44 pp, PB, 978-1-59473-152-5 **$8.99**

Wisdom in the Telling

Finding Inspiration and Grace in Traditional Folktales and Myths Retold
by Lorraine Hartin-Gelardi
6 x 9, 192 pp, HC, 978-1-59473-185-3 **$19.99**

Religious Etiquette / Reference

How to Be a Perfect Stranger, 5th Edition: The Essential Religious Etiquette Handbook *Edited by Stuart M. Matlins and Arthur J. Magida*

The indispensable guidebook to help the well-meaning guest when visiting other people's religious ceremonies. A straightforward guide to the rituals and celebrations of the major religions and denominations in the United States and Canada from the perspective of an interested guest of any other faith, based on information obtained from authorities of each religion. Belongs in every living room, library and office. Covers:

African American Methodist Churches • Assemblies of God • Bahá'í Faith • Baptist • Buddhist • Christian Church (Disciples of Christ) • Christian Science (Church of Christ, Scientist) • Churches of Christ • Episcopalian and Anglican • Hindu • Islam • Jehovah's Witnesses • Jewish • Lutheran • Mennonite/Amish • Methodist • Mormon (Church of Jesus Christ of Latter-day Saints) • Native American/First Nations • Orthodox Churches • Pentecostal Church of God • Presbyterian • Quaker (Religious Society of Friends) • Reformed Church in America/Canada • Roman Catholic • Seventh-day Adventist • Sikh • Unitarian Universalist • United Church of Canada • United Church of Christ

"The things Miss Manners forgot to tell us about religion."

—Los Angeles Times

"Finally, for those inclined to undertake their own spiritual journeys ... tells visitors what to expect." *—New York Times*

6 x 9, 432 pp, Quality PB, 978-1-59473-294-2 **$19.99**

The Perfect Stranger's Guide to Funerals and Grieving Practices: A Guide to Etiquette in Other People's Religious Ceremonies *Edited by Stuart M. Matlins*
6 x 9, 240 pp, Quality PB, 978-1-893361-20-1 **$16.95**

The Perfect Stranger's Guide to Wedding Ceremonies: A Guide to Etiquette in Other People's Religious Ceremonies *Edited by Stuart M. Matlins*
6 x 9, 208 pp, Quality PB, 978-1-893361-19-5 **$16.95**

Spiritual Poetry—The Mystic Poets

Experience these mystic poets as you never have before. Each beautiful, compact book includes a brief introduction to the poet's time and place, a summary of the major themes of the poet's mysticism and religious tradition, essential selections from the poet's most important works, and an appreciative preface by a contemporary spiritual writer.

Hafiz
The Mystic Poets
Translated and with Notes by Gertrude Bell
Preface by Ibrahim Gamard
Hafiz is known throughout the world as Persia's greatest poet, with sales of his poems in Iran today only surpassed by those of the Qur'an itself. His probing and joyful verse speaks to people from all backgrounds who long to taste and feel divine love and experience harmony with all living things.
5 x 7¼, 144 pp, HC, 978-1-59473-009-2 **$16.99**

Hopkins
The Mystic Poets
Preface by Rev. Thomas Ryan, CSP
Gerard Manley Hopkins, Christian mystical poet, is beloved for his use of fresh language and startling metaphors to describe the world around him. Although his verse is lovely, beneath the surface lies a searching soul, wrestling with and yearning for God.
5 x 7¼, 112 pp, HC, 978-1-59473-010-8 **$16.99**

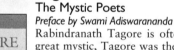

Tagore
The Mystic Poets
Preface by Swami Adiswarananda
Rabindranath Tagore is often considered the Shakespeare of modern India. A great mystic, Tagore was the teacher of W. B. Yeats and Robert Frost, the close friend of Albert Einstein and Mahatma Gandhi, and the winner of the Nobel Prize for Literature. This beautiful sampling of Tagore's two most important works, *The Gardener* and *Gitanjali,* offers a glimpse into his spiritual vision that has inspired people around the world.
5 x 7¼, 144 pp, HC, 978-1-59473-008-5 **$16.99**

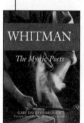

Whitman
The Mystic Poets
Preface by Gary David Comstock
Walt Whitman was the most innovative and influential poet of the nineteenth century. This beautiful sampling of Whitman's most important poetry from *Leaves of Grass,* and selections from his prose writings, offers a glimpse into the spiritual side of his most radical themes—love for country, love for others and love of self.
5 x 7¼, 192 pp, HC, 978-1-59473-041-2 **$16.99**

Sacred Texts—SkyLight Illuminations Series

Offers today's spiritual seeker an enjoyable entry into the great classic texts of the world's spiritual traditions. Each classic is presented in an accessible translation, with facing pages of guided commentary from experts, giving you the keys you need to understand the history, context and meaning of the text.

CHRISTIANITY

Celtic Christian Spirituality: Essential Writings—Annotated & Explained
Annotation by Mary C. Earle; Foreword by John Philip Newell
Explores how the writings of this lively tradition embody the gospel.
5½ x 8½, 176 pp, Quality PB, 978-1-59473-302-4 **$16.99**

Desert Fathers and Mothers: Early Christian Wisdom Sayings—Annotated & Explained
Annotation by Christine Valters Paintner, PhD
Opens up wisdom of the desert fathers and mothers for readers with no previous knowledge of Western monasticism and early Christianity.
5½ x 8½, 192 pp, Quality PB, 978-1-59473-373-4 **$16.99**

The End of Days: Essential Selections from Apocalyptic Texts—Annotated & Explained
Annotation by Robert G. Clouse, PhD
Helps you understand the complex Christian visions of the end of the world.
5½ x 8½, 224 pp, Quality PB, 978-1-59473-170-9 **$16.99**

The Hidden Gospel of Matthew: Annotated & Explained
Translation & Annotation by Ron Miller
Discover the words and events that have the strongest connection to the historical Jesus.
5½ x 8½, 272 pp, Quality PB, 978-1-59473-038-2 **$16.99**

The Infancy Gospels of Jesus: Apocryphal Tales from the Childhoods of Mary and Jesus—Annotated & Explained
Translation & Annotation by Stevan Davies; Foreword by A. Edward Siecienski, PhD
A startling presentation of the early lives of Mary, Jesus and other biblical figures that will amuse and surprise you.
5½ x 8½, 176 pp, Quality PB, 978-1-59473-258-4 **$16.99**

John & Charles Wesley: Selections from Their Writings and Hymns—Annotated & Explained
Annotation by Paul W. Chilcote, PhD
A unique presentation of the writings of these two inspiring brothers brings together some of the most essential material from their large corpus of work.
5½ x 8½, 288 pp, Quality PB, 978-1-59473-309-3 **$16.99**

The Lost Sayings of Jesus: Teachings from Ancient Christian, Jewish, Gnostic and Islamic Sources—Annotated & Explained
Translation & Annotation by Andrew Phillip Smith; Foreword by Stephan A. Hoeller
This collection of more than three hundred sayings depicts Jesus as a Wisdom teacher who speaks to people of all faiths as a mystic and spiritual master.
5½ x 8½, 240 pp, Quality PB, 978-1-59473-172-3 **$16.99**

Philokalia: The Eastern Christian Spiritual Texts—Selections
Annotated & Explained *Annotation by Allyne Smith; Translation by G. E. H. Palmer, Phillip Sherrard and Bishop Kallistos Ware*
The first approachable introduction to the wisdom of the Philokalia, the classic text of Eastern Christian spirituality.
5½ x 8½, 240 pp, Quality PB, 978-1-59473-103-7 **$16.99**

The Sacred Writings of Paul: Selections Annotated & Explained
Translation & Annotation by Ron Miller
Leads you into the exciting immediacy of Paul's teachings.
5½ x 8½, 224 pp, Quality PB, 978-1-59473-213-3 **$16.99**

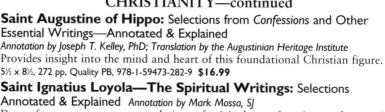

Sacred Texts—continued

CHRISTIANITY—continued

Saint Augustine of Hippo: Selections from *Confessions* and Other Essential Writings—Annotated & Explained
Annotation by Joseph T. Kelley, PhD; Translation by the Augustinian Heritage Institute
Provides insight into the mind and heart of this foundational Christian figure.
5½ x 8½, 272 pp, Quality PB, 978-1-59473-282-9 **$16.99**

Saint Ignatius Loyola—The Spiritual Writings: Selections
Annotated & Explained *Annotation by Mark Mossa, SJ*
Draws from contemporary translations of original texts focusing on the practical mysticism of Ignatius of Loyola.
5½ x 8½, 288 pp, Quality PB, 978-1-59473-301-7 **$16.99**

Sex Texts from the Bible: Selections Annotated & Explained
Translation & Annotation by Teresa J. Hornsby; Foreword by Amy-Jill Levine
Demystifies the Bible's ideas on gender roles, marriage, sexual orientation, virginity, lust and sexual pleasure.
5½ x 8½, 208 pp, Quality PB, 978-1-59473-217-1 **$16.99**

Spiritual Writings on Mary: Annotated & Explained
Annotation by Mary Ford-Grabowsky; Foreword by Andrew Harvey
Examines the role of Mary, the mother of Jesus, as a source of inspiration in history and in life today.
5½ x 8½, 288 pp, Quality PB, 978-1-59473-001-6 **$16.99**

The Way of a Pilgrim: The Jesus Prayer Journey—Annotated & Explained
Translation & Annotation by Gleb Pokrovsky; Foreword by Andrew Harvey
A classic of Russian Orthodox spirituality.
5½ x 8½, 160 pp, Illus., Quality PB, 978-1-893361-31-7 **$14.95**

GNOSTICISM

Gnostic Writings on the Soul: Annotated & Explained
Translation & Annotation by Andrew Phillip Smith; Foreword by Stephan A. Hoeller
Reveals the inspiring ways your soul can remember and return to its unique, divine purpose.
5½ x 8½, 144 pp, Quality PB, 978-1-59473-220-1 **$16.99**

The Gospel of Philip: Annotated & Explained
Translation & Annotation by Andrew Phillip Smith; Foreword by Stevan Davies
Reveals otherwise unrecorded sayings of Jesus and fragments of Gnostic mythology.
5½ x 8½, 160 pp, Quality PB, 978-1-59473-111-2 **$16.99**

The Gospel of Thomas: Annotated & Explained
Translation & Annotation by Stevan Davies; Foreword by Andrew Harvey
Sheds new light on the origins of Christianity and portrays Jesus as a wisdom-loving sage.
5½ x 8½, 192 pp, Quality PB, 978-1-893361-45-4 **$16.99**

The Secret Book of John: The Gnostic Gospel—Annotated & Explained
Translation & Annotation by Stevan Davies
The most significant and influential text of the ancient Gnostic religion.
5½ x 8½, 208 pp, Quality PB, 978-1-59473-082-5 **$16.99**

Sacred Texts—continued

JUDAISM

The Book of Job: Annotated & Explained
Translation and Annotation by Donald Kraus; Foreword by Dr. Marc Brettler
Clarifies for today's readers what Job is, how to overcome difficulties in the text, and what it may mean for us.
5½ x 8½, 256 pp, Quality PB, 978-1-59473-389-5 **$16.99**

The Divine Feminine in Biblical Wisdom Literature
Selections Annotated & Explained
Translation & Annotation by Rabbi Rami Shapiro; Foreword by Rev. Cynthia Bourgeault, PhD
Uses the Hebrew Bible and Wisdom literature to explain Sophia's way of wisdom and illustrate Her creative energy.
5½ x 8½, 240 pp, Quality PB, 978-1-59473-109-9 **$16.99**

Ecclesiastes: Annotated & Explained
Translation & Annotation by Rabbi Rami Shapiro; Foreword by Rev. Barbara Cawthorne Crafton
A timeless teaching on living well amid uncertainty and insecurity.
5½ x 8½, 160 pp, Quality PB, 978-1-59473-287-4 **$16.99**

Ethics of the Sages: *Pirke Avot*—Annotated & Explained
Translation & Annotation by Rabbi Rami Shapiro
Clarifies the ethical teachings of the early Rabbis.
5½ x 8½, 192 pp, Quality PB, 978-1-59473-207-2 **$16.99**

Hasidic Tales: Annotated & Explained
Translation & Annotation by Rabbi Rami Shapiro; Foreword by Andrew Harvey
Introduces the legendary tales of the impassioned Hasidic rabbis, presenting them as stories rather than as parables.
5½ x 8½, 240 pp, Quality PB, 978-1-893361-86-7 **$16.95**

The Hebrew Prophets: Selections Annotated & Explained
Translation & Annotation by Rabbi Rami Shapiro;
Foreword by Rabbi Zalman M. Schachter-Shalomi
5½ x 8½, 224 pp, Quality PB, 978-1-59473-037-5 **$16.99**

Maimonides—Essential Teachings on Jewish Faith & Ethics
The Book of Knowledge & the Thirteen Principles of Faith—Annotated & Explained
Translation and Annotation by Rabbi Marc D. Angel, PhD
Opens up for us Maimonides's views on the nature of God, providence, prophecy, free will, human nature, repentance and more.
5½ x 8½, 224 pp, Quality PB, 978-1-59473-311-6 **$18.99**

Proverbs: Annotated & Explained
Translation and Annotation by Rabbi Rami Shapiro
Demonstrates how these complex poetic forms are actually straightforward instructions to live simply, without rationalizations and excuses.
5½ x 8½, 288 pp, Quality PB, 978-1-59473-310-9 $16.99

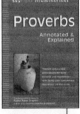

Tanya, the Masterpiece of Hasidic Wisdom
Selections Annotated & Explained
Translation & Annotation by Rabbi Rami Shapiro; Foreword by Rabbi Zalman M. Schachter-Shalomi
Clarifies one of the most powerful and potentially transformative books of Jewish wisdom.
5½ x 8½, 240 pp, Quality PB, 978-1-59473-275-1 **$16.99**

Zohar: Annotated & Explained
Translation & Annotation by Daniel C. Matt; Foreword by Andrew Harvey
The canonical text of Jewish mystical tradition.
5½ x 8½, 176 pp, Quality PB, 978-1-893361-51-5 **$16.99**

Sacred Texts—continued

ISLAM

Ghazali on the Principles of Islamic Spirituality
Selections from *The Forty Foundations of Religion*—Annotated & Explained
Translation & Annotation by Aaron Spevack, PhD
Makes the core message of this influential spiritual master relevant to anyone seeking a balanced understanding of Islam.
5½ x 8½, 338 pp, Quality PB, 978-1-59473-284-3 **$18.99**

The Qur'an and Sayings of Prophet Muhammad
Selections Annotated & Explained
Annotation by Sohaib N. Sultan; Translation by Yusuf Ali, Revised by Sohaib N. Sultan; Foreword by Jane I. Smith
Presents the foundational wisdom of Islam in an easy-to-use format.
5½ x 8½, 256 pp, Quality PB, 978-1-59473-222-5 **$16.99**

Rumi and Islam: Selections from His Stories, Poems, and Discourses—
Annotated & Explained *Translation & Annotation by Ibrahim Gamard*
Focuses on Rumi's place within the Sufi tradition of Islam, providing insight into the mystical side of the religion.
5½ x 8½, 240 pp, Quality PB, 978-1-59473-002-3 **$15.99**

EASTERN RELIGIONS

The Art of War—Spirituality for Conflict: Annotated & Explained
by Sun Tzu; Annotation by Thomas Huynh; Translation by Thomas Huynh and the Editors at Sonshi.com; Foreword by Marc Benioff; Preface by Thomas Cleary
Highlights principles that encourage a perceptive and spiritual approach to conflict.
5½ x 8½, 256 pp, Quality PB, 978-1-59473-244-7 **$16.99**

Bhagavad Gita: Annotated & Explained
Translation by Shri Purohit Swami; Annotation by Kendra Crossen Burroughs; Foreword by Andrew Harvey
Presents the classic text's teachings—with no previous knowledge of Hinduism required.
5½ x 8½, 192 pp, Quality PB, 978-1-893361-28-7 **$16.95**

Chuang-tzu: The Tao of Perfect Happiness—Selections Annotated & Explained
Translation & Annotation by Livia Kohn, PhD
Presents Taoism's central message of reverence for the "Way" of the natural world.
5½ x 8½, 240 pp, Quality PB, 978-1-59473-296-6 **$16.99**

Confucius, the *Analects:* The Path of the Sage—Selections Annotated
& Explained *Annotation by Rodney L. Taylor, PhD; Translation by James Legge, Revised by Rodney L. Taylor, PhD* Explores the ethical and spiritual meaning behind the Confucian way of learning and self-cultivation.
5½ x 8½, 192 pp, Quality PB, 978-1-59473-306-2 **$16.99**

Dhammapada: Annotated & Explained
Translation by Max Müller, revised by Jack Maguire; Annotation by Jack Maguire; Foreword by Andrew Harvey Contains all of Buddhism's key teachings, plus commentary that explains all the names, terms and references.
5½ x 8½, 160 pp, b/w photos, Quality PB, 978-1-893361-42-3 **$14.95**

Selections from the Gospel of Sri Ramakrishna: Annotated & Explained
Translation by Swami Nikhilananda; Annotation by Kendra Crossen Burroughs; Foreword by Andrew Harvey Introduces the fascinating world of the Indian mystic and the universal appeal of his message.
5½ x 8½, 240 pp, b/w photos, Quality PB, 978-1-893361-46-1 **$16.95**

Tao Te Ching: Annotated & Explained
Translation & Annotation by Derek Lin; Foreword by Lama Surya Das
Introduces an Eastern classic in an accessible, poetic and completely original way.
5½ x 8½, 208 pp, Quality PB, 978-1-59473-204-1 **$16.99**

Sacred Texts—continued

MORMONISM

The Book of Mormon: Selections Annotated & Explained
Annotation by Jana Riess; Foreword by Phyllis Tickle Explores the sacred epic that is cherished by more than twelve million members of the LDS church as the keystone of their faith. 5½ x 8½ , 272 pp, Quality PB, 978-1-59473-076-4 **$16.99**

NATIVE AMERICAN

Native American Stories of the Sacred: Annotated & Explained
Retold & Annotated by Evan T. Pritchard These teaching tales contain elegantly simple illustrations of time-honored truths. 5½ x 8½, 272 pp, Quality PB, 978-1-59473-112-9 **$16.99**

STOICISM

The Meditations of Marcus Aurelius: Selections Annotated & Explained *Annotation by Russell McNeil, PhD; Translation by George Long, revised by Russell McNeil, PhD* Ancient Stoic wisdom that speaks vibrantly today about life, business, government and spirit. 5½ x 8½, 288 pp, Quality PB, 978-1-59473-236-2 **$16.99**

Hinduism / Vedanta

The Four Yogas: A Guide to the Spiritual Paths of Action, Devotion, Meditation and Knowledge *by Swami Adiswarananda*
6 x 9, 320 pp, Quality PB, 978-1-59473-223-2 **$19.99**; HC, 978-1-59473-143-3 **$29.99**

Meditation & Its Practices: A Definitive Guide to Techniques and Traditions of Meditation in Yoga and Vedanta *by Swami Adiswarananda* 6 x 9, 504 pp, Quality PB, 978-1-59473-105-1 **$24.99**

The Spiritual Quest and the Way of Yoga: The Goal, the Journey and the Milestones *by Swami Adiswarananda* 6 x 9, 288 pp, HC, 978-1-59473-113-6 **$29.99**

Sri Ramakrishna, the Face of Silence
by Swami Nikhilananda and Dhan Gopal Mukerji; Edited with an Introduction by Swami Adiswarananda; Foreword by Dhan Gopal Mukerji II 6 x 9, 352 pp, Quality PB, 978-1-59473-233-1 **$21.99**

Sri Sarada Devi, The Holy Mother: Her Teachings and Conversations
Translated with Notes by Swami Nikhilananda; Edited with an Introduction by Swami Adiswarananda
6 x 9, 288 pp, HC, 978-1-59473-070-2 **$29.99**

The Vedanta Way to Peace and Happiness *by Swami Adiswarananda*
6 x 9, 240 pp, Quality PB, 978-1-59473-180-8 **$18.99**; HC, 978-1-59473-034-4 **$29.99**

Vivekananda, World Teacher: His Teachings on the Spiritual Unity of Humankind
Edited and with an Introduction by Swami Adiswarananda
6 x 9, 272 pp, Quality PB, 978-1-59473-210-2 **$21.99**

Sikhism

The First Sikh Spiritual Master: Timeless Wisdom from the Life and Teachings of Guru Nanak *by Harish Dhillon* 6 x 9, 192 pp, Quality PB, 978-1-59473-209-6 **$16.99**

Spiritual Biography

Spiritual Leaders Who Changed the World
The Essential Handbook to the Past Century of Religion
Edited by Ira Rifkin and the Editors at SkyLight Paths; Foreword by Dr. Robert Coles
An invaluable reference to the most important spiritual leaders of the past 100 years.
6 x 9, 304 pp, b/w photos, Quality PB, 978-1-59473-241-6 **$18.99**

Mahatma Gandhi: His Life and Ideas *by Charles F. Andrews; Foreword by Dr. Arun Gandhi*
Examines the religious ideas and political dynamics that influenced the birth of the peaceful resistance movement. 6 x 9, 336 pp, b/w photos, Quality PB, 978-1-893361-89-8 **$18.95**

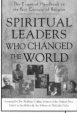

Bede Griffiths: An Introduction to His Interspiritual Thought
by Wayne Teasdale The first study of his contemplative experience and thought, exploring the intersection of Hinduism and Christianity.
6 x 9, 288 pp, Quality PB, 978-1-893361-77-5 **$18.95**

Spirituality & Crafts

Beading—The Creative Spirit: Finding Your Sacred Center through the Art of Beadwork *by Rev. Wendy Ellsworth*
Invites you on a spiritual pilgrimage into the kaleidoscope world of glass and color. 7 x 9, 240 pp, 8-page color insert, 40+ b/w photos and 40 diagrams, Quality PB, 978-1-59473-267-6 **$18.99**

Contemplative Crochet: A Hands-On Guide for Interlocking Faith and Craft *by Cindy Crandall-Frazier; Foreword by Linda Skolnik*
Illuminates the spiritual lessons you can learn through crocheting.
7 x 9, 208 pp, b/w photos, Quality PB, 978-1-59473-238-6 **$16.99**

The Knitting Way: A Guide to Spiritual Self-Discovery
by Linda Skolnik and Janice MacDaniels Examines how you can explore and strengthen your spiritual life through knitting.
7 x 9, 240 pp, b/w photos, Quality PB, 978-1-59473-079-5 **$16.99**

The Painting Path: Embodying Spiritual Discovery through Yoga, Brush and Color *by Linda Novick; Foreword by Richard Segalman*
Explores the divine connection you can experience through art.
7 x 9, 208 pp, 8-page color insert, plus b/w photos,
Quality PB, 978-1-59473-226-3 **$18.99**

The Quilting Path: A Guide to Spiritual Discovery through Fabric, Thread and Kabbalah *by Louise Silk*
Explores how to cultivate personal growth through quilt making.
7 x 9, 192 pp, b/w photos and illus., Quality PB, 978-1-59473-206-5 **$16.99**

The Scrapbooking Journey: A Hands-On Guide to Spiritual Discovery
by Cory Richardson-Lauve; Foreword by Stacy Julian Reveals how this craft can become a practice used to deepen and shape your life.
7 x 9, 176 pp, 8-page color insert, plus b/w photos, Quality PB, 978-1-59473-216-4 **$18.99**

The Soulwork of Clay: A Hands-On Approach to Spirituality
by Marjory Zoet Bankson; Photos by Peter Bankson
Takes you through the seven-step process of making clay into a pot, drawing parallels at each stage to the process of spiritual growth.
7 x 9, 192 pp, b/w photos, Quality PB, 978-1-59473-249-2 **$16.99**

Kabbalah / Enneagram
(Books from Jewish Lights Publishing, SkyLight Paths' sister imprint)

Cast in God's Image: Discover Your Personality Type Using the Enneagram and Kabbalah
by Rabbi Howard A. Addison, PhD 7 x 9, 176 pp, Quality PB, 978-1-58023-124-4 **$16.95**

Ehyeh: A Kabbalah for Tomorrow *by Rabbi Arthur Green, PhD*
6 x 9, 224 pp, Quality PB, 978-1-58023-213-5 **$18.99**

The Enneagram and Kabbalah, 2nd Edition: Reading Your Soul
by Rabbi Howard A. Addison, PhD 6 x 9, 192 pp, Quality PB, 978-1-58023-229-6 **$16.99**

The Gift of Kabbalah: Discovering the Secrets of Heaven, Renewing Your Life on Earth
by Tamar Frankiel, PhD 6 x 9, 256 pp, Quality PB, 978-1-58023-141-1 **$16.95**

God in Your Body: Kabbalah, Mindfulness and Embodied Spiritual Practice
by Jay Michaelson 6 x 9, 272 pp, Quality PB, 978-1-58023-304-0 **$18.99**

Jewish Mysticism and the Spiritual Life: Classical Texts, Contemporary Reflections
Edited by Dr. Lawrence Fine, Dr. Eitan Fishbane and Rabbi Or N. Rose
6 x 9, 256 pp, HC, 978-1-58023-434-4 **$24.99**

Kabbalah: A Brief Introduction for Christians
by Tamar Frankiel, PhD 5½ x 8½, 208 pp, Quality PB, 978-1-58023-303-3 **$16.99**

Zohar: Annotated & Explained *Translation & Annotation by Daniel C. Matt;*
Foreword by Andrew Harvey 5½ x 8½, 176 pp, Quality PB, 978-1-893361-51-5 **$15.99**

Women's Interest

Women, Spirituality and Transformative Leadership
Where Grace Meets Power
Edited by Kathe Schaaf, Kay Lindahl, Kathleen S. Hurty, PhD, and Reverend Guo Cheen
A dynamic conversation on the power of women's spiritual leadership and its emerging patterns of transformation. 6 x 9, 288 pp, Hardcover, 978-1-59473-313-0 **$24.99**

Spiritually Healthy Divorce: Navigating Disruption with Insight & Hope
by Carolyne Call A spiritual map to help you move through the twists and turns of divorce. 6 x 9, 224 pp, Quality PB, 978-1-59473-288-1 **$16.99**

New Feminist Christianity: Many Voices, Many Views
Edited by Mary E. Hunt and Diann L. Neu
Insights from ministers and theologians, activists and leaders, artists and liturgists who are shaping the future. Taken together, their voices offer a starting point for building new models of religious life and worship.
6 x 9, 384 pp, HC, 978-1-59473-285-0 **$24.99**

New Jewish Feminism: Probing the Past, Forging the Future
Edited by Rabbi Elyse Goldstein; Foreword by Anita Diamant
Looks at the growth and accomplishments of Jewish feminism and what they mean for Jewish women today and tomorrow. Features the voices of women from every area of Jewish life, addressing the important issues that concern Jewish women.
6 x 9, 480 pp, Quality PB, 978-1-58023-448-1 **$19.99**; HC, 978-1-58023-359-0 **$24.99***

Bread, Body, Spirit: Finding the Sacred in Food
Edited and with Introductions by Alice Peck 6 x 9, 224 pp, Quality PB, 978-1-59473-242-3 **$19.99**

Dance—The Sacred Art: The Joy of Movement as a Spiritual Practice
by Cynthia Winton-Henry 5½ x 8½, 224 pp, Quality PB, 978-1-59473-268-3 **$16.99**

Daughters of the Desert: Stories of Remarkable Women from Christian, Jewish and Muslim Traditions
by Claire Rudolf Murphy, Meghan Nuttall Sayres, Mary Cronk Farrell, Sarah Conover and Betsy Wharton
5½ x 8½, 192 pp, Illus., Quality PB, 978-1-59473-106-8 **$14.99** Inc. reader's discussion guide

The Divine Feminine in Biblical Wisdom Literature
Selections Annotated & Explained
Translation & Annotation by Rabbi Rami Shapiro; Foreword by Rev. Cynthia Bourgeault, PhD
5½ x 8½, 240 pp, Quality PB, 978-1-59473-109-9 **$16.99**

Divining the Body: Reclaim the Holiness of Your Physical Self
by Jan Phillips 8 x 8, 256 pp, Quality PB, 978-1-59473-080-1 **$18.99**

Honoring Motherhood: Prayers, Ceremonies & Blessings
Edited and with Introductions by Lynn L. Caruso
5 x 7¼, 272 pp, Quality PB, 978-1-58473-384-0 **$9.99**; HC, 978-1-59473-239-3 **$19.99**

Next to Godliness: Finding the Sacred in Housekeeping
Edited by Alice Peck 6 x 9, 224 pp, Quality PB, 978-1-59473-214-0 **$19.99**

ReVisions: Seeing Torah through a Feminist Lens
by Rabbi Elyse Goldstein 5½ x 8½, 224 pp, Quality PB, 978-1-58023-117-6 **$16.95***

The Triumph of Eve & Other Subversive Bible Tales
by Matt Biers-Ariel 5½ x 8½, 192 pp, Quality PB, 978-1-59473-176-1 **$14.99**

White Fire: A Portrait of Women Spiritual Leaders in America
by Malka Drucker; Photos by Gay Block 7 x 10, 320 pp, b/w photos, HC, 978-1-893361-64-5 **$24.95**

Woman Spirit Awakening in Nature: Growing Into the Fullness of Who You Are
by Nancy Barrett Chickerneo, PhD; Foreword by Eileen Fisher
8 x 8, 224 pp, b/w illus., Quality PB, 978-1-59473-250-8 **$16.99**

Women of Color Pray: Voices of Strength, Faith, Healing, Hope and Courage
Edited and with Introductions by Christal M. Jackson
5 x 7¼, 208 pp, Quality PB, 978-1-59473-077-1 **$15.99**

The Women's Torah Commentary: New Insights from Women Rabbis on the 54 Weekly Torah Portions
Edited by Rabbi Elyse Goldstein
6 x 9, 496 pp, Quality PB, 978-1-58023-370-5 **$19.99**; HC, 978-1-58023-076-6 **$34.95***

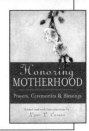

* A book from Jewish Lights, SkyLight Paths' sister imprint

Spirituality of the Seasons

Autumn: A Spiritual Biography of the Season
Edited by Gary Schmidt and Susan M. Felch; Illus. by Mary Azarian
Rejoice in autumn as a time of preparation and reflection. Includes Wendell Berry, David James Duncan, Robert Frost, A. Bartlett Giamatti, E. B. White, P. D. James, Julian of Norwich, Garret Keizer, Tracy Kidder, Anne Lamott, May Sarton.
6 x 9, 320 pp, b/w illus., Quality PB, 978-1-59473-118-1 **$18.99**

Spring: A Spiritual Biography of the Season
Edited by Gary Schmidt and Susan M. Felch; Illus. by Mary Azarian
Explore the gentle unfurling of spring and reflect on how nature celebrates rebirth and renewal. Includes Jane Kenyon, Lucy Larcom, Harry Thurston, Nathaniel Hawthorne, Noel Perrin, Annie Dillard, Martha Ballard, Barbara Kingsolver, Dorothy Wordsworth, Donald Hall, David Brill, Lionel Basney, Isak Dinesen, Paul Laurence Dunbar. 6 x 9, 352 pp, b/w illus., Quality PB, 978-1-59473-246-1 **$18.99**

Summer: A Spiritual Biography of the Season
Edited by Gary Schmidt and Susan M. Felch; Illus. by Barry Moser
"A sumptuous banquet.... These selections lift up an exquisite wholeness found within an everyday sophistication." — ★ *Publishers Weekly* starred review
Includes Anne Lamott, Luci Shaw, Ray Bradbury, Richard Selzer, Thomas Lynch, Walt Whitman, Carl Sandburg, Sherman Alexie, Madeleine L'Engle, Jamaica Kincaid.
6 x 9, 304 pp, b/w illus., Quality PB, 978-1-59473-183-9 **$18.99**
HC, 978-1-59473-083-2 **$21.99**

Winter: A Spiritual Biography of the Season
Edited by Gary Schmidt and Susan M. Felch; Illus. by Barry Moser
"This outstanding anthology features top-flight nature and spirituality writers on the fierce, inexorable season of winter.... Remarkably lively and warm, despite the icy subject." — ★ *Publishers Weekly* starred review
Includes Will Campbell, Rachel Carson, Annie Dillard, Donald Hall, Ron Hansen, Jane Kenyon, Jamaica Kincaid, Barry Lopez, Kathleen Norris, John Updike, E. B. White.
6 x 9, 288 pp, b/w illus., Deluxe PB w/ flaps, 978-1-893361-92-8 **$18.95**
HC, 978-1-893361-53-9 **$21.95**

Spirituality / Animal Companions

Blessing the Animals: Prayers and Ceremonies to Celebrate God's Creatures, Wild and Tame *Edited and with Introductions by Lynn L. Caruso*
5¼ x 7¼, 256 pp, Quality PB, 978-1-59473-253-9 **$15.99**; HC, 978-1-59473-145-7 **$19.99**

Remembering My Pet: A Kid's Own Spiritual Workbook for When a Pet Dies
by Nechama Liss-Levinson, PhD, and Rev. Molly Phinney Baskette, MDiv; Foreword by Lynn L. Caruso
8 x 10, 48 pp, 2-color text, HC, 978-1-59473-221-8 **$16.99**

What Animals Can Teach Us about Spirituality: Inspiring Lessons from Wild and Tame Creatures *by Diana L. Guerrero* 6 x 9, 176 pp, Quality PB, 978-1-893361-84-3 **$16.95**

Spirituality—A Week Inside

Lighting the Lamp of Wisdom: A Week Inside a Yoga Ashram
by John Ittner; Foreword by Dr. David Frawley
6 x 9, 192 pp, b/w photos, Quality PB, 978-1-893361-52-2 **$15.95**

Making a Heart for God: A Week Inside a Catholic Monastery
by Dianne Aprile; Foreword by Brother Patrick Hart, OCSO
6 x 9, 224 pp, b/w photos, Quality PB, 978-1-893361-49-2 **$16.95**

Waking Up: A Week Inside a Zen Monastery
by Jack Maguire; Foreword by John Daido Loori, Roshi
6 x 9, 224 pp, b/w photos, Quality PB, 978-1-893361-55-3 **$16.95**; HC, 978-1-893361-13-3 **$21.95**

Spirituality

Gathering at God's Table: The Meaning of Mission in the Feast of Faith
By Katharine Jefferts Schori
A profound reminder of our role in the larger frame of God's dream for a restored and reconciled world. 6 x 9, 256 pp, HC, 978-1-59473-316-1 **$21.99**

The Heartbeat of God: Finding the Sacred in the Middle of Everything
by Katharine Jefferts Schori; Foreword by Joan Chittister, OSB
Explores our connections to other people, to other nations and with the environment through the lens of faith. 6 x 9, 240 pp, HC, 978-1-59473-292-8 **$21.99**

A Dangerous Dozen: Twelve Christians Who Threatened the Status Quo but Taught Us to Live Like Jesus
by the Rev. Canon C. K. Robertson, PhD; Foreword by Archbishop Desmond Tutu
Profiles twelve visionary men and women who challenged society and showed the world a different way of living. 6 x 9, 208 pp, Quality PB, 978-1-59473-298-0 **$16.99**

Decision Making & Spiritual Discernment: The Sacred Art of Finding Your Way *by Nancy L. Bieber*
Presents three essential aspects of Spirit-led decision making: willingness, attentiveness and responsiveness. 5½ x 8½, 208 pp, Quality PB, 978-1-59473-289-8 **$16.99**

Laugh Your Way to Grace: Reclaiming the Spiritual Power of Humor
by Rev. Susan Sparks A powerful, humorous case for laughter as a spiritual, healing path. 6 x 9, 176 pp, Quality PB, 978-1-59473-280-5 **$16.99**

Bread, Body, Spirit: Finding the Sacred in Food
Edited and with Introductions by Alice Peck 6 x 9, 224 pp, Quality PB, 978-1-59473-242-3 **$19.99**

Claiming Earth as Common Ground: The Ecological Crisis through the Lens of Faith
by Andrea Cohen-Kiener; Foreword by Rev. Sally Bingham
6 x 9, 192 pp, Quality PB, 978-1-59473-261-4 **$16.99**

Creating a Spiritual Retirement: A Guide to the Unseen Possibilities in Our Lives
by Molly Srode 6 x 9, 208 pp, b/w photos, Quality PB, 978-1-59473-050-4 **$14.99**

Creative Aging: Rethinking Retirement and Non-Retirement in a Changing World
by Marjory Zoet Bankson 6 x 9, 160 pp, Quality PB, 978-1-59473-281-2 **$16.99**

Keeping Spiritual Balance as We Grow Older: More than 65 Creative Ways to Use Purpose, Prayer, and the Power of Spirit to Build a Meaningful Retirement
by Molly and Bernie Srode 8 x 8, 224 pp, Quality PB, 978-1-59473-042-9 **$16.99**

Hearing the Call across Traditions: Readings on Faith and Service
Edited by Adam Davis; Foreword by Eboo Patel
6 x 9, 352 pp, Quality PB, 978-1-59473-303-1 **$18.99**; HC, 978-1-59473-264-5 **$29.99**

Honoring Motherhood: Prayers, Ceremonies & Blessings
Edited and with Introductions by Lynn L. Caruso
5 x 7¼, 272 pp, Quality PB, 978-1-58473-384-0 **$9.99**; HC, 978-1-59473-239-3 **$19.99**

The Losses of Our Lives: The Sacred Gifts of Renewal in Everyday Loss
by Dr. Nancy Copeland-Payton 6 x 9, 192 pp, HC, 978-1-59473-271-3 **$19.99**

Renewal in the Wilderness: A Spiritual Guide to Connecting with God in the Natural World *by John Lionberger*
6 x 9, 176 pp, b/w photos, Quality PB, 978-1-59473-219-5 **$16.99**

Soul Fire: Accessing Your Creativity
by Thomas Ryan, CSP 6 x 9, 160 pp, Quality PB, 978-1-59473-243-0 **$16.99**

A Spirituality for Brokenness: Discovering Your Deepest Self in Difficult Times
by Terry Taylor 6 x 9, 176 pp, Quality PB, 978-1-59473-229-4 **$16.99**

A Walk with Four Spiritual Guides: Krishna, Buddha, Jesus, and Ramakrishna
by Andrew Harvey 5½ x 8½, 192 pp, b/w photos & illus., Quality PB, 978-1-59473-138-9 **$15.99**

The Workplace and Spirituality: New Perspectives on Research and Practice
Edited by Dr. Joan Marques, Dr. Satinder Dhiman and Dr. Richard King
6 x 9, 256 pp, HC, 978-1-59473-260-7 **$29.99**

Spiritual Practice

Fly-Fishing—The Sacred Art: Casting a Fly as a Spiritual Practice
by Rabbi Eric Eisenkramer and Rev. Michael Attas, MD; Foreword by Chris Wood, CEO, Trout Unlimited; Preface by Lori Simon, executive director, Casting for Recovery
Shares what fly-fishing can teach you about reflection, awe and wonder; the benefits of solitude; the blessing of community and the search for the Divine.
5½ x 8½, 160 pp, Quality PB, 978-1-59473-299-7 **$16.99**

***Lectio Divina*—The Sacred Art:** Transforming Words & Images into Heart-Centered Prayer *by Christine Valters Paintner, PhD*
Expands the practice of sacred reading beyond scriptural texts and makes it accessible in contemporary life. 5½ x 8½, 240 pp, Quality PB, 978-1-59473-300-0 **$16.99**

Writing—The Sacred Art: Beyond the Page to Spiritual Practice
By Rami Shapiro and Aaron Shapiro
Push your writing through the trite and the boring to something fresh, something transformative. Includes over fifty unique, practical exercises.
5½ x 8½, 192 pp, Quality PB, 978-1-59473-372-7 **$16.99**

Dance—The Sacred Art: The Joy of Movement as a Spiritual Practice
by Cynthia Winton-Henry 5½ x 8½, 224 pp, Quality PB, 978-1-59473-268-3 **$16.99**

Everyday Herbs in Spiritual Life: A Guide to Many Practices
by Michael J. Caduto; Foreword by Rosemary Gladstar
7 x 9, 208 pp, 20+ b/w illus., Quality PB, 978-1-59473-174-7 **$16.99**

Giving—The Sacred Art: Creating a Lifestyle of Generosity
by Lauren Tyler Wright 5½ x 8½, 208 pp, Quality PB, 978-1-59473-224-9 **$16.99**

Haiku—The Sacred Art: A Spiritual Practice in Three Lines
by Margaret D. McGee 5½ x 8½, 192 pp, Quality PB, 978-1-59473-269-0 **$16.99**

Hospitality—The Sacred Art: Discovering the Hidden Spiritual Power of Invitation and Welcome *by Rev. Nanette Sawyer; Foreword by Rev. Dirk Ficca*
5½ x 8½, 208 pp, Quality PB, 978-1-59473-228-7 **$16.99**

Labyrinths from the Outside In: Walking to Spiritual Insight—A Beginner's Guide
by Donna Schaper and Carole Ann Camp
6 x 9, 208 pp, b/w illus. and photos, Quality PB, 978-1-893361-18-8 **$16.95**

Practicing the Sacred Art of Listening: A Guide to Enrich Your Relationships and Kindle Your Spiritual Life *by Kay Lindahl* 8 x 8, 176 pp, Quality PB, 978-1-893361-85-0 **$16.95**

Recovery—The Sacred Art: The Twelve Steps as Spiritual Practice *by Rami Shapiro; Foreword by Joan Borysenko, PhD* 5½ x 8½, 240 pp, Quality PB, 978-1-59473-259-1 **$16.99**

Running—The Sacred Art: Preparing to Practice *by Dr. Warren A. Kay; Foreword by Kristin Armstrong* 5½ x 8½, 160 pp, Quality PB, 978-1-59473-227-0 **$16.99**

The Sacred Art of Chant: Preparing to Practice
by Ana Hernández 5½ x 8½, 192 pp, Quality PB, 978-1-59473-036-8 **$15.99**

The Sacred Art of Fasting: Preparing to Practice
by Thomas Ryan, CSP 5½ x 8½, 192 pp, Quality PB, 978-1-59473-078-8 **$15.99**

The Sacred Art of Forgiveness: Forgiving Ourselves and Others through God's Grace
by Marcia Ford 8 x 8, 176 pp, Quality PB, 978-1-59473-175-4 **$18.99**

The Sacred Art of Listening: Forty Reflections for Cultivating a Spiritual Practice
by Kay Lindahl; Illus. by Amy Schnapper 8 x 8, 160 pp, b/w illus., Quality PB, 978-1-893361-44-7 **$16.99**

The Sacred Art of Lovingkindness: Preparing to Practice
by Rabbi Rami Shapiro; Foreword by Marcia Ford 5½ x 8½, 176 pp, Quality PB, 978-1-59473-151-8 **$16.99**

Sacred Attention: A Spiritual Practice for Finding God in the Moment
by Margaret D. McGee 6 x 9, 144 pp, Quality PB, 978-1-59473-291-1 **$16.99**

Soul Fire: Accessing Your Creativity
by Thomas Ryan, CSP 6 x 9, 160 pp, Quality PB, 978-1-59473-243-0 **$16.99**

Spiritual Adventures in the Snow: Skiing & Snowboarding as Renewal for Your Soul
by Dr. Marcia McFee and Rev. Karen Foster; Foreword by Paul Arthur
5½ x 8½, 208 pp, Quality PB, 978-1-59473-270-6 **$16.99**

Thanking & Blessing—The Sacred Art: Spiritual Vitality through Gratefulness
by Jay Marshall, PhD; Foreword by Philip Gulley 5½ x 8½, 176 pp, Quality PB, 978-1-59473-231-7 **$16.99**

Prayer / Meditation

Men Pray: Voices of Strength, Faith, Healing, Hope and Courage
Created by the Editors at SkyLight Paths
Celebrates the rich variety of ways men around the world have called out to the
Divine—with words of joy, praise, gratitude, wonder, petition and even anger—
from the ancient world up to our own day.
5 x 7, 200 pp (est), HC, 978-1-59473-395-6 **$16.99**

Sacred Attention: A Spiritual Practice for Finding God in the Moment
by Margaret D. McGee
Framed on the Christian liturgical year, this inspiring guide explores ways to
develop a practice of attention as a means of talking—and listening—to God.
6 x 9, 144 pp, Quality PB, 978-1-59473-291-1 **$16.99**

Women of Color Pray: Voices of Strength, Faith, Healing, Hope and Courage
Edited and with Introductions by Christal M. Jackson
Through these prayers, poetry, lyrics, meditations and affirmations, you will share
in the strong and undeniable connection women of color share with God.
5 x 7¼, 208 pp, Quality PB, 978-1-59473-077-1 **$15.99**

The Art of Public Prayer, 2nd Edition: Not for Clergy Only
by Lawrence A. Hoffman, PhD 6 x 9, 288 pp, Quality PB, 978-1-893361-06-5 **$19.99**

A Heart of Stillness: A Complete Guide to Learning the Art of Meditation
by David A. Cooper 5½ x 8½, 272 pp, Quality PB, 978-1-893361-03-4 **$18.99**

Living into Hope: A Call to Spiritual Action for Such a Time as This
by Rev. Dr. Joan Brown Campbell; Foreword by Karen Armstrong
6 x 9, 208 pp, HC, 978-1-59473-283-6 **$21.99**

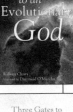

Meditation without Gurus: A Guide to the Heart of Practice
by Clark Strand 5½ x 8½, 192 pp, Quality PB, 978-1-893361-93-5 **$16.95**

Prayers to an Evolutionary God
by William Cleary; Afterword by Diarmuid O'Murchu
6 x 9, 208 pp, HC, 978-1-59473-006-1 **$21.99**

Praying with Our Hands: 21 Practices of Embodied Prayer from the World's
Spiritual Traditions *by Jon M. Sweeney; Photos by Jennifer J. Wilson; Foreword by Mother Tessa
Bielecki; Afterword by Taitetsu Unno, PhD*
8 x 8, 96 pp, 22 duotone photos, Quality PB, 978-1-893361-16-4 **$16.95**

Secrets of Prayer: A Multifaith Guide to Creating Personal Prayer in Your Life
by Nancy Corcoran, CSJ
6 x 9, 160 pp, Quality PB, 978-1-59473-215-7 **$16.99**

Three Gates to Meditation Practice: A Personal Journey into Sufism, Buddhism,
and Judaism *by David A. Cooper* 5½ x 8½, 240 pp, Quality PB, 978-1-893361-22-5 **$16.95**

Prayer / M. Basil Pennington, OCSO

Finding Grace at the Center, 3rd Edition: The Beginning of
Centering Prayer *with Thomas Keating, OCSO, and Thomas E. Clarke, SJ; Foreword by Rev.
Cynthia Bourgeault, PhD* A practical guide to a simple and beautiful form of medita-
tive prayer. 5 x 7¼, 128 pp, Quality PB, 978-1-59473-182-2 **$12.99**

The Monks of Mount Athos: A Western Monk's Extraordinary
Spiritual Journey on Eastern Holy Ground *Foreword by Archimandrite Dionysios*
Explores the landscape, monastic communities and food of Athos.
6 x 9, 352 pp, Quality PB, 978-1-893361-78-2 **$18.95**

Psalms: A Spiritual Commentary *Illus. by Phillip Ratner*
Reflections on some of the most beloved passages from the Bible's most widely
read book. 6 x 9, 176 pp, 24 full-page b/w illus., Quality PB, 978-1-59473-234-8 **$16.99**

The Song of Songs: A Spiritual Commentary *Illus. by Phillip Ratner*
Explore the Bible's most challenging mystical text.
6 x 9, 160 pp, 14 full-page b/w illus., Quality PB, 978-1-59473-235-5 **$16.99**
HC, 978-1-59473-004-7 **$19.99**

About SKYLIGHT PATHS Publishing

SkyLight Paths Publishing is creating a place where people of different spiritual traditions come together for challenge and inspiration, a place where we can help each other understand the mystery that lies at the heart of our existence.

Through spirituality, our religious beliefs are increasingly becoming a part of our lives—rather than *apart* from our lives. While many of us may be more interested than ever in spiritual growth, we may be less firmly planted in traditional religion. Yet, we do want to deepen our relationship to the sacred, to learn from our own as well as from other faith traditions, and to practice in new ways.

SkyLight Paths sees both believers and seekers as a community that increasingly transcends traditional boundaries of religion and denomination—people wanting to learn from each other, *walking together, finding the way.*

For your information and convenience, at the back of this book we have provided a list of other SkyLight Paths books you might find interesting and useful. They cover the following subjects:

Buddhism / Zen	Global Spiritual	Monasticism
Catholicism	Perspectives	Mysticism
Children's Books	Gnosticism	Poetry
Christianity	Hinduism /	Prayer
Comparative	Vedanta	Religious Etiquette
Religion	Inspiration	Retirement
Current Events	Islam / Sufism	Spiritual Biography
Earth-Based	Judaism	Spiritual Direction
Spirituality	Kabbalah	Spirituality
Enneagram	Meditation	Women's Interest
	Midrash Fiction	Worship

Or phone, fax, mail or e-mail to: SKYLIGHT PATHS Publishing
Sunset Farm Offices, Route 4 • P.O. Box 237 • Woodstock, Vermont 05091
Tel: (802) 457-4000 • Fax: (802) 457-4004 • www.skylightpaths.com
Credit card orders: (800) 962-4544 (8:30AM–5:30PM EST Monday–Friday)
Generous discounts on quantity orders. SATISFACTION GUARANTEED. Prices subject to change.